CAMBRIDGE STUDIES IN ECONOMIC HISTORY
PUBLISHED WITH THE AID OF THE ELLEN MCARTHUR FUND

GENERAL EDITOR: DAVID JOSLIN
Professor of Economic History in the University of Cambridge

Population and Society in Norway 1735-1865

T0381897

Population and Society in Norway 1735-1865

MICHAEL DRAKE
University of Kent at Canterbury

CAMBRIDGE
AT THE UNIVERSITY PRESS, 1969

CAMBRIDGE UNIVERSITY PRESS
Cambridge, New York, Melbourne, Madrid, Cape Town, Singapore, São Paulo, Delhi

Cambridge University Press
The Edinburgh Building, Cambridge CB2 8RU, UK

Published in the United States of America by Cambridge University Press, New York

www.cambridge.org
Information on this title: www.cambridge.org/9780521073196

© Cambridge University Press 1969

This publication is in copyright. Subject to statutory exception
and to the provisions of relevant collective licensing agreements,
no reproduction of any part may take place without the written
permission of Cambridge University Press.

First published 1969
This digitally printed version 2008

A catalogue record for this publication is available from the British Library

Library of Congress Catalogue Card Number: 69–14393

ISBN 978-0-521-07319-6 hardback
ISBN 978-0-521-08514-4 paperback

Contents

Figures

Tables

List of tables

viii

List of tables

TABLES IN APPENDIX I

List of tables

xii

xiii

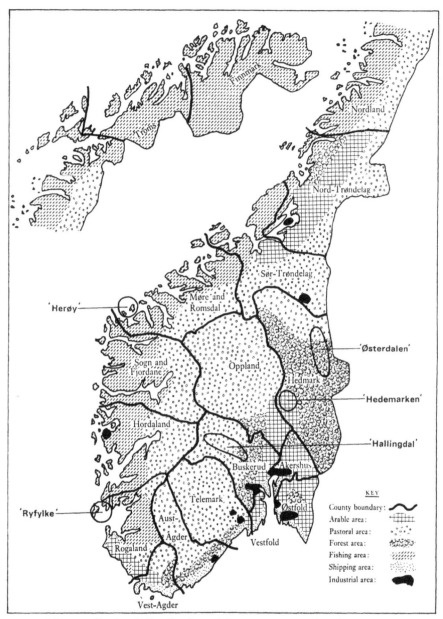

KEY

County boundary:
Arable area:
Pastoral area:
Forest area:
Fishing area:
Shipping area:
Industrial area:

Map 1   Regional distribution of dominant occupations in Norway
c. 1860.

xiv

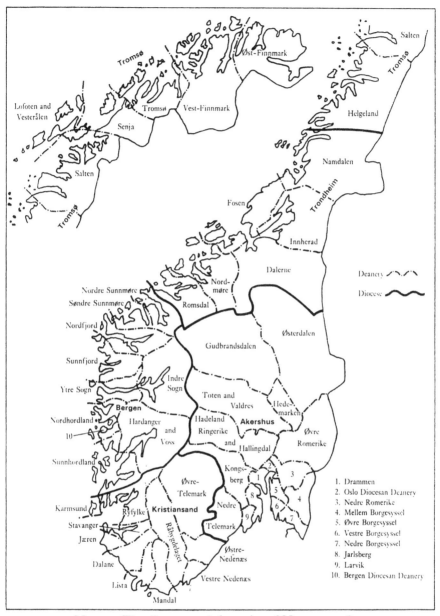

Map 2   The dioceses and deaneries of Norway c. 1850.

Labels on the map:

Salten
Tromsø
Øst-Finnmark
Tromsø
Lofoten and Vesterålen
Senja
Vest-Finnmark
Helgeland
Salten
Tromsø
Namdalen
Fosen
Trondheim
Innherad
Dalerne
Deanery
Diocese
Nordre Sunnmøre
Nord-møre
Søndre Sunnmøre
Romsdal
Østerdalen
Nordfjord
Gudbrandsdalen
Sunnfjord
Indre Sogn
Ytre Sogn
Toten and Valdres
Hede-marken
Bergen
Nordhordland
Hardanger and Voss
Hadeland Ringerike and Hallingdal
Akershus
Øvre Romerike
10
Sunnhordland
Kongs-berg
Øvre-Telemark
Karmsund
Ryfylke
Kristiansand
Nedre
Stavanger
Jæren
Råbygdelaget
Nedre Telemark
Dalane
Østre-Nedenæs
Lista
Vestre Nedenæs
Mandal

1. Drammen
2. Oslo Diocesan Deanery
3. Nedre Romerike
4. Mellem Borgesyssel
5. Øvre Borgesyssel
6. Vestre Borgesyssel
7. Nedre Borgesyssel
8. Jarlsberg
9. Larvik
10. Bergen Diocesan Deanery

Preface

Many of the currently underdeveloped countries have experienced a sharp population rise in recent years. In the past, high crude birth rates—of the order of 40 or more per 1,000 of the population annually—have been matched by almost equally high death rates. The widespread application of the products of western medical science has, however, brought about a dramatic fall in the death rate, especially during the last twenty years. Since birth rates have remained at their traditionally high levels, populations have grown rapidly.

It is still commonly assumed[1] that most western societies had similarly high birth and death rates until the late eighteenth century at least and that when these societies began to display a quickening rate of population growth, it too was caused by a fall in the death rate. Recently this view has been challenged. Studies of eighteenth- and early nineteenth-century population developments in England[2] and Ireland[3] have suggested that *high* birth and death rates were not a universal characteristic of the pre-industrial west, if by *high* we mean 40 or so per 1,000. Indeed, to use Malthusian terminology, it seems that the 'preventive' rather than the 'positive' check may have been the greatest obstacle to population growth: in western societies fertility being limited either through the postponement of marriage or the practice of birth control within marriage,[4] in order to maintain or raise living standards; this control of the birth rate leading in turn to higher per capita incomes and lower death rates.

Such a hypothesis is of more than academic interest for the under-

[1] Carlo Cipolla, *The economic history of world population* (1962), p. 86.
[2] J. T. Krause, 'Changes in English fertility and mortality, 1781–1850', *Economic History Review*, 2nd ser. **11** (1958), 52–70.
[3] K. H. Connell, *The population of Ireland 1750–1845* (1950), *passim*.
[4] E. A. Wrigley, 'Family limitation in pre-industrial England', *Economic History Review*, 2nd ser. **19** (April 1966), 91–8.

developed countries of today, since it suggests that the demographic characteristics of the pre-industrial west probably led to higher standards of living—associated with lighter burdens of dependency, a higher lifetime return from investment in children (since fewer died before they reached working age), and attitudes of mind more conducive to the creation of an industrial society—than do the population mechanisms of many of the countries now at the pre-industrial stage in their development. The high birth and death rates of the latter might be said to have hindered industrialisation, whereas the western demographic traits of two hundred years ago may well have favoured it.[1]

How true a reading this is of population behaviour in the pre-industrial western world *generally* has yet to be ascertained. It is difficult to do this because only occasionally do we have adequate statistical material, whilst that other main source of evidence, the impressions of contemporary observers can be misleading, as will be shown in this study. And even if the hypothesis is broadly confirmed, the details remain obscure. Little is known of the actual levels of the birth and death rate, of the relationship between them, and of their response to economic circumstances. Little is known of the more intimate domestic situations, which they reflect. Such matters as the size and composition of families and households, the age at which children left home and the fate of the aged have only occasionally been discussed in by far the most meaningful way—in quantitative terms. Surprisingly little is known too of the age at marriage, often considered to be the key mechanism determining fertility in pre-industrial western societies. To what extent this varied from region to region and between different social groups are questions that still await definitive answers. They may never be answered fully because they involve the dissection of a society in an area that is particularly hard to reach.

The concern of this present study is with these and allied questions. Norway has been chosen as the field of operations, because within this context it offers three major attractions to the demographic historian. The first lies in the considerable body of population

[1] J. T. Krause, 'Some neglected factors in the English industrial revolution', *Journal of Economic History*, **19** (1959), 528–40.

Preface
statistics in print relating to the pre-industrial period. Norway did
not begin to experience her industrial revolution until the late
1860s. Since the population statistics begin as early as 1735 we can
study in unusual detail and for an unusually long period the population developments of a pre-industrial western society. The second
is the large amount of unprinted material that can be employed to
reveal interesting supplementary information on population conditions. Much of it is used here for the first time, in particular the
exceptionally detailed returns of the 1801 census which enable us
to compare age and social structure as well as nuptiality, fertility
and marital age patterns in various parts of Norway. The third is
the work of Eilert Sundt, a pioneer of empirical sociology. During
the third quarter of the nineteenth century, Sundt made a large
number of studies of Norwegian society, both of a contemporary
and an historical character. These provide the historical demographer
with a rich source of statistical and literary material, most of it as
yet unknown outside Scandinavia.

Readers who are prepared to accept on trust my analysis of the
statistical and literary sources and my presentation of the broad
demographic trends, are invited to proceed immediately to the core
of the work, namely chapters 3–6. Here I attempt to show the inter-
play of marriage, economic circumstances, social custom and
fertility in the century before Norway's industrial revolution.
Summary tables appear in the body of the text. The figures from
which these are derived appear in the statistical appendix, which
also contains a more detailed examination of their strength and
weaknesses. No doubt many readers will be aware of the major
changes in Norwegian orthography over the past hundred years.
For the benefit of those who are not I have followed, in the text,
the somewhat anachronistic practice of using the modern form for
all proper names. References, however, are given in the spelling
of the time when the works appeared.

A large part of this study was presented to the University of
Cambridge as a doctoral thesis in 1964. I am particularly grateful
for the help received from Professor M. M. Postan and Professor
D. V. Glass who supervised this. I would also like to thank the many
people who helped to stimulate and maintain my interest in demo-

Preface

graphic history during and since my undergraduate days, in particular Professor J. D. Chambers, Professor K. H. Connell, Professor D. M. Joslin, Professor John Krause, Professor Oliver MacDonagh, Professor Peter Mathias, Professor Johan Vogt and Dr. E. A. Wrigley. Parts of chapter 1 and virtually the whole of chapter 3 appeared in the *Scandinavian Economic History Review*, for 1965. That part of chapter 2 covering the work of Malthus on Norway together with parts of chapters 4 and 6 appeared in *Population Studies* for 1966. I am grateful to the editors of both these journals for permission to use the same material here. My thanks too, go to the Norwegian and British governments and to the Scandinavian Studies Fund of the University of Cambridge for financial assistance over a number of years. This study was awarded the Ellen McArthur Prize in economic history by the University of Cambridge in 1967. I would like to thank the Managers of the Ellen McArthur Fund for the award and for generously subsidizing the publication of this book. For help and consideration on countless occasions I would like to express my gratitude to the staff of the riksarkiv, the statsarkiv, and the library of the statistisk sentralbyrå in Oslo; to Ingvald and Mary Sørum, Trygve and Unndis Bull, Sølvi Sogner, Ann Zammit and Helge Refsum. I am deeply indebted too to the staff of the Cambridge University Press for their care and understanding of a difficult manuscript. Finally, my thanks go to three people whose patience has been sorely tried by this study: my wife, my friend and colleague Dr J. A. Dowie, who has read the manuscript and done a great deal to improve its form and content, and my secretary, Mrs Carole Phillips, who can now add Norwegian orthography, in all its manifestations, to her many qualifications.

MICHAEL DRAKE

Canterbury, November 1968

I *Problems of the population historian*

History, traditionally viewed, is a literary exercise: 'charm and style'[1] are the hall marks of good historical scholarship. Population history, however, is more for the numerate than the literate, since numbers, not words, are the basic although, of course, not the only material. Without adequate quantitative evidence the demographic historian should not pick up his pen. If he does he will rarely be credible. He might well, of course, be more readable and this is his dilemma: the more statistics he has, the more authoritative his writing becomes and, not infrequently, the more unreadable. But to eschew statistics, to write in the traditional manner, is to contribute little or nothing to the understanding of our demographic past.

It is of course one thing to demand quantitative evidence, quite another to produce it. Population statistics are rarely, if ever, perfect and become less so the further back in time we probe. Yet it is because the success of population history depends so much on the representativeness and accuracy of the statistical material that the demographic historian must needs spend much of his time and energy in assessing its worth.

The value of any statistics depends upon the skill with which they are collected, processed and analysed. Errors are likely to be made during each of these stages and if not spotted may be compounded—possibly with horrendous results.

In the case of population statistics the primary material from which they are derived is collected in two ways: by a census or enumeration at a point in time and by a recording or registration process through time. The demographer takes a census in order to draw up a balance sheet of the various characteristics of the individuals making up the population: age, sex, marital status, occupation, place of residence

[1] Douglass C. North, 'The state of economic history', *American Economic Review*, **55**, no. 2 (May 1965), 86.

and so on. The registration process is used to record, as they happen, the events which bring about population change; births, marriages and deaths being the important ones for most purposes.

Censuses covering all, or almost all, a western country's population were not taken until the eighteenth century, the first being in Iceland in 1703. This was followed by Sweden in 1749, where a unique system was inaugurated which combined the registration and enumeration processes. The kingdom of Denmark–Norway carried out its first census in 1769, the United States in 1790, England and France in 1801. Most other European countries did not begin to take regular censuses until later in the nineteenth century.[1]

These first censuses were a great advance. Inevitably, however, they leave much to be desired. Neither the people who planned them nor those who actually carried them out had any experience of this kind of work. They tended to ask only a limited range of questions and even these were frequently ambiguous. Enumerators were sometimes recruited and paid in ways not likely to enhance their efficiency. The Irish census of 1831, for example, probably resulted in an over-count partly because it was spread over a considerable period of time and partly because the enumerators thought that 'their payment would be in proportion to the number of people included in the returns'.[2] Under, rather than over-enumeration was, however, the main problem of the early census takers. The populace was often suspicious and uncooperative. Poor communications made the task of the enumerators arduous and sometimes even dangerous. Children, particularly those under five years of age, were frequently missed. When ages were asked digital preferences were often very marked. The ages commonly given ended in either a nought or some other even number.

Eight censuses were taken in Norway between 1769 and 1865: two in these years and the others in 1801, 1815, 1825, 1835, 1845,

[1] Excepting the 1665 census of New France. A. M. Carr-Saunders, *World population: past growth and present trends* (Oxford, 1936), pp. 6–8. T. Thorsteinsson, 'The census of Iceland in 1703', *Nordic Statistical Journal*, **8** (1929), 362–70; H. Palmström, 'The census of population in Norway, August 15th 1769', *Nordic Statistical Journal*, **8** (1929), 371–80; H. Gille, 'The demographic history of the northern European countries in the eighteenth century', *Population Studies*, **3** (1949–50), 3–18.
[2] K. H. Connell, *The population of Ireland, 1750–1845* (Oxford, 1950), p. 3.

and 1855.[1] The best were undoubtedly those of 1801 and 1865 as they were the only ones where the enumerators had to record the *name* of each inhabitant together with his or her age, sex, marital status, occupation, position within the household and address.

For the 1801 census considerable pains were taken to see that the instructions were carried out properly, and completed sample forms were sent to each enumerator before the count was taken. The clergy acted as enumerators in the countrysides, the magistrates in the towns. On the question of marital status not only was the enumerator required to find out whether the person was single, married or widowed, but also whether he or she had been married more than once and if so how many times. People temporarily away from the household in which they normally lived, no matter if they were in some other part of the country or overseas, were to appear in the census as if they had been in their normal residence on census day, 1 February.

In the towns the magistrates, accompanied by local registrars, were to visit the heads of each household and obtain the requisite information directly from them. In the countryside the priests were not obliged to visit the different households, but were instead to announce from the pulpit a time and a place at which they would meet the heads of households. Priests were assisted in filling out the census forms by local school teachers and parish precentors.

It was obvious to the organisers of the census that not all these meetings could take place on the one day and that unless care was taken this might well spoil the census. They therefore warned the enumerators specifically to omit from the census children born after 1 February and to make sure not to omit those people who had died after that day. It was also realised that the returning of ages might easily lead to confusion. To avoid this two illustrations of how ages should be recorded were given to guide the enumerators. Thus a new-born child was to be entered as aged one year; a man in his 26th year was to appear as 26, not 25 (i.e. his last birthday).[2]

Despite these precautions, the general failings of census-taking

---

[1] For details of these see Kaare Ofstad, 'Population statistics and population registration in Norway: Part 3, Population censuses', *Population Studies*, 3 (1949–50), 66–75.

[2] A copy of the census schedule together with the instructions to the enumerators is in Wessel Berg, *Kongelige rescripter, resolutioner og collegial-breve for Norge i tidsrummet 1660–1813*, IV, 1797–1813 (Christiania, 1845), pp. 273–80.

in relatively primitive societies appear, although one supposes they were less evident than they might have been. A check of some burial registers for the years immediately after 1801 reveals the deaths of people not recorded in the census.[1] One finds, too, digital preferences leading to the bunching of the population around the ages 10, 20, 30, 40, etc. A large number of men in the valley of Hallingdal chose to return themselves as 36 years of age, possibly because liability for military service ended at that age![2] In spite of these shortcomings, the census of 1801 was far superior to any taken outside Scandinavia either by that date or for many years to come, and the range of detail it supplies allows us to dissect the Norwegian society of the time with considerable precision. It is a great pity that a census of this type was not to be taken again until 1865.

The remaining six censuses were much less satisfactory. None of them were nominative. The enumerators using tally sheets were merely required to return population totals broken down by age, sex, marital status, and occupation. Because no names were required the task of assessing the reliability of these censuses is very difficult. One can fairly safely assume, however, that they covered the population less completely than did the censuses of 1801 and 1865. The two least satisfactory of this non-nominative group of censuses were those of 1769 and 1815. The first of these was taken in August, a month when many people were likely to be away either on the fishing grounds or tending their animals on the high mountain pastures. There appears also to have been quite a widespread fear that the census was a prelude to higher taxation. It was, after all, the first census and it came shortly after a particularly onerous poll tax had been introduced in 1762.[3] This fear, we imagine, must have led to some under-enumeration.

The census of 1815 also appears to have suffered from its timing

[1] Ivar Myklebust, 'Svartedauden, pestår og reproduksjon', *Norsk Historisk Tidsskrift*, **37** (Oslo, 1954–6), 351–2.
[2] Census of Norway 1801. My analysis of enumerators' returns for parishes of Nes and Ål in Hallingdal. These are now in the Riksarkiv, Oslo. For liability for military service see T. R. Malthus, *An essay on population* (Everyman edition, London, 1914), book 2, p. 155.
[3] This led to a serious uprising in and around Bergen in 1765. Karen Larsen, *A history of Norway* (Princeton, 1948), pp. 322–3. About 4,000 regular soldiers were excluded from the census. For a further discussion of this census see notes in statistical appendix.

—just after the Napoleonic wars had ended and during the early days of Norwegian independence. The instructions sent to the enumerators were much less detailed than in 1801 and were sometimes misleading.[1] No particular effort appears to have been made to ensure an accurate count.

For the censuses of 1845 and 1855 the enumerators were provided with a list of all the farms in their district. This had been drawn up for rating purposes in 1839 and obviously reduced the likelihood of entire households being overlooked. The officials in the department of the interior responsible for the publication of these two censuses used the list to check the work of the census-takers. Their comment on the census of 1845 was that the returns showed 'care and accuracy'.[2] Their only comment on that of 1855 was that in the agricultural part of the census, the amount of seed sown and the number of animals on the farms appeared too low.[3] This agricultural section had first been attached to the population census in 1835 and was repeated in 1845 and 1855.[4]

Despite these strictures, leading figures among those who have worked on the early Norwegian censuses have not been sparing in their praise. Eilert Sundt remarked that the more he worked on them the

[1] The schedule and the instructions used in the rural districts appear in *Den norske rigstidende for 1815*, no. 9. The enumerators were asked to place the population in eight-year age groups. A footnote to the schedule—it looks very much like an afterthought—asked that a separate note be made of the number of male and female children under four years of age. An examination of the original returns (now in the riksarkiv, Oslo) reveals that in at least the following parishes the under four-year groups was not included in the under eight-year group: Røyken (Drammens deanery), Spydeberg (Øvre Borgesyssel); Gjerdrum (Øvre Romerike); Botne and Ramnes (Jarlsberg); Solum (Bamble); Manger and Hosanger (Nordhordland); Ona (Nordmøre); Hadsel (Vesterålen); Loppa and Alta-Talvik (Vest-Finnmark). In at least two of these parishes this under four-year group was not included in the population total for the parish as a whole. This made the total for the parish of Spydeberg, 1,656 instead of 1,822 and for Gjerdrum 1,186 instead of 1,297.

[2] Norges officielle statistik, ottende række, *Tabeller over folkemængden i Norge den 31te December 1845 samt over de i tidsrummet 1836–1845 ægteviede, fødte og døde* (Christiania, 1847).

[3] Norges officielle statistik, sextende række, *Tabeller over folkemængden i Norge den 31te December 1855 samt over de i tidsrummet 1846–1855 ægteviede, fødte og døde* (Christiania, 1857). Kaare Ofstad, *op. cit.* pp. 68–70.

[4] O. Vig, 'Nogle ord om folketælling m.m.', *Folkevennen*, 4 (Kristiania, 1855), 306 notes that farmers in 1835 thought the agricultural part of the census was a prelude to new taxation. These fears proved groundless as in 1836 the land tax was abolished. For this reason the agricultural census of 1845 was more complete.

5

stronger his impression of their reliability became.[1] When Anders
Kiær, the first director of the central statistical bureau in Norway,
came to revise the census totals he estimated that the most inaccurate of them all, that of 1815, was no more than 3 per cent
deficient.[2] Gunnar Jahn, another notable director of the bureau,
believes that the deficiency was probably even less than this modest
figure.[3]

The registration of births, deaths and marriages in eighteenth
and early nineteenth-century Europe was usually in the hands of
the clergy. The process of registration began much earlier than the
taking of censuses. In England, Thomas Cromwell ordered all
parish clergy to keep registers of births, deaths and marriages as
early as 1538. Quite a large number of the surviving registers do go
back as far as this, which suggests that his order was effective.
Registration began in France, the Netherlands and Scandinavia in
the seventeenth century.[4] Not until the eighteenth century, however,
were the clergy required to make annual returns of the number of
births, deaths or marriages taking place in their parishes. The first
country to do so was the dual kingdom of Denmark–Norway. Here
we have annual returns of births and deaths from as early as 1735
and, for some parts of the country, even earlier.[5] No attempt was
made to obtain returns in England until the nineteenth century,
although then Rickman sought to obtain retrospective returns from
as far back as the middle of the sixteenth century.[6]

Any registration process is inherently more subject to error than
a census, because it is a continuous process requiring constant
attention. Moreover, a registration system conducted by the clergy
involves snags of its own owing to its usually being based upon
registers of baptisms rather than births, of burials rather than deaths,

[1] Eilert Sundt, *Om dødeligheden i Norge* (Christiania, 1855), p. 23.
[2] Norges officielle statistik. Ældre række, C. no. 1, *Tabeller vedkommende folkemængdens bevægelse i aarene, 1856–1865* (Christiania, 1868-9), p. vii.
[3] Gunnar Jahn, 'Folketellingene 1801 og 1815 og befolknings-forholdene dengang', *Statsøkonomisk Tidsskrift*, **43** (Oslo, 1929), 202.
[4] Paul Harsin and Étienne Hélin, *Actes du colloque international de démographie historique*, Liège, 18–20 April 1963 (Paris, 1963), pp. 185–225.
[5] Manuscript returns for the diocese of Christiania beginning in 1733 are in the statsarkiv, Oslo.
[6] G. Talbot Griffiths, 'Rickman's second series of eighteenth century population figures', *Journal of the Royal Statistical Society*, **92** (1929), 265-8.

and of the marriages of that part of the population belonging to the religious denomination keeping the register. Any increase of non-conformity in a population, as for example occurred in late eighteenth, or perhaps even late seventeenth-century England,[1] will tend to reduce the completeness of registration. Much, too, depends upon the personal commitment of the clergy to what they might not regard as an essential part of their work and if there is a shortage of clergy the difficulty of covering the population effectively will be increased. Such a shortage might well occur if the population increases faster than the establishment of the church, or if it redistributes itself, for example through urbanisation, without a corresponding redeployment of the clergy.[2]

The registration of births, deaths and marriages in Norway from the seventeenth century to the present day has been the responsibility of the clergy of the State Church.[3] Some parsons began to keep registers in the early seventeenth century and all were ordered to do so by a law of 1687.[4] Their task was not easy. Parishes often covered a vast area and as compact nucleated villages were rare, apart from some areas in the west, the population was often widely dispersed.[5]

It was common for the clergy to perform services in different parts of their parishes on different Sundays,[6] but even then some communicants had to travel ten or fifteen miles or even, along the western and northern coasts where many scattered islands were included in the one parish, up to thirty miles.[7] Under such circumstances, it was frequently impossible, especially in the harsh winter months, for children to be baptised soon after birth, although it

---

[1] For eighteenth century, J. T. Krause, 'The changing adequacy of English registration, 1790–1837', in D. V. Glass and D. E. C. Eversley (editors), *Population in history* (London, 1965), pp. 379–93; for the seventeenth century, Michael Drake, 'An elementary exercise in parish register demography', *Economic History Review*, 2nd ser. **14**, no. 3 (April 1962), 427, note 7 and 437, note 2.

[2] J. T. Krause, *op. cit.* pp. 385–6.

[3] For an account of the system see Julie E. Backer, 'Population statistics and population registration in Norway. Part I. The vital statistics of Norway, an historical review', *Population Studies*, **2** (1947–8), 318–38.

[4] Norges officielle statistik, tredie række no. 106, *Oversigt over de vigtigste resultater af de statistiske tabeller vedkommende folkemængdens bevægelse 1866–1885* (Kristiania, 1890), p. 4.   [5] See table 1.1.

[6] H. D. Inglis, *A personal narrative of a journey through Norway, part of Sweden and the islands and states of Denmark* (4th ed. London, 1837), p. 143.

[7] *Ibid.* pp. 61, 144.

7

TABLE I.I   *Distribution of the population amongst the
parishes of southern Norway in 1801**

PARISHES					
Population per sq.km.	Number	Total population	Total area (sq.km.)	Percentage of total population	Percentage of total area
20 and over	20	52,676	2,097	7·8	1·4
15–20	32	88,876	5,187	13·2	3·5
10–15	36	92,439	7,550	13·7	5·1
5–10	74	198,161	28,400	29·4	19·2
1–5	90	241,733	104,762	35·9	70·8

* Calculated from figures of parish areas and populations in Jens Kraft, *Topographisk-statistisk beskrivelse over kongeriget Norge* (Christiania, 1820–35), I–VI. Kraft does not give the areas of parishes in the counties of Nord-Trøndelag, Nordland, and Troms and Finnmark. Even for the rest of the country it is not likely that the areas of the different parishes are strictly comparable, for, on occasion, Kraft excludes from his figures those parts of a parish that were mountainous or uninhabitable. Thus the table gives only the very roughest idea of the population densities of the parishes of southern Norway.

seems every effort was made to do this. Sometimes the baptismal journey proved fatal. On one occasion, for instance, thirty children born in the west coast parish of Volda during the hard winter of 1755 were said to have died because their parents insisted on taking them to church on the day they were born.[1] The clergy were also obviously unable to conduct burial services for all the newly deceased.[2] Sometimes the corpse was buried and the grave filled in, except for the space occupied by a wooden plank extending from the top of the coffin up to the surface of the ground above. On the parson's next visit the traditional Christian service took place with the parson withdrawing the plank and casting into the cavity the symbolic handful of soil.[3] Possibly the bulk of births and deaths were registered but that this was not always the case is indicated by complaints of clergy in the Kristiansand diocese in 1741, that

[1] Hans Strøm, *Physisk og økonomisk beskrivelse over fogderiet Søndmør* (Sorøe, 1762), part I, p. 567. The practice was still followed almost a hundred years after Strøm wrote. See Joh. Gotaas, 'Om spæde børn og om jordemødre', *Folkevennen*, 8 (Kristiania, 1859), 291.
[2] Ingrid Semmingsen, *Husmannsminner* (Oslo, 1960), p. 50.   [3] *Ibid.*

farmers in the more remote valleys were burying their dead without any form of religious service and without informing their priest.[1] To set against these difficulties the Norwegian clergy enjoyed certain advantages not shared, for instance, by the English clergy who were doing comparable work at this time. The Norwegian parson did not have to cope with the rapidly expanding urban populations of industrial workers that over-taxed the English parochial system in the late eighteenth and early nineteenth centuries,[2] for there was comparatively little urbanisation in Norway until the second half of the nineteenth century.[3] Although the population of the country increased from approximately 600,000 in 1735, to 1,700,000 in 1865, 84 per cent still lived in rural areas at the latter date.[4] What towns there were rarely held five-figure populations. Despite rapid growth during the 1840s and 1850s Oslo, the largest town, had only 57,382 inhabitants in 1865 compared with 11,923 in 1801, whilst Bergen, the second largest, had only 27,703 compared with 16,931 in 1801.[5] Together they accounted for one-third of Norway's urban population.[6] Of the thirty-seven other places classified as towns in 1835 only eight had populations over 3,000.[7]

The rapid population growth of the first half of the nineteenth century did, however, greatly exceed the rise in the number of clergy. In 1720 there were, on average, 1,300 people per parson.[8] By 1800 the number had increased to 1,884 and by 1855 to 3,164;

[1] Letter from Bishop Jakob Kærup of Kristiansand to Geheime-Conferentz-Raad J. L. von Holstein, 12 May 1741. A copy of this is to be found in the Christiania Bispearkiv, *Ministerielle forretninger. Innberetninger. Rekke 1. Biskopene 1733–1814*, box 6, now in the statsarkiv, Oslo. The same complaint was made by Niels Ribe, the vicar of Ål in Hallingdal in 1745. Letter in *Kjeldeskriftfondets manuscript No. 181*, Norsk historisk kjeldeskrift-institutt, Oslo.

[2] J. T. Krause, *op. cit.* pp. 385–6.

[3] Of the total population, 9 per cent lived in urban areas in 1769, 10 per cent in 1815, 13 per cent in 1855, 16 per cent in 1865 and 28 per cent in 1900. Norges offisielle statistikk, **10**, 178 *Statistiske oversikter*, 1948 (Oslo, 1949), table 8, p. 31.

[4] *Ibid.*

[5] O. J. Broch, *Kongeriget Norge og det norske folk, dets sociale forhold, sundhedstilstand, næringsveie, samfærdselsmidler og ekonomi* (Kristiania, 1876), tillæg 11, pp. 3–4.

[6] *Ibid.*

[7] Samuel Laing, *Journal of a residence in Norway during the years 1834, 1835 and 1836. Made with a view to inquire into the moral and political economy of the country and the conditions of its inhabitants* (2nd ed. London, 1851), p. 253.

[8] Dagfinn Mannsåker, *Det norske presteskapet i det 19 hundreåret* (Oslo, 1954), tables 5 and 7, pp. 70, 72.

TABLE I.2   *Inhabitants per priest in the*
*Norwegian dioceses 1800–55**

Year	Akershus	Kristian-sand	Bergen	Trondheim	Tromsø	NORWAY
1800	2,081	1,804	1,875	1,825	1,426	1,884
1815	2,263	2,181	2,314	2,297	1,753	2,214
1825	2,952	2,821	3,227	3,138	2,689	2,978
1835	2,588	2,741	2,619	3,026	2,139	2,632
1845	—	—	—	—	—	2,952
1855	3,232	3,492	3,328	2,878	2,645	3,164

* Dagfinn Mannsåker, *Det norske presteskapet i det 19 hundreåret* (Oslo, 1954), pp. 70, 72.

with, as in 1800, the north having a slightly higher proportion of parsons than the south.[1] The difference between north and south was not, however, sufficient to make up for the greater distances and harsher climate encountered by the clergy in the north. On the face of it the increase in population relative to the number of clergy would suggest that the effective registration of births and deaths was becoming more difficult in the second half of the eighteenth and the first half of the nineteenth centuries. Yet it never became an impossible task, for even with the vital rates current in mid-nineteenth-century Norway, one would not expect a population of 3,000 to produce much above 100 births and 60 deaths each year.

In carrying out their registration duties, the Norwegian clergy were not hampered by dissenting congregations, although it is true that from the closing years of the eighteenth century an increasing number of people turned to Hans Nielsen Hauge as he inveighed against the rationalism of many of the state clergy.[2] By the 1830s his followers were said to number 20,000 or 30,000[3] but, as a Scottish observer noted, they were not dissenters or sectarians in the English sense. They were more like 'the evangelical part of the community of the Church of England'.[4] Unlike the English dissenters, who by

[1] Mannsåker, *op. cit.* pp. 70, 72.
[2] Sverre Steen, *Det norske folks liv og historie gjennem tidene*, **7** (Oslo, 1933), 259, 261.
[3] H. D. Inglis, *A personal narrative*, pp. 145–6.   [4] Samuel Laing, *Journal*, p. 124.

absenting themselves from church were an important cause of the
under-registration of births and deaths during the late eighteenth
and early nineteenth centuries,[1] the followers of Hauge were keen
churchgoers and communicants.[2]

An important source of error in the registration system of countries
like England, where the clergy were required to return baptisms
and burials rather than births and deaths lay in the ambiguity surrounding the terms baptism and burial. As Professor Krause has
pointed out, many children in England were baptised privately at
home and not publicly in church. Sometimes these children were
entered in the baptismal registers, sometimes not. Furthermore,
non-baptised persons were not supposed to be given a Christian
burial service and should not therefore have been entered in the
burial registers, although there is plenty of evidence to show that on
occasions they were. The normal time of baptism varied from place
to place and from period to period; thus an indeterminate number
of children were, or were not, baptised before dying, giving rise to
another kind of variation in the completeness of the coverage
afforded by the registration system. Finally, in eighteenth-century
England many parishes had non-resident parsons or parsons holding
several livings. No doubt some of these managed the registration
system adequately, either because they were personally diligent or
because they employed efficient curates. The presumption is, however, that many neglected their duties, both spiritual and secular,
especially in the closing decades of the eighteenth and the opening
decades of the nineteenth centuries.[3]

The Norwegian registration system does not appear to have
suffered badly from such faults. First, the clergy themselves seem
on the whole to have been 'hard working, conscientious and
thoroughly competent'.[4] Samuel Laing, who lived in Norway during
the years 1834-6, accorded them 'the merits of being laborious,
zealous and effective',[5] whilst two other nineteenth-century observers, Andrew Chrichton and Henry Wheaton, remarked that 'the

[1] J. T. Krause, *op. cit.* pp. 387-8.
[2] Sverre Steen, *Det norske folks liv*, **7**, 264.
[3] J. T. Krause, *op. cit.* pp. 386, 388-9.
[4] Sverre Steen, *Det gamle samfunn* (Oslo, 1957), p. 250.
[5] Samuel Laing, *Journal*, p. 126.

Norwegian clergy are a well informed body of men possessing much influence over their flocks, conscientious in the discharge of their duties and diligent in superintending the interests of education'.[1] These testimonials are borne out by the present writer's own experience in examining many of the returns made by the clergy, either in their capacity as registrars of births, deaths and marriages or as census enumerators or respondents to questionnaires issued by government departments or research workers such as Eilert Sundt. These covered an ever-increasing range of subjects.[2]

The efficiency of any registration system also depends to a very large extent upon the support and co-operation of the people whose experiences are being recorded. One advantage of having the registration system in the hands of the clergy was that it then enjoyed the reflected glory of the church and became something of a religious experience. We might expect such a system to operate efficiently amongst people who were diligent in their observance of religious ceremonies. Anything that weakened the hold of religion, or of a particular kind of religion, would on the other hand adversely affect the registration system. This may have happened in England after the civil wars of the seventeenth century since these shook both the authority of the church of England and that of the monarchy.[3] Certainly the rise of new kinds of dissent in late eighteenth-century England reduced the hold of the established church. Quite apart from this, however, there seems to have been in England a decline in religious observance itself amongst some people, many for example being prepared to bury their dead in private burial grounds often without 'benefit of clergy'.[4] Burial in these grounds had the singular advantage of being cheaper than in ones belonging to the church of England. In some places the overwhelming majority of burials took place in private burial grounds. By 1830 for example, over 70 per cent of the burials in Manchester were in such places.[5]

As indicated earlier, the church in Norway does not appear to have lost its hold on the people to anything like the extent it did in

[1] Andrew Chrichton and Henry Wheaton, *Scandinavia ancient and modern: being a history of Denmark, Sweden and Norway* (Edinburgh, 1839), II, 319.
[2] See appendix 2 for examples of these questionnaires.
[3] Michael Drake, *op. cit.* pp. 427, 437.
[4] J. T. Krause, *op. cit.* pp. 389-90.   [5] *Ibid.*

England during the eighteenth and nineteenth centuries. Furthermore, the Norwegian state continued to use its power to support the
edicts of the church, whilst the church in its turn applied religious
sanctions to what would seem to be civil offences. For example, the
state could and did commit to prison with hard labour anyone not
presenting himself for instruction leading to confirmation.[1] Fortunately this rite appears to have been held 'in great consideration'[2]
by the mass of the population, so the sanctions were not invoked
very frequently. Another instance of the state using civil sanctions
for essentially religious offences is indicated by the number of times
Hans Nielsen Hauge and his followers were arrested and punished
under the vagrancy laws.[3] As early as 1682 legal sanctions were
placed on local authorities and the relatives of deceased persons to
ensure that all were given a Christian burial. With the introduction
of the registration of deaths in the eighteenth century further regulations appeared to make certain that all deaths were reported.[4] There
were no similar regulations for births, apart from still-births after
1802, but it has recently been suggested that 'it may be taken for
granted that in the eighteenth and the greater part of the nineteenth
centuries the majority of parents had their children baptised'.[5] The
most notable example of religious sanctions being imposed for civil
offences occurred in 1810. In April of that year a royal order made
vaccination compulsory for all Norwegians. No civil sanctions were
imposed but after that date the church refused either to confirm
or to marry anyone not holding a vaccination certificate.[6]

What has been said so far suggests, I think, that the registration
of births, marriages and deaths in Norway in the years 1735–1865
was reasonably accurate. Certainly it does not seem to have suffered
from any of the major disturbances that appear to have wreaked such
havoc on the English system during roughly the same period. There
is, however, one source of confusion that was not eliminated from
the Norwegian registration system until the present century: the
treatment of still-births. So far as the eighteenth century is con-

[1] H. O. Christophersen, *Eilert Sundt: en dikter i kjensgjerninger* (Oslo, 1962), p. 68.
[2] Samuel Laing, *Journal*, p. 124.
[3] Sverre Steen, *Det gamle samfunn*, p. 64.
[4] Julie Backer, *op. cit.* p. 219.   [5] *Ibid.* p. 218.
[6] O. J. Broch, *Kongeriget Norge*, tillæg v, p. 12.

cerned, we have no clear indication of the general practice. Anders Kiær at one time believed still-births to have been registered as both births and deaths. Later he thought them to have been omitted from both birth and burial registers.[1] Unfortunately, he gave no indication of the reasons for either his first or second opinion. More recently, Halvor Gille has argued that they were omitted from the birth but included in the death registers, basing his opinion upon the supposed position in Denmark.[2] The most recent and authoritative judgement is that of Aksel Lassen, who, after a most penetrating study, has come to the conclusion that while the Danish burial returns should be reduced by as much as 5 per cent or 6 per cent to account for still-births, this is not necessary with the Norwegian. Although he has not examined the Norwegian material as closely as the Danish, he suggests that still-births were kept out of both the birth and burial registers, if not completely, then at least to a much greater extent than in Denmark.[3] From 1802 the clergy were required to return still-births separately, these being defined as children dead at birth or dying within 24 hours of birth. The effect of this regulation was to lower the number of deaths recorded and raise the number of still-births as normally defined.[4]

The second point at which errors enter into population statistics occurs when the raw data are being processed. Often these errors arise from nothing more than simple mistakes of addition or subtraction. In Norway such mistakes were facilitated by the difficulties involved in getting returns sent up through the administrative hierarchy. We do not know the precise date when Norwegian bishops were required to obtain the number of births and of deaths occurring in their dioceses and to submit annual returns to the Økonomie-og-Commerce Collegiet in Copenhagen.[5] We have, however, from 1735 onwards annual totals of births and deaths for all the dioceses of the kingdom of Denmark–Norway. The diocesan totals for the years 1735–84 were first published in the *Materialien zur statistik der*

[1] Norges officielle statistik. Tredie række, no. 106, *op. cit.* p. 8, note 4.
[2] H. Gille, 'The demographic history of the northern European countries in the eighteenth century', *Population Studies*, **3** (1949–50), 16–17.
[3] Aksel Lassen, *Fald og fremgang: træk af befolkningsudviklingen i Danmark 1645–1960* (Aarhus, 1965), pp. 286–7.   [4] Julie Backer, *op. cit.* p. 215.
[5] Norges officielle statistik. Tredie række, no. 106, *op. cit.* p. 4.

Problems of the population historian

Dänischen staaten (Flensburg and Leipzig, 1784–6) (hereafter abbreviated, *Materialien*), whilst totals for the kingdom of Norway (but not for the individual dioceses), in the years 1785–99, first appeared in J. P. G. Catteau-Calleville's *Tableau statistique des états danois* (Paris, 1802). No figures have been published for 1800. From 1801, diocesan and national totals appear in a series of official publications beginning with *Statistiske tabeller for kongeriget Norge. Fjerde række* (Kristiania, 1839). The tables in the *Materialien* and in Catteau-Calleville have been incorporated into the current official Norwegian statistics without amendment. It has been possible to make a partial check of the accuracy of these tables from manuscript material in various Norwegian and Danish archives. Complete details of the errors discovered so far appear in the statistical appendix. Only a brief indication of their possible magnitude will be given here.

Correspondence between Norway and Copenhagen shows that the bishops sometimes sent incomplete returns. For instance, the bishop of Trondheim wrote in 1741, apologising for having sent no returns for 1738, 1739 or 1740 and excusing himself on the grounds that many of his deans had sent none to him.[1] Although still incomplete in 1741 he sent what he had. The return for 1738 was short of totals of both births and deaths for three of the thirteen deaneries, namely Storfosen, Namdalen and Vesterålen. This deficient return appears, however, without comment in the *Materialien* and, therefore, in the current official statistics. Also in 1741 the bishop of Kristiansand wrote to Copenhagen complaining of the difficulties he was encountering in getting returns. He pointed out that the dean of Dalarne had not been able to get figures from one parish because the incumbent had died, nor from another because the incumbent had been suspended from duty, whilst he himself, despite the 'serious reminders' issued, had had nothing whatsoever from the dean of Nedenæs.[2]

Several mistakes appear in the *Materialien*; the results of what is

[1] Letter from Bishop E. Hagerup of Trondheim to Geheime-Conferentz-Raad J. L. von Holstein, 2 June 1741. A copy of this is to be found in the Christiania Bispearkiv, *Ministerielle forretninger. Innberetninger. Rekke 1. Biskopene 1733–1814*. Box 6 in statsarkivet, Oslo.
[2] Bishop Jakob Kærup of Kristiansand, *loc. cit.*

15

sometimes a true 'comedy of errors'. We learn from the bishop of Kristiansand's *Kopibok* that in 1742 there were in his diocese (excepting the deanery of Upper Telemark, for which there was no return), 2,167 births and 3,525 deaths.[1] A manuscript table in the Danske rigsarkiv emanating no doubt from the commerce collegium, gives however, only 1,411 births and 2,578 deaths for that year.[2] On checking with the bishop's *Kopibok* it is clear that these are totals covering only seven of the deaneries in the diocese. In the *Materialien* we find 2,580 births and 14,011 deaths. The typographical link between this latter total and the partial total of births in the rigsarkiv manuscript is obvious. The correction 'reduces' the crude death rate in Norway from over 70 to about 50 per 1,000 mean population in this year.[3]

One other clerical error will suffice to indicate the degree of inaccuracy possible at this particular stage in the compilation of the Norwegian population statistics. The bishop of Bergen enclosed his return of births and deaths for 1741 in a letter sent to Copenhagen in March 1742.[4] There were, it appears, in that year, 2,784 births and 5,030 deaths in the Bergen diocese. The table in the *Materialien* records, however, 2,784 births and 2,746 deaths: the latter figure being, simple arithmetic shows, not the total of deaths but the excess of deaths over births!

Anders Kiær, the first person to calculate birth and death rates for eighteenth-century Norway, was not immune from mistakes when transcribing data from the *Materialien*. One of these occurred when he inadvertently included the totals of births and deaths of the two Icelandic bishoprics (at that time Iceland was a dependency of Denmark) in his Norwegian national totals. Thus, for the years

[1] Kristiansand bispearkiv. *Kopibok no. 10, 1742–44*, pp. 101–2 in statsarkivet, Kristiansand.
[2] Dansk rigsarkiv. *Rtk. 352. 27. Tabelvæsen og statistik.*
[3] See statistical appendix, table 7. Eli Heckscher, 'Swedish population trends before the industrial revolution', *Economic History Review*, 2nd ser. 2 (1950), 268 was unwittingly nearer the truth than he imagined when he observed that in 1742 'in Norway the death rate reached the *almost incredible* figure of 69·3 per 1,000 as compared with the Swedish top figure of 43·7' (my italics).
[4] Bishop O. C. Bornemann of Bergen to Johan Ludvig von Holstein, Copenhagen, 20 March 1742. A copy of this letter is to be found in the Christiania bispearkiv. *Ministerielle forretninger. Innberetninger. Rekke 1. Biskopene 1733–1814.* Box 6 in statsarkivet, Oslo.

1761-9 the current official Norwegian birth and death rates are inflated by between 5 per cent and 10 per cent, and because of the way Kiær calculated rates for the years 1735-60 the error was pushed back in time.[1]

The third and final point at which population statistics are liable to mislead occurs when they are subjected to analysis; for here, unless very great care is taken, much more is read into them than they will bear. Examples of mistakes of this sort abound, since few demographic historians avoid them. An illustration of such an error from a study by Christian Henriksen Pram (1756-1821) indicates how easy and how fatal such mistakes can be. Pram, apart from being a poet and co-editor of *Minerva*, Copenhagen's leading literary magazine, wrote on current population developments in the Scandinavian countries: a task for which, as an important member of the Danish administration concerned with economic affairs, he appeared well qualified.[2] In one study, which appeared in 1809, Pram drew attention to the startling difference in the rate of population growth of two contiguous Norwegian dioceses during the years 1769-1801. According to Pram the censuses held at these dates revealed that whereas the population of the diocese of Bergen rose from 1769-1801 by a mere 0·065 per cent, that of the diocese of Trondheim increased by 52·52 per cent. He ascribed the absence of growth in the Bergen diocese to the mountainous character of the area and the general shortage of cultivable land. The startling increase in Trondheim, he thought, must have been the product of the 'spirit of the people', together with a notable rise in the consumption of potatoes.[3] On the question whether these factors caused the population to grow through a raising of the birth rate or a lowering of the death rate, Pram remained silent. It was perhaps well that he did for the explanation of the gross disparity between the rates of population growth in the two dioceses was neither economic nor social. Pram failed to

[1] Curiously enough, Kiær realised that he had made this mistake for certain years and corrected it, but for the years 1761-9 he failed to see a mistake had been made. See Norges officielle statistik. Tredie række, no. 106, *op. cit.* p. 8, note 4.

[2] *Biographie universelle ancienne et moderne*, **36** (Paris, 1823), 8; Sverre Steen, *Det norske folks liv og historie gjennem tidene*, **8** (Oslo, 1933), 123, 211, 213, 218.

[3] Christian Henriksen Pram, *Om befolkningen i Skandinavien og dens tilvæxt i tidsløbet 1769-1800* (Kjøbenhavn, 1809), pp. 38, 46 and table II at end of Pram's text.

realise that the discrepancy was due to a mistake in the presentation of the results of the 1801 census. Thus the population of the Bergen diocese increased in fact from about 130,000 to 150,000 between 1769 and 1801 instead of, as Pram believed, remaining stationary at the former figure. On the other hand, the population of the Trondheim diocese did not increase from 105,000 to 160,000 between 1769 and 1801, as Pram thought, but only to 138,000.[1]

This review has shown that the Norwegian data are by no means free of the weaknesses commonly found in the population statistics of the pre-industrial western world. On the other hand, our examination of the Norwegian material suggests that in general we can build upon it with some confidence. The smallness of the population, the relative efficiency of the administration and the co-operation of the public appear on the whole to have ensured comparatively complete population statistics and to have reduced the effect of such obvious drawbacks as a harsh climate and a mountainous terrain. This is not to say, of course, that the Norwegian statistics should not be exposed at all times to critical scrutiny. Experience has shown all too conclusively that every new look at them, as indeed with all population statistics, reveals fresh shortcomings.

[1] In presenting the results of the 1801 census the population of the deanery of Sunnmøre was inadvertently included in that of the Trondheim rather than the Bergen diocese. See note on p. 98, C. no. 1. *Tabeller vedkommende folketællingerne i aarene 1801 og 1825* (Christiania, 1874).

2 T. R. Malthus and Eilert Sundt

The demographic historian is rarely satisfied with just presenting the processes of population change in statistical terms. He seeks to explain them; to find out why a population rises or falls; to discover the determinants of the levels and trends of birth and death rates; to understand why in some societies, or in some periods, marriage occurs earlier than in others. To do this he must necessarily draw on the writings and reported opinions of people living in the society and at the time he has chosen to study. Thus, the demographic historian comes up against his second major problem; that of assessing the reliability of contemporary literary, as opposed to statistical evidence.

That there are good reasons for approaching literary evidence cautiously needs to be stressed. In order to indicate the sort of criteria to be adopted in vetting this kind of evidence, the *modus operandi* of two notable commentators on Norwegian population conditions of the period covered by this study will be considered. One, the Reverend T. R. Malthus, enjoys an international reputation. The other, Eilert Sundt, is little more than a name outside Scandinavia. Because some of Sundt's findings are crucial to later sections of this study, and because so little is known of him outside Scandinavia, a few biographical details seem appropriate.

Eilert Sundt was born on 8 August 1817 in Farsund, a small town on the south-west coast of Norway.[1] According to the census of 1815 the town had in that year a population of 560. Sundt's father had been a sailor and for twenty years a ship's captain. By the time Eilert was born—the last of thirteen children—his father had long been settled in Farsund as a small trader and shop-keeper. Eilert's father was neither a particularly successful nor an inspiring

---

[1] The biographical details on Sundt are taken from H. O. Christophersen, *Eilert Sundt: en dikter i kjensgjerninger* (Oslo, 1962), *passim*.

sort of man; certainly not by comparison with his brothers, who had established themselves as merchants a little further along the coast, in Flekkefjord and Stavanger. Fortunately, Eilert's mother was a woman of tremendous energy, allied with an indomitable spirit. A list of her activities makes exhausting reading. With the aid of a single servant girl she cared for her large family, ran a little shop, took in lodgers 'of the better sort', conducted the only bakery in the town, and brewed beer for sale both in the neighbourhood and to the ships that came to it. She had a small farm and a vegetable garden. Each autumn she made sausage and salted meat for the entire year and produced candles both for her own household and for sale. On top of all this she even organised a literary circle, for which Eilert's father acted as librarian.

It seems that Eilert's mother was the driving force behind him. Determined that one of her sons should join the ranks of the Norwegian Lutheran clergy, she made the necessary sacrifices to get him educated, at first privately and then at the grammar school at Stavanger. Sundt proved to be a good scholar and in 1835 came top of the 132 candidates drawn from the entire country, who sat the university entrance examination.

Sundt's university years were eventful. He played a prominent role in the students' union, being twice elected its chairman. He was soon caught up in the surge of national feeling which pervaded student circles in the 1840s. Norway's release from the 400 years of Danish domination in 1814 was still recent. There was a hectic interest in all things Norwegian; in the language, especially the dialects and Old Norse, as well as in history and the literature of the past. This interest was suffused with a love of and a faith in the Norwegian people. Nowhere were these emotions better expressed than in the poetry of Henrik Wergeland. But it was equally strong in Sundt, a disciple and friend of Wergeland, and provided the motive force behind his long series of writings on the customs and conditions of the Norwegian people. It would be wrong, however, to think of Sundt as the narrow nationalist, blind to the world outside Norway and carried away by a romantic attachment to his people and his country. As a student leader he played a major role in 'Scandinavianism', a movement designed to bring together the peoples of the Nordic countries. Against the argument that this would destroy the characteristics of the individual nations, Sundt argued that on the contrary, it would heighten them and bring them into relief. 'Historical conditions', argued Sundt, 'provided a basis for the belief in a living Nordic spirit which, if all the Nordic peoples united together, would be capable of making a contribution both for the benefit of mankind and the Scandinavian countries.'[1] In November 1844 the Norwegian students' union urged the students of Denmark and Sweden to arrange new meetings and celebrations to mark their common values. The text of the invitation largely written, it is believed, by Sundt, is interesting in showing the breadth of his interests and lifts from him the charge of bearing a narrow antiquarian spirit.

Among the students of the Nordic universities there is an ever more living recognition of the fact that their profession as scientific workers calls on them to establish mutual connections so that they may be able, in this modern age, to collaborate and thereby assure to Nordic learning an independent development, and safeguard it from being a mere apprentice of powerful foreign scholarship. In such a mutual connection each single strand will be far from losing its significance—on the contrary, it would make gains for its own country. For the consciousness of its calling will become clearer in this effort to develop the spirit inherited from our fathers, and in the interaction with related peoples—all three seeking to bring the fruits gained into their joint treasure house, and to acquire what the good powers of their brethren had produced—one-sidedness is prevented, and our own strength felt more strongly. If we therefore work on with courage, strength and unity, we may with good confidence hope to be able to contribute not only to the enlightenment of our Nordic fatherlands and to their happiness, but also, in a larger context, to the victory of truth.[2]

Before Sundt launched himself into a comprehensive series of studies of conditions amongst the Norwegian lower classes, he made a thorough survey of much native and foreign literature. He kept up these contacts with the outside world throughout his career. The records of the Oslo University Library show that among the books borrowed by Sundt were the 25-volume *Topographisk journal for*

[1] Martin S. Allwood, *Eilert Sundt, a pioneer in sociology and social anthropology* (Oslo, 1957), pp. 16–17.   [2] *Ibid.* pp. 17–18.

Population and Society in Norway 1735–1865

Norge which came out in the 1790s and Jens Kraft's five-volume *Topographisk-statistisk beskrivelse over kongeriget Norge*, a work of over 4,500 pages which was published at intervals between 1820 and 1835, and remains a major source for Norwegian social and economic historians. Sundt supplemented these writings with a number of regional studies and travellers' accounts dating from the eighteenth and early nineteenth centuries. Amongst foreign statistical works Sundt read Carl af Forsell's *Statistik öfver Sverige* and *Anteckninger öfver Sverige* as well as the *Bidrag til kundskaben om de danske provindser* and Gaspari's *Materialien zur statistik der Dänischen staaten*. He was also an 'ardent reader of the *Journal of the Statistical Society*', *The reports of the registrar general* and of statistical publications from other European countries, particularly Germany, France and Belgium.[1]

Sundt made a particular study of the poor laws of different countries. Notable amongst his reading in this field was the Swedish work *Betänkande angående fattigvården* (1839); the *Reports of the Poor Law Commission* in England; Robert Paschley's *Pauperism and poor laws* (1852); Joseph Kay's *The social condition of the people in England and Europe* (1850). He also borrowed from the University Library C. Th. v. Kleinschrod's *Die neue armengesetzgeburg Englands und Irlands*; Carl Godeffroy's *Theorie der armuth* (1836) and M. T. Duchatel's and F. M. L. Naville's *Das armenwesen* (1842).

Sundt's study of Norwegian demographic problems must be seen against his reading of foreign writings. He studied von Bicke's *Die bewegung der bevölkerung mehrerer europäischer staaten* (1883); Francis d'Ivernois, *Sur la mortalité proportionelle des peuples considerée comme mesure de leur aisance et leur civilisation* (1833); J. Edouard Horn's *Bevölkerungswissenschaftliche studien aus Belgien* (1854) and a number of works by Adolphe Quetelet including his *De l'influence des saisons sur la mortalité aux différents ages dans la Belgique* (1838) and *De la statistique considerée sous la rapport du physique, du moral et de l'intelligence de l'homme*.[2] This list could be lengthened, even from the records of the University Library which, one assumes, was not Sundt's only source of literature.

Sundt did not graduate from the university until 1846, his studies

[1] Christophersen, *op. cit.* p. 107.   [2] *Ibid.* pp. 107–8.

22

having been interrupted by illness and by a certain disinclination to face up to the choice of a career. His course of studies was intended to fit him for a position in the church, but the life of a parish priest did not attract him nor did he wish to follow a purely academic career at the university; although the quality of his work and the result of his degree examination certainly opened the way for him. He wanted something greater, more in keeping with the ideals he had so often expressed in the students' union. He wanted to strike out in new directions, to somehow fulfil the promise of the new independent Norway. 'Are there not energetic young men in Norway', he wrote, 'who are longing for work, who are thinking of something else than following the beaten road of routine living, young and courageous men, whose desire it is to be put before a high and worthy aim?'[1]

The beginning of Sundt's career as a sociologist was inauspicious. He was teaching a sunday school class in the Christiania prison. Amongst the prisoners he noticed one man with 'hair, beard and bushy eyebrows as black as a raven's and a skin...of a darker hue than one finds on a normal sun burned Norwegian face'.[2] This man was a gypsy. He had been sent to prison to be prepared for his confirmation, a punishment at that time for anyone who did not voluntarily present themselves for instruction. Sundt became interested in the man and from him, in the gypsies as a group, in their language and way of life. He began at once to read a large number of foreign works on gypsies, mostly in German, but also including George Borrow's *The Zincali: or an account of the gypsies in Spain with an original collection of their songs and poetry and a copious dictionary of their language.*[3] During the summer of 1847, Sundt took two trips into the Norwegian countryside seeking information about the gypsies. Then, in the spring of 1848, he asked the Norwegian parliament for a research grant so as to continue his studies. Fortunately, the time was propitious. The parliament of 1848 already had two propositions before it concerning gypsies; one demanding a law to curb their activities, the other suggesting a comprehensive enquiry into their condition. The government was, therefore, favourably inclined towards Sundt's proposal and on 12 July 1848

[1] Allwood, *Eilert Sundt*, p. 22.
[2] Cited Christopherson, *op. cit.* p. 68.   [3] *Ibid.* p. 70.

granted him 100 spd. (about £22) for a four-week study tour. Sundt did not confine himself to this short period. He continued his studies and on 3 November 1849 sent his report to the government. The authorities were so impressed by it that they ordered it to be printed at public expense. It appeared under the title *An account of the gypsy or itinerant population of Norway.*

Sundt subtitled his study *A contribution to the understanding of the condition of the lowest orders of society.*[1] This reflected a basic conclusion of the work, namely that the gypsies were part of the Norwegian lower class and that their problems should be seen in this context. It also indicated the nature of his academic and social aspirations. Already in the autumn of 1850 he had made a further application to the government for money to support a long-term enquiry into the conditions of the Norwegian lower classes. Although he did not get the promise of long-term finance—like all governments, that of Norway was loath to commit itself very far ahead—he accepted a grant to run for one year in the first instance. Again, Sundt's application was timely. The census of 1845 had revealed that 46,000 people were either wholly or partly supported by public funds.[2] Although this was less than 3½ per cent of the population, the government was concerned. It was also disturbed by increasing signs of unrest among the lower classes generally, particularly among the cottar class.

Norway had escaped any serious disturbances in the revolutionary year 1848, but the ruling class had nevertheless been shaken by the growth of a radical socialist movement led by Marcus Thrane, onetime editor of the newspaper *Drammens Adresse.* Drawing much inspiration from the English Chartists[3] Thrane travelled throughout Norway in the late 1840s addressing large meetings and forming local socialist societies. At its height, there were over 20,000 members in the movement—the largest Labour party in the world looked at in relation to the population of the country, as Thrane himself remarked.[4] Eventually in the summer of 1851 Thrane was arrested,

---

[1] Eilert Sundt, *Beretning om Fante- eller landstrygerfolket i Norge. Et bidrag til kundskab om de laveste samfundsforholde* (Christiania, 1850).
[2] Christophersen, *op. cit.* p. 81.
[3] Oddvar Bjørklund, *Marcus Thrane: en stridsmann for menneskerett og fri tanke* (Oslo, 1951), p. 25.   [4] *Ibid.*

and remained in prison until July 1858.[1] Although the government crushed the movement—other leaders received even heavier sentences—this did not mean that it was not concerned about the reason for the unrest. Furthermore, the government agreed with Sundt that satisfactory legislation must be based on a thorough knowledge of lower-class conditions, although, as we have seen, it believed that these could be adequately examined in less time than Sundt thought possible.

There were, however, other reasons why Sundt's request was sympathetically received and quickly acted upon. In a speech at Eidsvoll on 17 May 1849, the Norwegian National Day, Sundt had shown himself to be out of sympathy with the Thranist movement. As a Norwegian patriot he could not bear the setting of class against class.

If the tone which is used by several of our popular writers, even by those who have the largest audiences and are perhaps most believed in, if this tone is to permeate from them to the parties, in whose name they claim to be acting, the result will be that every person in the country will consider his neighbour to the right or left as a madman, an unreliable person, a self-seeker, a traitor to his country; if the rich seed of suspicion which is ceaselessly sewn into the soul of the people is to bear as rich a harvest, then there will no longer be trust or faith between man and man—then the nation is demoralised. If this is to happen, I would not hesitate to say: grant that my people had never been brought out of the condition of political innocence that prevailed under Christian VII! Would that May 17, 1814, and all its work had never taken place![2]

On top of this, Sundt disapproved of the materialism of the movement, partly on Christian grounds, but partly perhaps because he himself had a certain ascetic temperament. All his life he spurned the accepted social goals, the professorial chair, the rich parish living. Yet Sundt had a tremendous empathy for the Norwegian people, especially for the small farmers, the poverty-stricken cottars, the fishermen of the west coast, the growing, if still small, proletariat of the towns. This feeling was recognised by the objects of his concern, so that by travelling thousands of miles and conducting hundreds of interviews, Sundt was able to get a much deeper understanding of lower-class culture than perhaps any Norwegian before or since.

[1] *Ibid.* p. 318.   [2] Cited in Allwood, *Eilert Sundt*, p. 28.

Several aspects of Sundt's mode of enquiry have already been mentioned. First he read widely in the secondary literature on whatever subject concerned him, not only amongst Scandinavian authors, but also amongst French, German and English. Second, he was very conscious of the need for all possible quantitative precision. In all his writings, the statistical analysis provides a basic framework. The abundance of statistical material in Sundt's work, invaluable as it was, unfortunately reduced his readership and this was a major source of disappointment to him. It is indicative, however, of the high standards of scholarship he set himself, that despite his deep desire to educate ordinary men and women through his writing (to which end he indulged in a simple style lardered with analogies drawn from everyday life) he never gave way to the temptation of glossing over the complications, of making easy generalisations or propounding jejune solutions. A further element in Sundt's method was his belief in field work. During the six and a half years from December 1850 to the summer of 1857 Sundt reckoned that he was travelling for 754 days.[1] He wandered across the entire country, interviewing farmers, cottars, labourers, teachers, clergy, indeed anyone who might throw some light on the problems he was examining. Sometimes he stayed with members of the clergy, or other government officials but often he lodged in farms and labourers' cottages. Finally, and perhaps the most important feature of Sundt's work was the eagerness with which he approached his task and the devotion he accorded to it. This is illustrated by his reaction on hearing that his request for a research grant had been met.

On 19 December [1850] I learnt of the royal edict granting me 500 spd. for a year. On 20 December I set out on my travels with a knapsack on my back. I journeyed to Bærum's ironworks and visited some of the workers there; that first night I slept with them. At that time Marcus Thrane's labour agitation was in full spate and I talked about it with all the members of the working class that I met. From Bærum I went to the vicarage at Asker and the reverend Lange was the first who extolled my undertaking: namely to go around, using my own eyes and ears, to satisfy myself about the condition of the common people.[2]

[1] Christophersen, *op. cit.* p. 97.   [2] Cited in Christophersen, *op. cit.* pp. 95–6.

T. R. Malthus and Eilert Sundt

Sundt published his first major work—*An account of the gypsy or itinerant population of Norway*—in 1850. His last—*On domestic life in Norway*—appeared in 1873.[1] To classify the large number of studies written between these dates is difficult because Sundt whilst ostensibly writing on one subject would always draw attention to its links with others. The close interdependence of all facets of human culture was a point made over and over again by Sundt. Thus in his studies on marriage in Norway he not only drew attention to the more obvious factors affecting the number of marriages and the age at marriage at any one time, e.g. contemporary happenings (war, food shortages, business conditions); the underlying age structure of the population and its causes; or the economic and social demands of a prospective 'groom or bride in different communities (fishing, pastoral, arable) and occupational groups (farmers, farm labourers); he also demonstrated how the design of houses and the means of heating them had an influence on the relations between the sexes and how in turn this affected the marital age pattern.[2] His works on the state of morality in Norway, whilst they reflect the general concern at the number of unmarried mothers and illegitimate children in the country, do not have that censorious tone that was so common in the writings of Sundt's contemporaries. Rather Sundt tries to explain why illegitimacy or drunkenness was so much higher in some districts than in others in terms of working conditions, domestic life and social heritage.[3] Even in such a study as that of the prevalence of foreign and double-barrelled christian names amongst the farming community Sundt attempts to show the links between the differences in this regard and those of other social or economic phenomena.[4]

Much of Sundt's work appeared either as articles in, or supplements to, *The People's Friend*, a journal published by the *Society for the promotion of popular enlightenment*. Sundt had helped to found this society, which began its work in 1852, although he was

---

[1] For a list, in English, of Sundt's major writings see Allwood, *Eilert Sundt*, pp. 110–11.
[2] Eilert Sundt, *Om giftermaal i Norge* (Christiania, 1855): 'Bygde-skikke', *Folkevennen*. 11 (Kristiania, 1862). *Om sædeligheds-tilstanden i Norge* (Christiania, 1857).
[3] Eilert Sundt, *Om sædeligheds-tilstanden i Norge* (Christiania, 1857, 1864, 1867); *Om ædrueligheds-tilstanden i Norge* (Christiania, 1859).
[4] Eilert Sundt, 'Sprogets bygde-skikke', *Folkevennen*, 13 (Kristiania, 1864).

not a prominent member for some years.[1] In 1858 however he
became chairman of the society and editor of its journal. The circulation of *The People's Friend* rose to over 4,000 under Sundt's
editorship.[2] Its readership was overwhelmingly middle class.[3] That
it never reached the 'ordinary' farmers and work people was a
source of much regret to Sundt, as indeed it was to many members of
the society.[4] Sundt, like the first editor Ole Vig, had difficulty in
finding copy for the journal with the result that in some issues
half or more of the contents had to be written by him. Sometimes
he produced extended essays over several issues, as for example his
detailed analysis of life in the west coast parish of Haram.[5] Often,
however, Sundt wrote masterly vignettes covering only a few pages,
as for example his analysis of the position of some hand sawyers
near Mandal facing the competition of the steam-driven saw,[6] or his
examination of politeness amongst the farming population of
Guldalen,[7] a parish in the Trondheim diocese.

Sundt's work was financed by regular grants from the Norwegian
parliament from 1850 to 1869. In the latter year a motion that the
grant should be continued was defeated by four votes (51–47).[8] It
was felt by many that Sundt had done all that was needed, and what
remained could be looked after by government departments. More
important, perhaps, was the growing animosity towards Sundt
amongst many professional people, particularly doctors.[9] They felt

[1] He was elected to the committee in 1852 and again in 1854. In the latter year he polled
the least number of votes of those elected (*Folkevennen*, 4, Kristiania, 1855, p. 52).
Sundt took a leading part in a discussion organised by the Society on elementary
schools in Kristiania on 24 April 1855 (*Folkevennen*, 4, Kristiania, 1855, pp. 199–200).
He topped the poll in elections for the committee and became chairman on the
incumbent, Hartvig Nissen, declining to continue (*Folkevennen*, 6, Kristiania, 1857,
p. 65).
[2] The society had 2,518 members in 1853, 2,962 in 1857 and 4,266 in 1862. 'Om vort
selskab', *Folkevennen*, 11 (Kristiania, 1862), p. 576.
[3] *Ibid.* p. 569 for a breakdown of membership by occupation.
[4] 'Eilert Sundt, "Folkevennens første ti Aar"', *Folkevennen*, 10 (Kristiania, 1861),
p. 646.
[5] Eilert Sundt, 'Harham. Et exempel fra fiskeri-distrikterne', *Folkevennen*, 7 (Kristiania,
1858), pp. 329–424; *Folkevennen*, 8 (Kristiania, 1859), pp. 2–47.
[6] Eilert Sundt, 'Arbeidsvæsen. 1. Haandsagen', *Folkevennen*, 13 (Kristiania, 1864),
pp. 329–40.
[7] 'Eilert Sundt, "Bygde-skikke. Første stykke"', *Folkevennen*, 7 (Kristiania, 1857),
pp. 17–56.
[8] Christophersen, *op. cit.* p. 310.   [9] *Ibid.* pp. 284 ff.

that his analysis of lower-class conditions in rural Norway gave support to reactionary elements. By explaining habits and customs, by setting them in a comprehensive cultural context, Sundt appeared often to be defending the indefensible. To this Sundt could only reply that throughout his career he had tried to understand lower-class behaviour and had come, after painstaking study, to the view that much of it was far less reprehensible than the urban middle class supposed. That he failed to swing influential public opinion to his view not only explains the rather abrupt and ignominious ending to his life's work, but also the fact that he had no immediate followers. Nineteenth-century Norwegian sociology blossomed and died prematurely with Sundt.[1] The subject can hardly be said to have revived until after the second world war.

Setting Malthus off against Sundt serves to spotlight both the weaknesses of the Malthusian mode of enquiry and the strengths of Sundt's own methods. An examination of Malthus's views on Norway is also of interest for its own sake. For in Norway Malthus discovered the enormous power of the 'preventive' check to population growth. This helped to make the second and subsequent editions of his *Essay on the principle of population* somewhat less sombre than the first.

The entry of Malthus into the field of population studies is well known. The son of a moderately prosperous landowner, Malthus took exception to his father's endorsement of the views of Godwin and Condorcet on the perfectability of man. In 1798 he produced his *Essay on the principle of population as it affects the future improvement of society with remarks on the speculation of Mr Godwin, M. Condorcet and other writers*. It was brief and polemical, but it had an immediate appeal to an England harassed both intellectually and politically by the French revolution and concerned at rising food prices and soaring poor rates. The core of the Malthusian position appears in the following quotations from the first edition of the Essay.

I think I may fairly make two postulata. First, that food is necessary to the existence of man. Secondly, that the passion between the sexes is necessary and will remain nearly in its present state.

[1] For a recent view of Sundt's place in Norwegian sociology see Nils Christie, *Eilert Sundt som fanteforsker og sosialstatistiker*, Institute of Sociology, University of Oslo, Stencil series (Oslo, 1958).

29

Assuming then, my postulata is granted, I say, that the power of population is indefinitely greater than the power in the earth to produce subsistence for man. . .Population when unchecked, increases in a geometrical ratio. Subsistence increases only in an arithmetical ratio. A slight acquaintance with numbers will shew the immensity of the first power in comparison of the second.

By that law of our nature which makes food necessary to the life of man the effects of these two unequal powers must be kept equal.[1]

These two unequal powers were kept in equilibrium by what Malthus called 'positive' and 'preventive' checks. By the positive check Malthus meant 'the check that represses an increase which is already begun',[2] e.g. war, epidemics, famine. On the other hand 'a foresight of the difficulties attending the rearing of a family'[3] and the fear of dependent poverty acted as a 'preventive' check, in that it delayed entry into marriage and, therefore, the period of time in which a married couple were exposed to having children.

Malthus admitted in the preface to his first edition that 'the essay might, undoubtedly, have been rendered much more complete by a collection of a greater number of facts in elucidation of the general argument'.[4] To remedy this omission Malthus began to read extensively and when books were not available, to travel in the areas concerned. Thus in 1799 he joined a small party of friends from Jesus College, Cambridge, of which he was a fellow, in a 'summer excursion'[5] to northern Europe. The countries to be visited were, in the words of William Otter, one of Malthus's travelling companions and at that time senior tutor of Jesus, 'precisely those in which the state of society was less known and the details required [for Malthus's researches] less likely to be obtained from native authors'.[6]

The party of four left England in May 1799 and reached the Wenner Lake in central Sweden by 20 June having travelled via Hamburg, Copenhagen and Gothenburg. There Malthus and Otter decided they had neither the time nor the money to complete the

---

[1] Kenneth E. Boulding (ed.), *Thomas Robert Malthus, Population: the first essay* (Ann Arbor, 1959), pp. 4, 5.   [2] *Ibid.* p. 25.
[3] *Ibid.* p. 31.   [4] *Ibid.* p. xiii.
[5] T. R. Malthus, *An essay in the principle of population* (Everyman edition, 1914), book 2, chapter 1, p. 153, note 3.
[6] William Otter, *The life and remains of the Rev. Edward Daniel Clark LL.D., professor of mineralogy in the University of Cambridge* (London, 1824), p. 338.

journey they had originally planned with Daniel Clarke, another fellow of Jesus, and John Marten Cripps, his pupil. So the party divided, Clarke and Cripps carried on through Sweden to Lapland; Malthus and Otter proceeded directly into Norway, entering by the fortress town of Halden. From there they travelled through Østfold to Moss, where they took a boat up the fjord to Oslo, then a small provincial town of about 10,000 people. From Oslo they went north to Trondheim by the road which runs along the eastern shore of Lake Mjøsa, up Gudbrandsdalen and over the Dovrefjell. After spending some time in Trondheim they turned south-eastward to Røros and Østerdalen, finally entering Sweden near Kongsvinger.[1]

During his six-week stay, Malthus travelled through some 600 miles of Norway. He saw some of the richest parts of the country but none of the coastal areas, where a large proportion of the population lived, apart from the small parts of the Oslo and Trondheim fjords near the two towns from which they take their names. His stay, then, was comparatively short and his itinerary somewhat circumscribed.

Malthus gathered a great deal of information about Norway from the people he met. In assessing the value of this information it is necessary to ascertain both the background and the attitudes of these informants. Fortunately, we now know a great deal about them through the recent discovery and publication of the diary kept by Malthus during his journey.[2] As one might have anticipated, Malthus's contacts were limited by linguistic and social factors. He spoke English and French, but not Norwegian, Danish or German. His letters of introduction were to the heads of the military and civil administration as well as to certain merchants and gentry with English connections. Most of the conversations which are recorded in the *Journal* and transcribed, often virtually verbatim, into the second and subsequent editions of the *Essay* took place in either Oslo or Trondheim. Thus in Oslo he talked with the prominent merchant, Bernt Anker and his brother Peder Anker, who at that time was the superintendent of roads in southern Norway. He also met

[1] A detailed account of the tour is to be found in Patricia James (ed.), *The travel diaries of T. R. Malthus* (Cambridge, 1966), pp. 24–219.

[2] And the meticulous editing of Patricia James, *ibid.* pp. 24–219.

John Collett, who had a model estate on the outskirts of Oslo and who was one of the more important representatives of that small band of gentry in Norway given to agricultural improvement. Malthus stayed just over a week in Trondheim and there met Count Gerhard Moltke, the provincial governor; General Georg Frederick von Krogh, commandant in Trondheim; Mr Knutson, a merchant, and Madam Lysholm, a merchant's widow who spoke 'middling French'.[1] Both in Oslo and in Trondheim Malthus met a number of other people who appear in the *Journal* simply as 'a Major of the Chasseurs',[2] an army officer who spoke English 'remarkably well',[3] the 'daughter of the landlord of our inn',[4] 'another gentleman',[5] or 'a merchant to whom we had a letter'.[6] He does not appear to have met a single clergyman. Possibly this was because whereas the merchants had connections with England and probably spoke some English, whilst the military men and the civil servants would normally speak French, the Lutheran clergy of the Norwegian state church spoke German, a language Malthus did not understand, and moreover had few if any contacts with England. That Malthus did not meet the clergy was singularly unfortunate for, as we have noted, they were responsible for making population returns and probably knew more than anyone about Norwegian demographic behaviour.

The final, and potentially most fruitful of his contacts, was Frederick Thaarup, who had been professor of statistics at the university of Copenhagen from 1793 to 1797. After a quarrel with his academic colleagues there, he had taken the post of sheriff of Solør and Odalen. It was here that Malthus, on the eve of his departure for Sweden, met him. Malthus had bought a copy of Thaarup's work *Udførlig veiledning til det Danske monarkies statistik* (Kjøbenhavn, 1794), possibly in the German translation, *Versuch einer statistik der Dänischen monarchie* (Kjøbenhavn, 1796), for Malthus confessed to Thaarup that 'he had purchased his work... even though we did not understand Danish or German'. As we shall see, Malthus was to use Thaarup's work in his analysis of

[1] Patricia James, *op. cit.* p. 150. [2] *Ibid.* p. 174.
[3] *Ibid.* p. 95. [4] *Ibid.* p. 102.
[5] *Ibid.* p. 172. [6] *Ibid.* p. 158.

Norwegian population conditions. The actual meeting with Thaarup was, however, a disappointment and at the end Malthus confessed that he 'could not get much out of the professor in the way of information'.[1]

This disappointment with the results of his conversations was not confined to the one case of Professor Thaarup. On another occasion in the *Journal* Malthus remarked ruefully that 'in general I have found the gentlemen whom I have talked with either unable, or unwilling to answer the questions I have asked; but very willing to run on into long discussions of their own'.[2]

Although these 'upper-class' figures were the main source of Malthus's information on Norway they were supplemented by some conversation with farmers, post-house keepers and even a family of Lapps. With these people Malthus had to draw on the services of his servant as interpreter. On the whole Malthus was satisfied with this man's work, but he admitted with particular reference to his talks with the Lapps (though one suspects it had a wider relevance) that 'there were many more questions that we wished to ask, but our servant naturally thought so many questions trifling & foolish & shewed a little unwillingness to repeat them'.[3]

In reading the *Journal*, one cannot help marvelling at Malthus's energy and inquiring spirit. He not only talked with and listened to a great number of people, he also kept his eyes open noting the changing nature of the landscape, the conditions of the people he met, what they were eating, how they were dressed, and what their houses were like, what they were growing in their fields, and so on. On the other hand, he made no systematic quantitative study. His pages are filled with odd prices or weights, the numbers of sheep or cattle on particular farms, but they appear rather haphazardly, the product, one suspects, of the half-hour wait for horses or of a chance meeting.

Apart from these conversations and impressions, Malthus's account of Norwegian population conditions is informed by two other sources; first, the statistical data gleaned from Thaarup's work, and second, his conviction of the rightness of the 'principle

---

[1] *Ibid.* pp. 208–9.   [2] *Ibid.* p. 117.
[3] *Ibid.* p. 195.

of population' which provided the organisational framework of his study.

Malthus began his chapter entitled 'Of the checks to population in Norway' with the statement that:

In reviewing the states of modern Europe, we shall be assisted in our enquiry by registers of births, deaths and marriages, which when they are complete and correct, point out to us with some degree of precision whether the prevailing checks to population are of the positive or preventive kind...

Norway during nearly the whole of the last century [the eighteenth], was in a peculiar degree exempt from the drains of people by war. The climate is remarkably free from epidemic sicknesses; and, in common years, mortality is less than in any other country in Europe, the registers of which are known to be correct. The proportion of the annual deaths to the whole population, on an average throughout the whole country, is only 1 to 48. Yet the population of Norway never seems to have increased with great rapidity. It has made a start within the last ten or fifteen years; but till that period its progress must have been very slow, as we know the country was peopled in very early ages, and in 1769 its population was only 723,141.

Before we enter upon an examination of its internal economy, we must feel assured, that as the positive checks have been so small, the preventive checks must have been proportionately great...[1]

Malthus appears to have made this diagnosis almost before reaching Norway, for early on in his *Journal* he writes of the Norwegian population 'increasing so slowly though the people live so long'.[2] It is not surprising therefore that the burden of Malthus's chapter on Norway should be the operation of the preventive check in that country. Nor, in view of the large number of military men he met, is it surprising that he should begin his analysis with a consideration of the role played by the regulations governing recruitment to the Norwegian army.

According to Malthus, the sons of all Norwegian farmers and farm labourers were liable for military service. Commanding officers could pick men of any age below 36 years. Usually they preferred to take men between the ages of 25 and 30, in the belief that

[1] T. R. Malthus, *An essay on the principle of population*, book 2, chapter 1, p. 155.
[2] Patricia James, *op. cit.* p. 89. Malthus entered Norway on 23 June. This entry appeared in the *Journal* on 24 June.

Norwegians did not attain their full strength until then. Once enrolled a man could not marry without the permission of his commanding officer and his parish priest, both of whom had to be satisfied that he could support a wife and family. The length of service was ten years and, as the eldest were customarily taken first, 'it would often be late in life before they could feel themselves at liberty to settle'.[1] There was no law to prevent a man from marrying before he was drafted, but in such a case a priest might refuse to marry him if he thought he was unable to support a family. Malthus obviously approved of these arrangements and was distressed to find that just before his visit they had been abandoned: the youngest men were to be drafted first and there were to be no restrictions on marriage. Many Norwegians whom he met apparently shared his concern and were of 'the opinion that the peasants will now marry too young and that more children will be born than the country can support'.[2]

There may have been some substance in the view that the old system of army recruitment discouraged some people from marrying at an early age. But it is also possible to argue that it had exactly the opposite effect, for Malthus did not tell the whole story. According to another source the bulk of the Norwegian army in the eighteenth century was organised on a militia basis.[3] Training occupied a number of weeks each year usually in the summer, over a period of twenty years. Round the year training in barracks was unusual. To obtain the required number of troops all the Norwegian farms were divided into small groups, known as *legder*. Each *legd* had to produce one soldier.[4] Single men were usually enrolled first, to obviate the possibility that the families of married men would become a public charge. Naturally, farmers had no desire to lose their sons or their more experienced farm labourers just at the time of year when they were most useful. To avoid this, they would, on occasion, provide them with land so that they might marry and have a family, so encouraging earlier marriage. One writer,[5] indeed, has ascribed at least a part of the allegedly rapid increase in the number

[1] T. R. Malthus, *op. cit.* p. 155. [2] *Ibid.* p. 156.
[3] S. Skappel, *Husmandsvæsenet i Norge* (Kristiania, 1922), p. 58.
[4] *Norway. Official publication for the Paris exhibition 1900* (Kristiania, 1900), p. 295.
[5] S. Skappel, *op. cit.* p. 58.

of crofts in Norway during the eighteenth century to this system of army recruitment. What statistical evidence we have, however, suggests that neither the old nor the new system had much effect on nuptiality or fertility. The prominence given to this factor by Malthus, as we have noted already, can probably be ascribed to the frequency with which his military hosts brought up the matter in conversation.[1]

The impact of Malthus's itinerary and of his rather eclectic method of collecting information is apparent in other parts of his analysis. For example, he noted that there was 'in every establishment [a] proportion of servants...two or three times as great as in England; and a farmer who is not to be distinguished from any of his labourers will sometimes have a household of twenty persons including his own family'.[2] The source of this figure twenty appears in the *Journal*. It came from the one farm where Malthus made a count! He did so because he happened to notice on this particular farm, where he had taken a night's lodging, 'seven men eating a most comfortable breakfast of fried bacon & veal, some fried fish, large bowls of milk & oat cake & butter...'[3] Malthus 'enquired of the master of the house afterwards whether they were all his men—he said they were, and lived in his house, besides others. He had, he said, 20 altogether in family, tho he had but little ground round the house, but a farm higher up the country. None of the men that lived with him were married. We did not learn how they were employed. The appearance of the master was quite that of a common peasant.'[4] As will be shown later, a household of this size, with as many as seven unmarried male servants was quite exceptional in Norway at this time. Certainly it was so outside the ranks of the gentry or of the civil or ecclesiastical members of the administration. A survey of 1,738 households in 1801, drawn from three different areas of Norway (the parishes of Nes and Ål in Hallingdal; Nes and Ringsaker in Hedmark and Herøy in Sunnmøre),

---

[1] Patricia James, *op. cit.* pp. 89, 103, 119, 152, 169, 173. However, one officer, Peter Vogt Nielsen, who commanded a detachment of the Danish hussars in Christiania, told Malthus that the asking permission 'to marry of the officer was merely a ceremony, and that it was hardly ever refused' (p. 119).

[2] T. R. Malthus, *op. cit.* pp. 157–8.

[3] Patricia James, *op. cit.* p. 142.   [4] *Ibid.*

revealed not one household with as many as twenty members. Furthermore, 60 per cent of the Hallingdal farmers, 49 per cent of those in Nes and Ringsaker and 44 per cent of those in Herøy had no servants living in, either male or female. (Table 5.16 below.)

Since Malthus was convinced, almost before reaching Norway that the positive check was weak in that country, he paid little attention to it. The source of his conviction was the ratio taken from Thaarup of deaths to total population, namely 1:48. He failed, however, to look at this ratio in conjunction with that of births to total population (1:34) which was also given by Thaarup.[1] Had he done so he would have realised that the combination of the two would have led to a doubling of Norway's population within 77 years. In other words, the population was growing by 0·9 per cent per annum. This rate of growth makes nonsense of Malthus's claim that 'the population of Norway never seems to have increased with great rapidity'. It makes even greater nonsense of his assertion in the first edition of the *Essay* that 'the principal states of modern Europe...require at present...three or four hundred years or more' to double their numbers.[2]

The origin of Malthus's error here appears to be the failure to recognise or, if he recognised, to draw the obvious conclusion: that the ratio 1:48 applied only to the years 1775–84. As it happens, these were years when the death rate in Norway was below normal. Furthermore, these years were free from the sharp fluctuations in the death rate, so characteristic of eighteenth-century Norway. A ratio of 1:48 gives a rate of just under 21 per 1,000 per annum. The most recent calculation of the mean crude death rate in the years 1775–84 is 23 per 1,000. In none of these years did the death rate rise above 27. Yet, in 1741 it had risen as high as 41, in 1742 even higher to 52, and had touched 36 in 1763 and 47 in 1773. It was over 30 per 1,000 in 1748, 1785 and 1789. The death rate was generally low in the 1790s but rose in the opening years of the nineteenth century, touching 36 per 1,000 in 1809. These are national aggregates and regional figures reveal even greater fluctuations and higher levels. For ex-

[1] Fr. Thaarup, *Udførlig veiledning til det Danske monarkies statistik* (2nd ed. Kjøbenhavn, 1794), p. 447.
[2] Boulding, *op. cit.* p. 22.

ample, in 1742 the crude death rate in the south-eastern diocese of Akershus, which covered most of the country where Malthus did his travelling and which at the time embraced approximately 40 per cent of the country's population, reached 67 per 1,000. In 1773—barely twenty-five years before Malthus's visit—this same area experienced a death rate of 64 per 1,000 and was to suffer one of 56 per 1,000 as late as 1809.[1]

That Malthus failed to see the important role of the positive check in Norway's demographic history is doubly ironical. First, because it was a fall in mortality which propelled Norway into half a century of very rapid population growth after 1815. Second, and perhaps more important, because it exposed the weakness of his research method. This is brought out clearly in the one passage where Malthus indicates that in at least some parts of Norway the positive check operated with some force. In a lengthy and in many ways perceptive analysis of the difficulty of making a livelihood sufficient to maintain a family in the interior of the country, Malthus pointed out that Norway had no large towns offering industrial employment whilst in the countryside pastoral and forest interests opposed the setting up of new households. This was because a new household would necessarily involve a reduction of the forests as wood was taken for building or fuel, as well as an encroachment on the lowland areas used for growing hay.[2] However, Malthus argued, 'on the sea coast where on account of the hope of an adequate supply of food from fishing the preventive check does not prevail in the same degree, people are very poor and wretched; and they are in comparison in a worse state than the peasants in the interior of the country'.[3] Malthus did not, in fact, visit the western or the northern coasts of Norway where it is true fishing was the main source of livelihood. His information on the matter came from an after-dinner conversation in Trondheim, possibly with Count Gerhard Moltke.[4] He did not use any statistical material to support

---

[1] Statistical appendix, table 7.
[2] T. R. Malthus. *op. cit.* p. 161.   [3] *Ibid.* p. 158.
[4] Patricia James, *op. cit.* p. 153. Malthus wrote in his journal—'the people on the sea coast are the poorest & suffer the most. They in general marry very young & have large families which they hope to support by fishing, and in a bad year, when the fisheries are unsuccessful they are reduced to extreme poverty. The people in the interior parts

his assertion and had he had such material he would have found his *a priori* assumptions shaken in several ways. First, he would have discovered that neither the evidence of the census of 1769 nor of that of 1801 showed marriage to be earlier or nuptiality and fertility higher along the western coasts from Hordaland to Sunnmøre than in the landlocked areas of the east through which he had travelled.

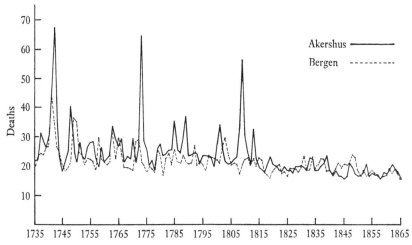

Fig. 1. Deaths per 1,000 mean population in the dioceses of Akershus and Bergen 1735–1865.*

* Statistical appendix, table 7.

Second, he would have discovered that the crude death rate in the diocese of Akershus—an area covering mostly inland areas—had been much higher in certain years than in the primarily coastal area embraced by the Bergen diocese.[1] Between 1735 and 1815 the crude death rate in the Bergen diocese never rose above 45 per 1,000 and seldom above 30. By contrast, it rose in the Akershus diocese to about or above 60 per 1,000 in three years (1742, 1773 and 1809) and was above 30 in another eleven (Fig. 1).

Some years after Malthus's visit, a Scottish resident in Norway

of the country seldom marry till they can get a place in which they can support a family, and this does not happen while they are very young, particularly as they in general wish to be quite free with respect to the military before they settle themselves.'

[1] See below, chapter 4.

39

remarked that travellers were 'very like the swallow, skimming over the land by day, roosting under the roofs by night, and returning home very little the wiser for [their] flight'.[1] This might seem an unnecessarily harsh judgement on Malthus's visit. Yet his writing in the *Essay* and more particularly in the *Journal*, suggests that he missed essential features of the Norwegian demographic experience and so misinterpreted it, by failing to overcome the bias of his itinerary, his contacts, his preconceived notions and his qualitative approach to an essentially statistical problem.

Eilert Sundt began his life's work almost half a century after Malthus. He was thus able to draw on a much wider range of authorities and upon a far more complete set of statistical sources. Inevitably, his interpretation of the Norwegian demographic scene was more accurate and more detailed than that of Malthus, but this was not simply due to the difference in the timing of the two men's work or to the fact that Malthus spent but six weeks in Norway whilst Sundt spent a lifetime. The basic difference lies in the fact that as Professor Hillman has pointed out, Sundt's work was 'empiric; not that of building a theoretical system'.[2] Malthus approached Norway with a theory; an explanation of population change. For him, Norway was essentially a source of material to illustrate a theoretical system already arrived at by essentially deductive processes. Although Alfred Marshall credited Malthus's work with 'the merit of being the first thorough application of the inductive method to social science',[3] he in fact showed little of that 'dogged honesty in pursuing facts and not taking surface explanations for what he observed, disciplined curiosity and imagination, respect for people as sources of social data, and...careful use of documentary and statistical evidence'[4] which lies at the roots of social scientific method and which can justly be ascribed to Sundt.

[1] Samuel Laing, *Journal of a residence in Norway during the years 1834, 1835 and 1836. Made with a view to inquire into the moral and political economy of the country and the condition of its inhabitants* (2nd ed. London, 1851), p. 76.
[2] Arthur Hillman, 'Eilert Sundt, social surveyor extraordinary', *Sociological Review*, **43** (1951), 49.
[3] Cited in William Petersen, 'Malthusian theory: a commentary and critique', *The Politics of Population* (Anchor Books, New York, 1965), p. 45.
[4] Hillman, *op. cit.* p. 49.

3 The growth of population

The population of Norway almost doubled in the half century after 1815, a rate of growth which the figures in table 3.1 suggest was high by the standards of contemporary Europe. It was high too by those of eighteenth-century Norway. In the years 1735–55 the population increased by only 0·4 per cent per annum; in the following twenty years by 0·5 per cent; in the years 1775–95 by 0·7 per cent and in the twenty years before 1815 by 0·4 per cent (table 3.2). Then came the explosion: a rate of 1·4 per cent per annum in the years 1815–35 followed by one of 1·1 per cent in the period 1835–55 and 1·3 per cent from 1855–65. If we move back beyond 1735 we leave the era of relative statistical security. We have estimates of population for the years 1665[1] and 1701,[2] based on partial censuses, but no more. These estimates suggest that the population of Norway numbered 444,000 in 1665 and 504,000 in 1701. If we accept these figures as broadly accurate we calculate that the population grew by 0·4 per cent per annum in the years 1665–1701 and 0·6 per cent per annum in the years 1701–35. In 1735 the population was about 616,000.

The four Norwegian dioceses evidenced a remarkably similar pattern of population growth throughout the period 1735–1865 (table 3.2). In each of them the population grew relatively slowly before 1815, with rates of increase fluctuating one or two points above or below 0·5 per cent per annum. All the dioceses experienced the sharp upward swing in the years 1815–35 with the lowest rate of growth in these years being that of Bergen at 1·2 per cent per annum and the highest that of Akershus at 1·4 per cent. Although each of the dioceses failed to maintain its 1815–35 rate during the

[1] T. H. Aschehoug, 'Om Norges folkemængde i aarene 1664–66', *Norsk Tidsskrift for Videnskab og Litteratur*, **2** (Christiania, 1848), 305–407.
[2] T. Lindstøl, *Mandtallet i Norge 1701* (Kristiania, 1887).

TABLE 3.1   *The growth of population in various European states from approximately 1815 to 1865**

State	Population c. 1815 (actual date in brackets)	Population c. 1865 (actual date in brackets)	Annual average rate of growth c. 1815 to c. 1865 per cent
Norway	885,431 (1815)	1,701,756 (1865)	1·30
Sweden	2,465,066 (1815)	4,114,141 (1865)	1·03
Denmark	1,018,180 (1815)	1,600,551 (1860)	1·01
Russia	45,000,000 (1815)	61,061,801 (1863)	0·64
Prussia	10,349,031 (1816)	19,675,990 (1867)	1·27
Hanover	1,680,285 (1836)	1,937,637 (1867)	0·46
Saxony	1,558,153 (1832)	2,423,587 (1867)	1·25
Bremen	47,797 (1812)	109,572 (1867)	1·52
Bavaria	3,707,966 (1818)	4,824,421 (1867)	0·54
Austria	26,000,000 (1818)	35,500,000 (1867)	0·64
Holland	2,613,487 (1829)	3,293,577 (1859)	0·74
Belgium	3,785,814 (1831)	4,984,351 (1865)	0·81
England and Wales	10,454,529 (1811)	20,066,224 (1861)	1·31
France	30,461,875 (1821)	37,394,000 (1866)	0·46
Spain	12,286,941 (1833)	15,658,531 (1860)	0·90
Portugal	3,412,500 (1841)	3,693,363 (1861)	0·40
Switzerland	2,188,009 (1837)	2,510,494 (1860)	0·60

* *Norges officielle statistik. Ældre række.* C. no. 1, *Tabeller vedkommende folkemængdens bevægelse i aarene 1856–65* (Christiania, 1868–9), p. viii.

next three decades, in none did the rate slip back to the pre-1815 level.

What caused the sudden rise in the rate of population growth after 1815? The end of the Napoleonic wars was marked in Norway by a sharp increase in the birth rate and a sharp fall in the death rate (fig. 2). Such a rise in the birth rate after a period of distress was not without precedent. It occurred in the 1740s and the 1770s after the exceptionally high mortality of 1742 and 1773. Nor was the level to which the birth rate rose in the late 1810s and the 1820s very different from what it had been in the eighteenth century. More than this, however, the rise of the birth rate in 1815 can be seen as

TABLE 3.2 *Average annual percentage growth of population in the kingdom of Norway and its constituent dioceses, Akershus, Kristiansand, Bergen and Trondheim in the years 1735–1865.**

Period	Akershus	Kristian-sand	Bergen	Trondheim	Norway
1735–55	0·4	0·5	0·5	0·3	0·4
1755–75	0·7	0·5	0·5	0·5	0·5
1775–95	0·7	0·6	0·5	0·8	0·7
1795–1815	0·3	0·7	0·4	0·2	0·4
1815–35	1·4	1·4	1·2	1·3	1·4
1835–55	1·2	1·1	0·8	1·2	1·1
1855–65	1·6	1·1	1·0	1·4	1·3
1735–1865	0·8	0·8	0·7	0·7	0·7

* Statistical appendix, table 1.

part of a pattern going back into the first half of the eighteenth century and forward into the second half of the nineteenth. A wave-like movement can be discerned with troughs in the 1740s, 1770s, 1800s and 1830s and crests in the 1750s, 1790s, 1820s and 1850s (fig. 2a). As Eilert Sundt pointed out a century ago[1] this wave-like movement was largely the product of changes in the age composition of the population initiated by distress in the early 1740s. This not only delayed marriages and conceptions, but also decimated the number of children that were born. With the return of better times, marriages that had been delayed took place, more births occurred and fewer children died young. Thirty years later, however, the deficient cohort of the early 1740s reached marriageable age. Even without the distress of the early 1770s, we might have expected a fall in the number of births, although this distress obviously reduced the number and took its toll of those that did take place. By the 1800s a doubly-deficient cohort reached marriageable age and again contemporary distress reduced still further the number of expected births. As tables 4 and 6 in the statistical appendix show, this wave-like movement of the birth rate was mirrored in the marriage rate.

[1] Eilert Sundt, *Om giftermaal i Norge* (Christiania, 1855), pp. 53–64.

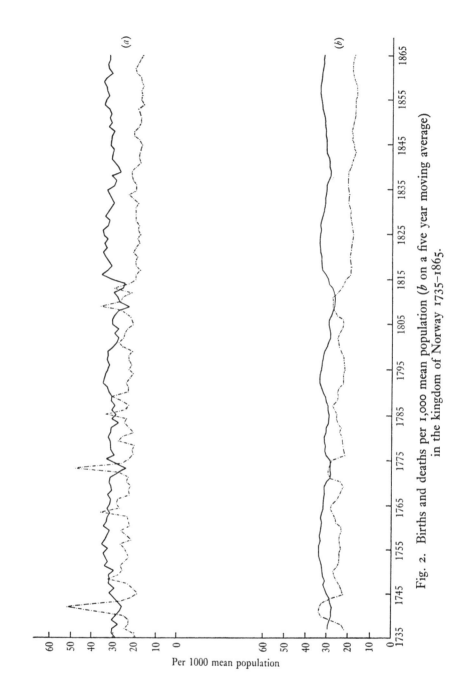

Fig. 2. Births and deaths per 1,000 mean population (b on a five year moving average) in the kingdom of Norway 1735–1865.

TABLE 3.3 *Intercensal rates of growth of various age groups in the Norwegian population 1801–65**

	Percentage changes between censuses				
Age group	1801–25	1825–35	1835–45	1845–55	1855–65
0–9	23·5	10·7	3·2	20·4	16·7
10–19	8·6	39·7	10·6	2·3	23·2
20–29	28·1	−1·8	38·8	8·5	−1·1
30–39	27·0	6·6	−0·3	31·5	10·1
40–49	2·2	22·6	5·3	−2·5	39·8
50–59	9·9	10·7	22·1	6·8	−2·5
60–	30·4	6·6	4·1	17·7	13·9

* Calculated from Johan Vogt, 'En generasjonsstatistikk for det norske folk', *Memorandum fra Oslo universitets sosialøkonomiske institutt*, Oslo, 29 January 1957.

Contemporary happenings then, according to Sundt, only served to reinforce the underlying trend.[1]

It is unfortunately not possible to measure changes in the age composition of the population until the nineteenth century. Then they were indeed dramatic. Table 3.3 reveals that between 1825 and 1835 the 30–39 year age group (the one that probably contributed most to the Norwegian birth rate), increased by a mere 6·6 per cent or only half the increase of the population as a whole. In the following decade it actually fell by 0·3 per cent. Not surprisingly, the birth rate fell in the 1830s. It began to rise in the 1840s as the 20–29 year group increased sharply—by 38·8 per cent between 1835 and 1845. Not till the next decade, however, did the birth rate reach its peak with the 30–39 year group rising by 31·5 per cent (1845–55) or three times as fast as the population as a whole.

When we examine the fall in the death rate which occurred towards the end of the Napoleonic wars we discover a rather different situation. The sharpness of the fall itself was not exceptional; there had been far greater reductions on a number of occasions during the eighteenth century (fig. 2). What was exceptional was that the death rate fell to an historically low level and, even more important, that this level was maintained. As we have seen, the general level of the

[1] Eilert Sundt, *op. cit.* p. 40.

birth rate and its year-to-year fluctuations were substantially the same in the half-century before, as in the half-century after 1815. The pattern of the death rate, however, changed completely at that date. Before 1815 its level was moderately high with major peaks every decade or so. After 1815 the fluctuations were slight and the level low by previous standards. This fall in the crude death rate in the second decade of the nineteenth century was reflected in the specific mortality rates. Unfortunately we can only calculate age specific mortality rates for a short period before 1815, namely in the years around 1801. In 1801—a year in which the crude death rate was the highest for any year between 1789 and 1809—some 46 boys under 10 years of age died for every 1,000 in that age group. In the years 1816–40 the average number was 32 per 1,000 and in the period 1841–65 it was 28 per 1,000. Deaths of youths aged 11–20 years amounted to 7 per 1,000 in 1801 and 5 per 1,000 in the years 1816–40 and again in 1841–65. For men aged 21–30 the corresponding figures were 12, 8 and 8. A similar pattern emerges in the case of the higher male age groups as well as in the case of women of all age groups. As one would expect, the contrast between the age specific mortality rates for 1801 and for the years after 1815 was more marked than that between the years 1802–5 and the post-1815 period (table 3.4). Again, as one might expect from these age specific mortality figures, the expectation of life at all ages remained fairly constant in the years 1821–65 (table 3.5).

To explain the sudden increase in the rate of growth of the Norwegian population attention should, it seems, be concentrated on the death rate. Furthermore, the picture emerging from the national aggregates would suggest that we look particularly closely at events in the first and second decades of the nineteenth century, near to when the change occurred. However, if we go behind the national aggregates, a number of interesting features emerge (fig. 3). First, although each of the four dioceses had high death rates in the 1740s, only Akershus and Trondheim had comparable rates in the early 1770s. Second, the two dioceses occupying the south-western part of the country (Bergen and Kristiansand) begin to develop what we might call the post-1815 death rate pattern before Trondheim in the north and Akershus in the south-east. Too much should

TABLE 3.4   *Age specific mortality in Norway 1801–65**

	Deaths per 1,000 men aged					Deaths per 1,000 women aged				
	0–10	11–20	21–30	31–40	41–50	0–10	11–20	21–30	31–40	41–50
1801	46·2	7·2	11·9	13·8	17·9	42·6	5·8	8·8	12·6	15·3
1802–5	37·7	6·9	11·4	12·5	17·2	32·6	6·0	7·9	10·9	13·8
1816–40	31·6	4·7	8·2	9·7	13·5	27·7	4·3	6·4	9·1	11·7
1841–65	28·1	4·8	8·3	8·8	12·4	25·1	4·4	6·0	8·5	10·6

* Figures for the years 1816–40 and 1841–65 from O. J. Broch, *Kongeriget Norge og det norske folk* (Kristiania, 1876), tillæg x, p. 25. My calculations for 1801 and 1802–5 based on totals of deaths in *Tabeller over ægteviede, fødte og døde i Norge i aarene 1801–1835 inclusive*, N.O.S. fjerde række (Christiania, 1839) and of 1801 age distribution in *Tabeller vedkommende folketællingerne i aarene 1801 og 1825*, N.O.S. Ældre række C, no. 1 (Christiania, 1874). The published total of deaths for 1801 have been corrected to remove the error discussed below in the statistical appendix, p. 180.

TABLE 3.5   *Expectation of life in Norway at various ages in the years 1821–65**

	Average number of years remaining for									
	Men					Women				
Age	1821–1830	1831–1840	1841–1850	1846–1855	1856–1865	1821–1830	1831–1840	1841–1850	1846–1855	1856–1865
0	45·0	41·8	44·5	44·9	47·4	48·0	45·6	47·9	47·9	50·0
1	—	—	—	—	52·4	—	—	—	—	54·2
5	53·9	50·9	52·6	52·4	53·7	56·0	53·9	55·0	55·0	55·6
10	50·3	47·4	49·4	49·4	50·8	52·4	50·4	51·8	52·0	52·8
20	42·5	39·5	41·5	42·0	43·2	44·5	42·4	43·9	44·5	45·3
30	35·6	32·9	34·6	34·8	36·3	37·0	35·1	36·2	36·9	37·8
40	28·3	26·2	27·5	28·0	29·1	29·8	28·2	29·4	29·7	30·7
50	21·4	19·6	20·7	21·0	22·0	22·4	21·4	22·2	22·5	23·4
60	15·2	13·8	14·4	14·6	15·2	15·8	14·8	15·2	15·5	16·2
70	9·7	8·8	9·1	9·0	9·4	10·0	9·3	9·5	9·4	10·1

* *Statistisk årbok for Norge 1940* (Oslo, 1940), table 35, p. 31.

not, perhaps, be made of these regional differences for all areas show greater and more regular population growth after 1815 than before. Nevertheless, the fact that 1785 was effectively the last year in the Bergen and Kristiansand dioceses in which deaths exceeded births

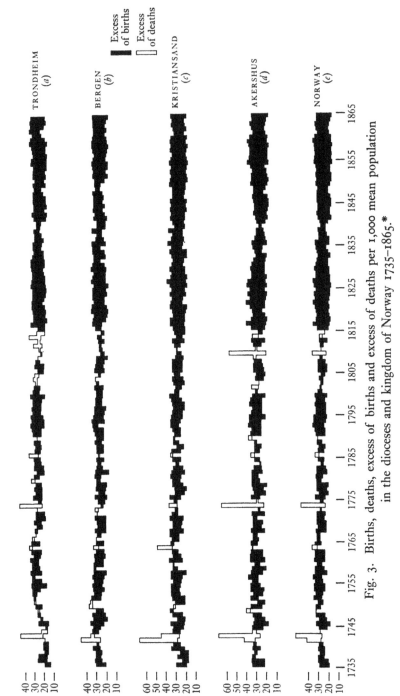

Fig. 3. Births, deaths, excess of births and excess of deaths per 1,000 mean population in the dioceses and kingdom of Norway 1735–1865.*

* The lines under the shaded and above the unshaded areas of the histogram indicate the level of the death rate. The birth rate is indicated by the lines running above the shaded and below the unshaded areas.

TABLE 3.6   *Births and deaths per 1,000 mean population in the kingdom of Norway and the dioceses of Akershus, Kristiansand, Bergen and Trondheim 1736–1865*

	Akershus		Kristiansand		Bergen		Trondheim		Norway	
	Births	Deaths	Births	Deaths	Births	Deaths	Births	Deaths	Births	Deaths
1736–55	33·3	29·2	31·1	26·0	31·5	26·2	24·7	21·6	30·5	26·3
1756–75	33·1	27·4	32·9	27·1	29·1	22·9	28·9	25·2	31·4	26·0
1776–95	33·1	25·2	31·8	24·0	28·9	21·7	28·7	22·9	31·1	23·8
1796–1815	30·3	26·2	30·9	22·2	27·5	22·0	25·9	24·2	28·9	24·3
1816–35	34·2	19·6	33·2	19·1	31·3	19·0	30·6	18·6	23·7	19·2
1836–55	31·3	18·2	32·3	18·3	29·7	19·5	28·9	18·7	30·6	18·6
1856–65	34·3	17·6	31·9	17·9	30·8	17·2	31·3	18·1	32·6	17·7

* Statistical appendix, tables 5 and 7.

(Bergen had a small excess in 1803) would suggest that in seeking to explain the national experience we bear in mind this regional variation. This evidence of a change in the pattern of the death rate occurring earlier in one part of the country than in another, appears more clearly when we look at the rates themselves (table 3.6). In both the Bergen and Kristiansand dioceses the shifts to a lower average death rate after 1815 was much less abrupt than in either the Akershus or the Trondheim dioceses.

Several explanations for this fall in mortality were put forward by contemporaries or near contemporaries.[1] The most plausible of these appear to be first, the widespread adoption of vaccination against smallpox and second, the great increase in the cultivation of potatoes.

Vaccination was made compulsory by a royal edict of 3 April 1810.[2] No civil penalty was imposed on those who refused to be vaccinated but, as we noticed earlier, the church would neither

[1] Professor D. Fredrik Holst, 'Om folketællingen i Norge i aaret 1825', *Budstikken* (Christiania, 1827), pp. 663–4; Professor A. Schweigaard, *Norges statistik* (Christiania, 1840), pp. 197, 203–4.
[2] O. J. Broch, *Kongeriget Norge og det norske folk, dets sociale forhold, sundhedstilstand, næringsveie, samfærdselsmidler og ekonomi* (Kristiania, 1876), tillæg I, p. 12.

confirm nor marry them.[1] A governmental enquiry in 1816 reported that there was no active opposition on the part of the public to the practice, though there was some apathy.[2] The main obstacles to a complete coverage of the country were said to be a shortage of doctors and nurses, together with difficulties encountered in preserving the vaccine.[3] This shortage of trained personnel was alleviated only gradually. By 1827 the King Frederik university, founded in Oslo in 1811, had produced only forty-six doctors, although it had trained 158 midwives, who were taught how to vaccinate.[4] The number of doctors per head of the population fell after 1814 and did not exceed the figure for that year until the 1840s. There was one doctor for every 5,634 inhabitants in 1814, one for every 8,167 in 1824 and one for every 7,690 in 1834. By 1844, however, the number of inhabitants per doctor had fallen to 4,966 and the ratio remained at about this until the 1860s.[5]

Country parsons were active in the practice of vaccination,[6] indeed, it was one they had pioneered. Already in the autumn of 1802 Nils Hertzberg, the vicar of Kvinnherad in the Bergen diocese, together with the young theology graduate, Nils Griis Alstrup Dahl, had vaccinated 402 people including almost all the children in the parish, not one of whom had died.[7] Yet this was only one year after vaccination had been introduced into Norway.[8] In 1803, some fifty-four people, of whom eighteen were clergymen, reported having carried out vaccinations.[9]

An interesting feature of the early history of vaccination in Norway was that much of it took place in the Bergen diocese. For it was here too that inoculation seems to have had a certain following. In 1772 the *Bergenske adresse-contoirs efterretninger* carried an account of the

[1] O. J. Broch, *op. cit.* tillæg 1, p. 12.
[2] 'Om vaccinationens tilstand i Norge i aaret 1816', *Budstikken* (Christiania, 1817), no. 41, pp. 334–6. The evidence for this was collected from parsons throughout the country.
[3] *Ibid.* pp. 334–6.   [4] Holst, *op. cit.* p. 647.
[5] There was one doctor for every 4,594 inhabitants in 1854 and for every 4,736 in 1864. I. Reichborn-Kjennerud, Fr. Grøn, I. Kobro, *Medisinens Historie i Norge* (Oslo, 1953), p. 289.
[6] Otto Lous Mohr, 'Geistlige pionerer i vaksinasjonen i Norge: Nils Hertzberg og Nils Griis Alstrup Dahl', *Aftenpostens aftennummer*, Oslo. 26 and 27 July 1961.
[7] *Ibid.* 27 July 1961.   [8] *Ibid.* 26 July 1961.
[9] O. Malm, *Kopper og vaccinationen i Norge* (Kristiania, 1915), p. 61.

The growth of population

TABLE 3.7 *Number of reported vaccinations as a percentage of live births and of total population in Norway 1802–60**

		Vaccinated as a percentage of	
Years	Total vaccinated	Population	Live births
1802–10	34,729	0·43	15·6
1811–20	85,066	0·92	30·7
1821–30	167,834	1·59	47·9
1831–40	205,339	1·72	58·1
1841–50	306,278	2·31	75·3
1851–60	401,249	2·69	81·5

* O. Malm, *Kopper og vaccinationen i Norge* (Kristiania, 1915), p. 95.

inoculations performed by J. A. Krogh, the incumbent of Davik in Nordfjord. Krogh reported that in a single week he had performed 200 and that his house had 'swarmed' with people bringing their children to him. Of late, he noted, the demand had slackened as quacks spread false rumours that those he had treated were not protected against later attacks. Krogh, together with a fellow parson and a farmer inoculated 562 people, of whom four died. In neighbouring parishes during the same period 326 people who had not been inoculated were said to have contracted smallpox and according to Krogh eighty-seven of these died.[1]

What little evidence we have suggests that inoculation did not spread much beyond the western parts of Norway.[2] It appears to have been practised hardly at all in the Akershus diocese.[3] Is it possible that the more gradual fall in mortality in the Bergen than in the Akershus diocese during the late eighteenth and early nineteenth centuries resulted from the wider prevalence, first of inoculation then of vaccination in the Bergen diocese?

Vaccination spread throughout Norway during the first half of the nineteenth century. In the 1800s the number of vaccinations

[1] *Ibid.* pp. 25–7.
[2] *Ibid.* pp. 21, 25. A doctor Wasmuth was reported to have inoculated about 200 people around Trondheim in the years 1762–3. In 1771 some seventy-five children and young people in Stavanger were said to have been inoculated. Sverre Steen. *Det norske folks liv og historie gjennem tidene* (Oslo, 1938), VI, 157.
[3] Malm. *op. cit.* p. 31.

51
4-2

amounted to about 16 per cent[1] of live births. By the 1850s the percentage had risen to 82 (table 3.7).

Whether vaccination on this scale was sufficient to make a major impact on the death rate in Norway during the early decades of the nineteenth century depends upon the extent and virulence of the disease. Unfortunately, we have little evidence on either score though what we do have suggests that on occasion smallpox was a major killer. For instance, it was reported that 1,376 people died in the town of Bergen in 1741 and that of this number 743 were children, most of whom had died from smallpox.[2] As the number of deaths in Bergen in 1738, 1739 and 1740 were respectively 648, 575 and 749 we might plausibly credit a considerable part of the increase in 1741 to smallpox.[3] In 1793 smallpox was prevalent in the town of Kristiansand and sixty-seven people were alleged to have died from it. They accounted for exactly one-third of the total deaths in that year.[4] Again, if we look at the number of deaths in the immediately preceding years—143, 113 and 143 in 1790, 1791 and 1792 respectively[5]—we can credit at least some of the sharp rise to smallpox.

Swedish medical statistics add some support to the contention that vaccination speedily reduced deaths from smallpox in the early decades of the nineteenth century. Deaths attributed to smallpox among Swedes of one year of age and upwards fell from 41,000 in the decade 1791–1800 to 20,000 in the following decade and to about 4,000 in each of the decades 1811–20 and 1821–30.[6] The effect on child mortality generally was nullified to some extent, however, by a sharp increase in deaths from measles. These rose from 7,650 in the decade 1781–90 (during this period smallpox accounted for 45,970 deaths) to 19,880 in the decade 1821–30.[7]

[1] O. Malm, *op. cit.* p. 95. Reported vaccinations probably less than the actual number, especially in the years 1802–20.
[2] Bishop O. C. Bornemann of Bergen to Johan Ludvig von Holstein, Copenhagen, 20 March 1742. Copy of letter in Christiania bispearkiv, *Ministerielle forretninger. Innberetninger. Rekke 1. Biskopene 1733–1814.* Box 6, statsarkivet, Oslo.
[3] For deaths in the Bergen deanery in the years 1736–1814 see the bishop's returns in the Bergen bispearkiv, statsarkivet, Bergen.
[4] O. Malm, *op. cit.* p. 97.
[5] For deaths in the Kristiansand deanery see bishop's returns in the Kristansand bispearkiv, statsarkivet, Kristiansand.
[6] G. Utterstrøm, 'Some population problems in pre-industrial Sweden', *Scandinavian Economic History Review*, **2** (1954), 160–5.   [7] *Ibid.* p. 164.

TABLE 3.8   *Deaths from smallpox in Copenhagen 1750–1811**

Period	Total deaths	Period	Total deaths
1750–9	4,059	1780–9	2,068
1760–9	2,208	1790–1801	3,172†
1770–9	1,288	1802–11	163

* C. W. Wendt, *Bidrag til børnekoppernes og vaccinationens historie i Danmark og om de sidste herskende koppeepidemier* (Kjøbenhavn, 1836), pp. 4, 7.
† Of which 486 occurred in 1801.

There was also a very sharp fall in smallpox deaths in Copenhagen during the first decade of the nineteenth century immediately after the introduction of vaccination in 1801 (table 3.8).

Although smallpox deaths fell in Scandinavia about the time vaccination was introduced, the disease by no means disappeared. Malm reported in 1915 that smallpox had been present in some part of Norway in every single year since 1815 and had sometimes proved fatal. For instance, 4,499 cases were reported in the years 1853–60 of which 446 were fatal; whilst of 7,929 cases which were reported in the period 1861–70, 560 were fatal.[1] This might perhaps suggest that the decline in deaths attributable to small-pox was more the result of a shift in the character of the disease, towards a milder form, than to vaccination.[2] Support for this view would come from the fact that only a small proportion of the Nor-wegian population was protected by vaccination (table 3.7) during the early decades of the nineteenth century.[3] The same was true in Copenhagen, where smallpox deaths dropped dramatically from 3,172 in the years 1790–1801, to 163 in the years 1802–11.[4] Between 1801 and 1811 vaccination was carried out on 16,790 people. This,

[1] Malm, *op. cit.* pp. 122, 144.
[2] The suggestion has been made by Thomas McKeown and R. G. Record, 'The reasons for the decline in mortality in England and Wales during the nineteenth century', *Population Studies*, 14 (1962), 97.
[3] Possibly, however, a partial coverage might have a more than proportionate effect on reducing the impact of the disease, as the presence of some vaccinated persons would inhibit its spread to the non-vaccinated. I am indebted for this suggestion to Professor D. M. Joslin.
[4] C. W. Wendt, *Bidrag til børnekoppernes og vaccinationens historie i Danmark og om de sidste herskende koppeepidemier* (Kjøbenhavn, 1836), pp. 4, 7.

Population and Society in Norway 1735–1865

however, represented less than half the number of births (35,840) occurring in the same period.[1]

But whatever the cause of the fall in deaths from smallpox, the fall itself is hardly sufficient to explain the marked change in character of the Norwegian death rate after 1815. It is highly unlikely that smallpox accounted for a greater proportion of deaths in Norway than in Sweden, yet in no decade during the period 1751–1800 were probably more than 8 per cent of deaths amongst Swedes attributable to it[2] and, as we have seen, some of those who were saved from smallpox succumbed to measles. Some other agency must have been at work. The most obvious one, though not necessarily the most important, is food supply and here the advent of the potato appears the most striking innovation.

The potato came to Norway in the 1750s probably from England or Scotland.[3] The earliest references are to its cultivation by two parsons in the Bergen diocese, H. C. Atke of Kinsarvik and Peter Harboe Hertzberg of Finnås, about 1758.[4] As with inoculation and vaccination against smallpox, the clergy not only introduced the cultivation of the potato into many parts of Norway, but continued to advocate its virtues over many years.[5] For example, the vicar of Gausdal in southern Gudbrandsdalen (Akershus diocese) harvested 460 bushels in 1775 and in the following year distributed them as seed potatoes to all the 120 cottars in the parish.[6] Not only the clergy,

[1] C. W. Wendt, *op. cit.* pp. 7–8.
[2] This is the percentage of smallpox deaths amongst the population one year of age and over to total deaths. Since many children in their first year of life have a certain immunity to smallpox derived from having a high proportion of their mother's blood, smallpox deaths were probably relatively small under age one. From Utterström, *op. cit.* pp. 162–5 one can calculate that smallpox deaths amongst the population one year of age and over did not account for more than 16 per cent of total deaths in this same age group in any decade between 1751 and 1800.
[3] The Norwegian word for the potato is the same as the English. Had the plant arrived by way of Denmark or Germany we would expect to find a variation of the Danish word *Kartoffel*. See F. C. Schübeler, *Viridarium norvegicum. Norges væxtrige. Et bidrag til nord Europas natur- og culturhistorie* (Christiania, 1886–9), II, 143.
[4] Jens Kraft, *Topographisk-statistisk beskrivelse over kongerigt Norge* (Christiania, 1829), IV, 456. Hertzberg wrote a book on how to plant and use potatoes: *Underretning for bønder i Norge om den meget nyttige jordfrugt, potatos at plante og bruge*, the third edition of which was published in Bergen in 1774. F. C. Schübeler, *op. cit.* II, 143.
[5] F. C. Schübeler, *op. cit.* II, 146–7; Kraft, *op. cit.* I, 119, 629–30; II, 13–14; V, 459–72.
[6] F. C. Schübeler, *op. cit.* II, 146.

54

but all servants of the Danish crown living in the countryside were urged to encourage the planting of the potato by 'the poor common people'.[1] The *Norske intelligenz-seddeler* carried three articles between December 1764 and March 1765 explaining how to grow potatoes, how to make them into flour and how to use them for animal feed.[2] Credit for the introduction of the potato to Norway cannot, however, be confined solely to governmental action. German immigrant workers at the Biri glassworks had brought the plant to the north-western shores of Lake Mjøsa by the 1770s,[3] whilst soldiers returning from service in Holstein in the years 1758–62 brought it to Odalen in southern Hedmark.[4]

The Norwegian clergy were particularly well placed to quicken the diffusion of the potato, since all had farms attached to their livings. These glebes varied greatly in size and quality; the best were in the south and east of the country, the poorest in the west and north. We are fortunate in being able to measure with unusual accuracy, not only the number of clergy planting potatoes (table 3.9) but also the amount planted relative to other crops (table 3.10), in the two decades after the Napoleonic wars. For this we are indebted to the detailed survey of Norway carried out at this time with government help by Jens Kraft.[5]

In the districts where potatoes were cultivated by the clergy, the quantities planted were large, relative to the amount of grain that was sown. In no county was the volume planted less than 19 per cent

---

[1] Anon. 'Efterretning om potatos-avling og brug', *Norske intelligenz-seddeler*, 20 March 1765.
[2] *Ibid.* 19 December 1764, 20 December 1764 and 20 March 1765.
[3] Kraft, *op. cit.* I, 629–30. [4] F. C. Schübeler, *op. cit.* II, 146.
[5] Jens Kraft, *Topographisk-statistisk beskrivelse over kongeriget Norge* (Christiania, 1820–35), I–VI. The assistance of the government was acknowledged in vol. I in a preface inserted immediately before p. 311. This stemmed from a resolution of the Norwegian government dated 12 November 1814, granting Kraft unrestricted access to the official archives. Much of the information was gathered via an extensive correspondence with civil servants throughout the country. The work consists of a systematic and comprehensive account of every parish in the country under the following heads: topography; administrative structure; tax values and yield; population; number of farms, farmers and cottars; soil, climate and suitability for agriculture; character of agriculture; flax, hemp, hop, garden and fruit tree culture; forestry; pastoral farming; hunting and shooting; fisheries; mineral deposits and workings; useful soils and rocks; mines and forges; factories; notable farms and homes; natural curiosities; historical and pre-historical notes. A great deal of the data is given in statistical form.

55

TABLE 3.9 *Number of glebes in rural districts of Norwegian counties on which pototaes planted by various dates 1820-35**

| County | Year | Number of glebes where | | |
		Potatoes planted	Possibly not planted	No crop data
Østfold	1820	6	13	—
Akershus	1820	1	15	1
Hedmark	1820	0	12	5
Oppland	1821	0	18	—
Buskerud	1821-2	0	13	—
Vestfold	1822	10	6	—
Telemark	1824	12	6	—
Aust-Agder	1826	10	1	—
Vest-Agder	1826	8	4	—
Rogaland	1829	17	5	—
Hordaland	1829	15	3	1
Sogn and Fjordane	1830	11	7	3
Møre and Romsdal	1831	12	6	5
Sør-Trøndelag	1831-2	9	4	2
Nord-Trøndelag	1835	9	7	—
Nordland	1835	13	12	2
Troms and Finnmark	1835	5	3	2
Norway	1820-35	138	135	21

* Jens Kraft, *Topographisk-statistisk beskrivelse over kongeriget Norge* (Christiania, 1820-35), I-VI. Kraft gives no information about what was done in the *fogderier* of Øst and Vest Finnmark.

of all seed although it never rose above 50 per cent (table 3.10). The potato was probably more widely disseminated in the south-western part of the country at this time than in the south-east or the extreme north (tables 3.9 and 3.10) The difference is, however, exaggerated for the probable explanation of the apparently small number of glebes on which potatoes were planted in Østfold, Akershus, Hedmark, Oppland and Buskerud (the counties that make up the bulk of the Akershus diocese) is that Kraft's survey of these areas was less complete, particularly, as he admitted, on the statistical side.[1] However, an alternative source suggests that in so far as the potato

[1] Jens Kraft, *Det søndenfjeldske Norge topographisk-statistisk beskrevet* (Christiania, 1840), preface.

TABLE 3.10 *Quantities of grain and potatoes sown on certain glebes in rural districts of Norwegian counties by various dates 1820–35**

County	N	Year	Grain	Potatoes	Potatoes as a percentage of all seed
			Bushels sown of		
Østfold	6	1820	784	182	19
Vestfold	10	1822	835	448	35
Telemark	9	1824	300	236	44
Aust-Agder	7	1826	292	272	48
Vest-Agder	7	1826	284	196	41
Rogaland	17	1829	878·5	366	29
Hordaland	14	1829	632·5	386	38
Sogn and Fjordane	10	1830	616·5	334	35
Møre and Romsdal	10	1831	536	246	31
Sør-Trøndelag	8	1831–2	870	538	38
Nord-Trøndelag	9	1835	768	572	43
Nordland	10	1835	362	146	29
Troms and Finnmark	3	1835	128	48	27
Norway	120		7,286·5	3,970	35

* Jens Kraft, *Topographisk-statistisk beskrivelse over kongeriget Norge* (Christiania, 1820–35), I–VI.—N is the number of glebes used in the analysis. It is occasionally smaller than in table 3·9 as not all the clergy specified the quantity of potatoes planted. Where Kraft gives more than one figure for the amount of grain and potatoes sown I have averaged them for the purpose of this analysis. Where he gives only the amounts of grain and potatoes harvested, I have used his evidence on crop yields to estimate the amounts sown. Kraft used the *tønde* (about 4 bushels) for all his measurements. I presume it was the same measure for potatoes and grain.

was grown at all in the first decades of the nineteenth century, it was mainly in the south-western part of the country, covered by the dioceses of Bergen and Kristiansand. In the spring of 1809 the Danish government feared a major food crisis in Norway following on the failure of the grain harvest in the previous year. To get some idea of the shortages in various parts of the country, the government sent the authorities in every parish a form on which was to be entered the kind and amount of seed sown both during a normal

TABLE 3.11 *Hectolitres of potatoes planted in a 'normal' year during the first decade of the nineteenth century and in 1835 in the counties of Norway, per 1,000 mean population**

Counties	Hectolitres of potatoes planted		Hectolitres planted per 1,000 mean population	
	1800s	1835	1800s	1835
Østfold	2,869	34,542	58	528
Akershus	1,432	39,199	22	413
Hedmark	3,312	39,751	55	498
Oppland	838	28,288	13	298
Buskerud	2,252	30,779	35	400
Vestfold	6,227	30,216	157	532
Telemark	7,689	32,160	162	474
Aust-Agder	6,404	19,770	180	415
Vest-Agder	10,907	19,354	277	349
Rogaland	5,641	17,080	134	252
Hordaland	7,463	21,758	95	200
Sogn and Fjordane	4,556	21,522	86	304
Møre and Romsdal	3,718	16,608	64	228
Sør Trøndelag ⎰ Nørd-Trøndelag ⎱	6,793	{28,984 {31,443	65	{363 {526
Nordland	643	11,038	12	188
Finnmark	103	3,139	4	84
Norway	71,201	425,999	81	353

* S. Hasund, *Vårt landbruks historie* (Oslo, 1932), table 3, p. 109 for totals of potatoes planted in 1800s and mid-1830s. The latter are taken from the first agricultural census of 1835. For calculating the amount of potatoes planted per 1,000 mean population I have used the population totals recorded at the 1801 and 1835 censuses. See *Statistisk årbok for Norge 1940* (Oslo, 1940), table 6, p. 5. A hectolitre is about 2·75 bushels. It will be noted that Hasund's county totals do not add up to his national totals. I presume this is due to rounding off when converting from *tønder* to hectolitres.

spring and during that of 1809.[1] Naturally we would expect the quantities to be understated. The farmers fearing, as usual, higher taxes would be unlikely to make a full return.[2] There is, however, no reason to believe that the degree of inaccuracy varied substantially from one part of the country to another.

[1] Jakob S. Worm-Müller, *Norge gjennem nødsaarene. Den norske regjeringskommission 1807–1810* (Kristiania, 1918), p. 85.   [2] *Ibid.* p. 85.

Part of the results of the 1809 survey appear in table 3.11. They suggest that in a normal year towards the end of the first decade of the nineteenth century the south-western part of the country centred on the county of Vest-Agder was the heartland of potato cultivation, just the area, in fact, where potatoes were grown 'extensively' on the parsons' glebes, at a relatively early date (table 3.9).

A striking feature of table 3.11 is the very sharp increase in the cultivation of potatoes between the 1800s and the 1830s particularly in those areas of the south-east and north of the country which made up the dioceses of Akershus and Trondheim. Even if we make a generous allowance for deficiencies in the returns there can be no doubt of the picture portrayed. By 1835 the potato was a major crop in Norway, providing a harvest to feed, on Schweigaard's calculation, 270,000 or more than one-fifth of the country's population.[1]

This tremendous increase in potato cultivation did more than anything else to raise the productivity of Norwegian farms and Norwegian farm workers. As Fartein Valen-Sendstad has recently demonstrated, the per capita output (of arable produce) of the agricultural population in Norway rose by 70 per cent in the first three decades of the nineteenth century and the output per farm unit by almost the same amount (table 3.12).

Can we account for this increase, and is it possible to define more narrowly the point at which the breakthrough came? Jens Kraft repeatedly stresses the war of 1807–14 as a major force behind the development of Norwegian agriculture generally, and of the growing of potatoes in particular.[2] On a number of occasions during this period the English fleet prevented the import of corn into Norway.[3] This was a serious matter as Norway was probably more dependent upon imports of grain than any other country in Europe. In a normal year about 25 per cent of her needs were said to be met from abroad, mostly from Denmark.[4] Unfortunately, a number of the years 1807–14 were by no means normal. The grain harvest failed

[1] A. Schweigaard, *Norges statistik* (Christiania, 1840), p. 64.
[2] Jens Kraft. *Topographisk-statistisk beskrivelse over kongeriget Norge* (Christiania, 1820–35), I, 92, 116–17, 256, 357–8, 416, 484; II, 12, 359, 625, 627, 823; III, 265, 332, 454; IV, 62, 456–7, 600; VI, 174, 318.
[3] Magnus Jensen, *Norges historie fra 1660 til våre dager* (Oslo, 1938), p. 134.
[4] Jakob S. Worm-Müller, *op. cit.* p. 82.

TABLE 3.12   *Rise of input and output of Norwegian agriculture reckoned in hectolitres of barley, c. 1800–1865**

	Normal year before 1809	1835	1855	1865
Seed				
(*a*) Corn and peas (hl)	334,000	380,000	555,000	551,000
(*b*) Potatoes (hl)	27,000	163,000	296,000	360,000
(*c*) Corn, peas and potatoes (hl)	361,000	543,000	851,000	911,000
Gross harvest (hl)	1,520,000	3,336,000	6,096,000	6,155,000
Agricultural population	710,000	920,000	1,030,000	1,090,000
(*a*) Average amount sown per head (hl)	*c.* 0·5	*c.* 0·6	*c.* 0·8	*c.* 0·8
(*b*) Average harvest per head (hl)	*c.* 2·1	*c.* 3·6	*c.* 5·9	*c.* 5·7
Enrolled farms	79,000	105,000	128,000	148,000
(*a*) Average amount sown per farm (hl)	*c.* 4·5	*c.* 5·2	*c.* 6·6	*c.* 6·2
(*b*) Average gross harvest per farm (hl)	*c.* 19	*c.* 32	*c.* 47	*c.* 42
Average yield	4·2	6·1	7·1	6·7

* Fartein Valen-Sendstad, *Norske landbruksredskaper, 1800–1850 årene* (De Sandvigske samlinger, Lillehammer, 1964), p. 272.

over wide areas of the south and east in 1807, 1808 and 1812.[1] On top of this, the sharp fall in timber exports during the war resulted in a considerable loss of employment and income for large numbers of farmers and labourers, particularly in southern and eastern Norway. Each of these factors made imperative an increase in the yield of the Norwegian soil. One way of bringing this about was to plant potatoes since the potato was usually more prolific than oats, the main Norwegian grain.[2]

If the failure of the grain harvest and the dislocation of trade in

[1] Sverre Steen, *Det norske folks liv og historie gjennem tidene* (Oslo, 1933), VII, 286, 288, 339.

[2] From an analysis of sixty-four examples of the yield of oats and thirty-four of potatoes, taken from all parts of the country, I have calculated that oats usually yield five-fold and potatoes eleven-fold in the years 1820–35. For these and other crop yields see Kraft, *op. cit.* I, 61–3, 93, 116–20, 256–7, 355–7, 416, 568, 626–8; II, 10, 12–13, 80–2, 187–9, 297–8, 359–61, 502–4, 622–6, 822–4; III, 50–1, 135–9, 265, 331–3, 454; IV, 65, 131, 133–5, 455, 738–9, 741, 843, 888; V, 72, 74, 161–4, 232–5, 455–6, 458–9, 572, 574, 695; VI, 78–9, 174, 261, 318, 365, 470, 472.

The growth of population

the war years is seen as a stimulus to agriculture[1] and especially to potato cultivation in the south and east of the country, can we find any similar stimulus for the apparently somewhat earlier adoption of the potato in western areas? Tentatively we might answer this question in the affirmative for the herring and cod fisheries, which normally provided the bulk of the livelihood of the west coast populations, failed badly in the closing years of the eighteenth century and throughout the first decade of the nineteenth.[2] Lacking the main element of both their usual diet and of their cash incomes, many people in this area were obliged to turn to agriculture for a living,[3] even though it was a way of life they despised[4] and in normal times neglected.[5]

Immediately after the war, other factors strengthened the hold of the potato. The rise in population encouraged people to make the most of the soil. The post-war depression in the shipping and timber industries[6] meant continued difficulty in importing grain and this situation was not eased by the protective tariffs imposed by the newly independent Norwegian government.[7] As the potato proved

[1] Magnus Jensen, *Norges historie Norge under eneveldet, 1660–1814* (Oslo–Bergen, 1962), p. 131. Sverre Steen, *Det gamle samfunn*, p. 266, whilst conceding that more attention was paid to agriculture during the war years, nevertheless maintains that shipbuilding, lumbering, commerce and the herring fisheries remained powerful counter-attractions.
[2] Sverre Steen, *Det gamle samfunn*, pp. 126–7; A. Schweigaard, *op. cit.* pp. 97, 102; O. J. Broch, *op. cit.* p. 112.
[3] Kraft, *op. cit.* IV, 452, remarks of Sunnhordland and Hardanger *fogderi* that 'the ending of the cod fisheries in 1796 gave agriculture in the district its first push forward, since then the war years have contributed much to its advance'. See also Kraft, IV, 134 and V, 231.
[4] Jens Rathke, 'Indberetning til Commerce Collegiet', Kjøbenhavn, 1801 (*Selskabet for de norske fiskeriers fremme*, Bergen, 1907), p. 19, observes that it was a commonly held opinion amongst the inhabitants of the west coast of Norway that agriculture was 'more difficult and less honourable than fishing'.
[5] Kraft, *op. cit.* V, 71; A. Helland, *Norges land og folk: statistisk og topografisk beskrevet: Romsdals amt* (Kristiania, 1885 ff.), pp. 991–2; B. C. de Fine, 'Beskrivelse over Stavanger amt 1745', *Norske magazin. Skrifter og optegnelser angaaende Norge og forfattede efter Reformationen, samlede og udgivne af. N. Nicolaysen* (Christiania, 1870), p. 142; Hans Strøm, *Physisk og œconomisk beskrivelse over fogderiet Søndmør* (Sorøe, 1762), I, 569; Jens Rathke, *op. cit.* p. 19 and his *Afhandling om de norske fiskerier* (Kjøbenhavn, 1797–8), pp. 4, 14.
[6] Edvard Bull, 'Norway: Industrialisation as a factor in economic growth', *Contributions to the first international conference of economic history, Stockholm, 1960* (Paris, The Hague, 1960), pp. 262–3.
[7] This tariff, of course, stimulated Norwegian grain production too. See Sverre Steen, *Det gamle samfunn*, p. 27.

61

itself a more reliable crop[1] than grain and one that could be grown
on land which would support little else,[2] it was natural that it should
be more widely cultivated. Its values as a means of checking weed
growth on land left fallow or of cleaning the soil of land just brought
into cultivation further enhanced its appeal.[3] One other factor
stimulating the planting of potatoes in the immediate post-war years
was a government order of 1816 permitting farmers and cottars
freely to distil potatoes or grain into spirits.[4] Consumption of spirits
produced largely, it would seem from potatoes, is estimated to have
risen from $3\frac{1}{2}$ to 8 litres per head per year between 1815 and 1830.
In the peak year of 1833 no less than 19 million litres were distilled.[5]
One result of this was that the potato became an important cash
crop sold by farmers either directly or indirectly in the form of
spirits.[6]

How quickly and to what extent did the potato enter the everyday
Norwegian diet? Here there is little or no reliable evidence. Christian
Pram reckoned that the potato met as much as one-quarter of the
need for 'bread corn' in the Trondheim diocese by 1800.[7] There is,
however, little other evidence to suggest that the potato had made
such an impact in the area as early as this. Had it done so, one would
imagine it to have made a far better showing in table 3.11 in the
counties of Sør-Trøndelag, Nord-Trøndelag, Nordland and
Finnmark.

Jens Kraft uses language similar to Pram's to indicate the extent
to which the potato had entered the ordinary diet. He speaks of the
potato making 'an important contribution'[8] in upper Telemark by
the 1820s and that, a little earlier, it was 'a considerable part of the

[1] Jens Kraft, *op. cit.* II, 825; VI, 365, 472. Kraft points out, however, that after the
potato had been introduced to Vadsø in Øst-Finnmark in 1829, it yielded very well
and was as much as 13–14 fold in 1831. But it failed partially in 1832 and completely
in 1833.
[2] D. Fredrik Holst, *op. cit.* p. 642; Peter Holm, 'Forsøg til en beskrivelse over Lister
og Mandals amter i Norge', *Topographisk journal for Norge* (Christiania, 1793–4),
II, 8, 104.
[3] Kraft, *op. cit.* II, 11–12, 504; IV, 64.
[4] O. J. Broch, *op. cit.* p. 32.
[5] *Norway. Official publication for the Paris exhibition 1900* (Kristiania, 1900), p. 207.
[6] Kraft, *op. cit.* II, 504; III, 49; V, 161; VI, 79.
[7] Christian Henriksen Pram, *Om befolkningen i Skandinavien og dens tilvæxt i tidsløbet
1769–1800* (Kjøbenhavn, 1809), p. 82.   [8] Kraft, *op. cit.* II, 137.

The growth of population

people's food'[1] in Vestfold. By 1820, according to Kraft, the potato was providing as much as one-third of the farmers' daily food in Solør and Odalen,[2] whilst by the mid-1820s the proportion in parts of Aust-Agder was higher and may even have been as great as one half.[3] Perhaps a more significant indicator of the role of the potato after 1815 is Kraft's oft repeated comment[4] that many parts of Norway previously dependent upon grain imports were able, by the 1820s and early 1830s to reduce their purchases or dispense with them altogether because they now had homegrown potatoes. In some areas a brisk internal trade in potatoes developed.[5]

Malthus noted in his *Essay* that 'almost everywhere the cultivation of potatoes has succeeded and they are growing more and more into general use, though in the distant parts of the country they are not relished by the common people'.[6] This comment stemmed, of course, from his journey through Norway in the summer of 1799. From the *Journal* we are able to trace the comments which underlie this judgement. Malthus, it seems, was told by a country gentleman, Mr Collett, who lived near Christiania, that 'potatoes thrive remarkably well. They have been introduced into Norway about 30 years and are coming daily more into use.'[7] Malthus himself noticed potato patches near Lake Mjøsa[8] and a little further north in Gudbrandsdalen his landlord told him that potatoes were 'much in use & much liked'.[9] On the other hand, in the same area, Malthus learned from a cottar that 'potatoes has been but lately introduced, & were not generally used. He liked them himself but many people did not. They have increased much in general use about Christiania during

[1] *Ibid.* II, 623.   [2] *Ibid.* I, 485–6.   [3] *Ibid.* II, 332.
[4] *Ibid.* I, 92, 485–6; II, 189–90, 623, 628; III, 49, 51, 454, 515; IV, 600, 843–4; V, 72–3; VI, 79, 261, 365, 473–4. These areas included parts of Østfold.
[5] *Ibid.* I, 119, 567; II, 359, 502, 623, 626, 824; III, 516; IV, 65–6, 131, 456–7, 888; V, 75, 232–3, 234, 456–7, 573; VI, 14 (note printed on pp. 617–18). Places selling potatoes included Rygge, Råde, (Østfold), Tynset (Hedmark), Lier, Sandsvær (Buskerud), Hof, Ramnes, Borre, Tjølling (Vestfold), Lyngdal, Vanse (Vest-Agder), Jæren, Rennesøy (Rogaland), Stord, Tysnes, Kvinnherad, Fjelberg, Skånevik, Os, Finnås (Hordaland), Gloppen (Sogn and Fjordane), Hjørundfjord, Sykkylven, Ørskog, Haram, Borgund, Ulstein, Sunndal, Ranes, Øye, (Møre and Romsdal), Støren, Byneset, Børsa (Sør-Trøndelag), and Frosta (Nord-Trøndelag).
[6] T. R. Malthus, *Essay on the principle of population*, Everyman edition (London, 1914), p. 162.
[7] Patricia James (ed.), *The travel diaries of T. R. Malthus* (Cambridge, 1966), p. 101.
[8] *Ibid.* p. 124.   [9] *Ibid.* p. 133.

the last 7 or 8 years, & now form a considerable part of the food
of the common people in that part of the country, but are probably
not much in use in the interior parts of the country'.[1]

The Danish traveller, Jens Rathke, noted in 1800 that in parts of
southern Norway people were beginning to 'love potatoes' although
there were still many farmers who did not know how to cultivate
them properly.[2] In an area such as Hallingdal around 1800 potatoes
were still a rarity as is indicated by the fact that the few that were
grown were washed as soon as they were dug and spread over the
floor to dry.[3] Daniel Clarke, who travelled through parts of Norway
in the same year as Malthus, does not appear to have considered
potatoes as part of the ordinary Norwegian diet. He believed the
diet of the better class of labourer consisted of 'black rye bread and
salted butter or cheese for breakfast; boiled barley and herring or
some other fish with beer for dinner. Once a week, and sometimes
twice...fresh meat. The common people in general live nearly in
the same way, only not quite so well; instead of beer they have sour
milk.'[4] But by the 1820s Inglis noted one change in this diet; the
fish was always eaten with 'a plentiful supply of potatoes'.[5]

No accurate assessment of the place of the potato in the diet of
Norwegians is possible until towards the end of the nineteenth
century. It appears from a survey carried out at the beginning of the
1870s that the annual per capita consumption of potatoes was then
450 lb.[6] The other main ingredients in the Norwegian diet of the
time were corn (420 lb), meat and bacon (55 lb), fish (at least
55 lb) and milk and milk products (700 pints).[7] Out of a total
cultivated area of 2,700 sq.km at the same date some 350 sq.km
were devoted to potatoes, 50 to wheat, 130 to rye, 500 to barley,
920 to oats, 190 to a hybrid of barley and oats (*blandkorn*) and 40–50
to peas and beans. The rest of the cultivated area was under other
root crops, artificial grass or was laying fallow.[8] In some areas the

[1] Patricia James, *op. cit.* pp. 137–8.
[2] Jens Rathke, 'Indberetning til commerce-collegiet om reiser i Norge i aarene 1800–02',
Kjøbenhavn, 1805, *Selskabet for det norske fiskeriers fremme* (Bergen, 1907), p. 46.
[3] Lars Reinton, *Folk og fortid i Hol, ii. Fra 1815 til vår tid* (Oslo, 1943), p. 53.
[4] Cited by H. D. Inglis, *A personal narrative of a journey through Norway, part of
Sweden and the islands and states of Denmark* (4th edn., London, 1837), pp. 159–60.
[5] *Ibid.* pp. 159–60.   [6] O. J. Broch, *op. cit.* pp. 29–30.
[7] *Ibid.* pp. 29–30.   [8] *Ibid.* pp. 11–13.

cultivation of potatoes was naturally much more important than the aggregate figures would suggest. For instance, in the north of Norway, from the Lofoten islands northwards, as much as half of the arable land was planted with potatoes in the early 1870s.[1] Also, as one might have expected, cottars devoted a greater proportion of their arable land to potatoes than did farmers.[2]

It is possible to draw three tentative conclusions from the evidence presented so far. First, although the potato was introduced into western Norway about 1760 there is little evidence to suggest that it made much headway amongst the general public before 1800, except perhaps in the south-west. By that date, however, the plant was probably known throughout the country mainly as a result of the activities of the 'potato-priests'.[3] Second, the collapse of the herring and cod fisheries along the west coast in the years around the turn of the century, together with the failures of the grain harvest, the disruption of the shipping and timber trades and the coastal blockade by the English fleet in the war years (1807–14), brought the potato into general use very rapidly. Third, the sharp increase in the rate of population growth in the decade after 1815; the combined depression in the shipping and timber industries; the high price of grain because of the tariff and unsatisfactory harvests; the removal of legal restrictions on distilling and the growing recognition of the value of the potato in crop rotations all accelerated its advance and may well have embedded it firmly in the Norwegian diet by the mid-1820s over wide areas of the country.

The question now arises, to what extent we can attribute the change in the mortality pattern after 1815 to an improved food supply. In so far as the potato provided this and in so far as the death rate began to fall earliest in those areas where it was first introduced, the presumption is strong that mortality in eighteenth and early nineteenth-century Norway was a function of food supply.

---

[1] *Ibid.* p. 12.

[2] For a detailed account of the cottar's economy and place in society in the early 1870s see J. N. Mohn, *Statistiske meddelelser om husmandsklassens betydning i samfundet og husmændenes økonomiske stilling* (Kristiania, 1880); see also Daniel Dybvik, 'Husmanns-vesenet i Numedal', *Norsk Geografisk Tidsskrift*, **14**, 7–8 (1954), 390.

[3] This was a contemporary nickname. See Wilhelm Keilhau, *Det norske folks liv og historie gjennem tidene*, **8** (Oslo, 1929), 32; O. Vig, 'Om landalmuens næringsdrift og levemaade', *Folkevennen*, **1** (Kristiania, 1852), 169.

Nevertheless, much depends upon whether or not harvest failures in earlier years can be correlated with increases in the death rate. So far as increases due to smallpox are concerned there would appear to be little correlation. For, as Utterstrøm has effectively demonstrated in Sweden, smallpox followed its own cycle apparently unaffected by food shortages.[1] Dysentery and typhus, however, seem on the Swedish evidence more closely tied to harvest failures[2] and certainly eighteenth-century Norwegian opinion attributed the prevalence of these diseases to malnutrition and the eating of infected food.[3] It is of course true that neither typhus nor dysentery is caused directly by lack of food, although in the case of the latter it has been pointed out recently that whilst 'an attack cannot develop except through the agency of the specific bacillus...anything causing an intestinal upset, unsuitable food for example, predisposes to infection'.[4]

One is inclined to feel that if the harvest failures had not had such dire consequences, the eighteenth-century Norwegian farmer would not have gone to such lengths to try to avoid them, nor been forced to make do with barely palatable surrogates when they occurred. Crops were grown high up the valley sides on barely accessible patches of land to avoid the cold air which tended to lie in the valley bottoms. Fires were lit so that their smoke might shield the crops from frost.[5] If the snow lay too long in the spring it had to be laboriously swept aside so that ashes could be strewn on the ground to attract the sun's rays, melt the frozen soil and make it fit for ploughing.[6] Sour milk, cheese, butter, dried fish and meat, salted

[1] G. Utterstrøm, 'Some population problems in pre-industrial Sweden', *Scandinavian Economic History Review*, **2**, 2 (Copenhagen, 1954), 137.

[2] Although Utterstrøm does not support this view see *ibid.* pp. 126–31, 135, 137, 152 and 160.

[3] B. C. de Fine, *op. cit.* p. 137. See too the large number of replies from parish priests to a government enquiry in 1743, which embraced questions on diseases. For a copy of the scheme see Reidar Djupedal, 'Den store innsamlinga av topografisk, historisk og språkleg tilfang ved embetsmennene 1743 og "Det Kongerige Norge"', *Heimen* (1955–7), **10**, 304–6. Copies of a large number of replies are to be found in the *Norsk historisk kjeldeskrifts-institutt* (Oslo).

[4] Sir William P. MacArthur, 'Medical history of the famine' in R. Dudley Edwards and T. Desmond Williams (eds.), *The great famine* (Dublin, 1956), p. 269.

[5] Lars Reinton, *Folk og fortid i Hol* (Oslo, 1943), II, 53–4, 58.

[6] *Ibid.* II, 58; Kraft, *op. cit.* II, 299.

herring, even bread (*flatbrød*)[1] were made to be stored over long periods with the aim of avoiding food shortages. But when the herring shoals by-passed the coast or when the spring was late and the summer short, so that the rich mountain pastures could be only partially exploited, food shortages occurred. Fish and fish bones were ground into flour whilst what grain there was might be mixed with 'straw', *Rumex crispus, Anagallis, Brassica oleracea* and *rapa, Lichen islandicus and rangiferinus, polypodium filix mas*, and the bark of *Betula alba*.[2] More extreme measures sometimes proved necessary. For example, it was reported from Hallingdal in the early 1740s, how accurately we cannot say, that so acute was the food shortage that straw was taken from the dungheaps, washed, mixed with meal and baked![3]

The behaviour of the birth rate in eighteenth-century Norway also appears to be closely associated with the success or failure of the harvest. Indeed it seems that Norwegians attempted to control their fertility in order not to fall to subsistence level or below and not to succumb, if possible, to a run of bad harvests. During a series of bad harvests, it is obvious that the controls on fertility which were built into the institutions of Norwegian society were sharpened, in an attempt to reduce fertility still further. Marriages and conceptions were prudently delayed. That this should have been so lends further support to the argument that the harvest was a crucial mechanism controlling the rate of population increase. Had a bad harvest not brought such suffering and premature death to eighteenth-century Norway it is difficult to see why the population should have sought so strenuously to limit its numbers during the years of food shortage.

To illustrate the demographic impact of food shortages we might look at the behaviour of the crude birth, death and marriage rates in the Akershus diocese during the early 1770s. This was a period of acute distress throughout Scandinavia. The population of Denmark

[1] For an account of Norwegian diet during the last four hundred years see Fredrik Grøn 'Om Kostholdet i Norge fra omkring 1500 tallet og op til vår tid', *Norsk videnskapsakademis skrifter*, II. *Historisk-filosofisk Klasse* (Oslo, 1941).
[2] D. Fredrik Holst, *op. cit.* p. 642.
[3] Ivar Wiel, 'Beskrivelse over Ringeriges og Hallingdals fogderi, 1743', *Topographisk journal for Norge* (Christiania, 1802–5), 9, 30–2, 152–3.

Population and Society in Norway 1735–1865

fell in 1771, 1772 and 1773;[1] that of Sweden in 1772 and 1773;[2] that of Norway in 1773 and 1774.[3] The usually accepted Danish index of food prices was especially high in 1770, 1771 and 1772. The Swedish harvest index showed dearth conditions in 1771 and 1773. Few areas within Scandinavia escaped the crisis. In the Danish diocese of Aarhus, twenty-two of twenty-six communes showed an excess of deaths over births in 1771. In 1772 the number doing so was eighteen and in 1773 it was twenty-four. In 1774 none did.[4] In Norway the Bergen diocese had more deaths than births in 1772 and in 1773 this was true of the dioceses of Akershus, Kristiansand and Trondheim.[5] Within the Kristiansand diocese, four of the eleven deaneries had an excess of deaths over births in 1771, five had in 1772 and seven in 1773. No deanery had more deaths than births in the Akershus diocese in 1771, but in 1772 seven out of the fifteen, and in 1772 every deanery had. In 1774 six were in this position and two were in 1775.[6]

The birth, marriage and death rates moved sharply in the years 1771–6 in the Akershus diocese, as indeed, they did in other parts of Norway and at other times when similar conditions of distress prevailed.[7] Perhaps not surprisingly the death rate moved the most sharply: from a low of 21 deaths per 1,000 mean population in 1771 to a high of 64 per 1,000 in 1773. It then declined to 20 by 1776. The marriage rate declined only slightly, from 7 to 6 per 1,000 between 1771 and 1772. It had, however, been declining relatively steadily for sometime before 1771; in fact from a high of 9·4 in 1764. This steady decline was partly a reflection of changes in the population's age composition—as the deficient cohort of the early 1740s reached the marriageable age groups. But it also reflected a compensatory movement to more normal levels following the sharp rise

[1] Aksel Lassen, *Fald og fremgang; træk af befolkningsudviklingen i Danmark 1645–1960* (Aarhus, 1965), table o, 2a, p. 527.
[2] The population entered in the *mandtal* actually fell each year from 1769 to 1775, *ibid.* p. 528.   [3] See below, statistical appendix, table 1.
[4] The *kapitaltakst* for rye, in rdlr. and skilling was 3·40 in 1770, 4·40 in 1771 and 3·80 in 1772. Over the five years 1765–9 it averaged 2·88 and in the period 1773–7, 2·36. Lassen, *op. cit.* p. 528.
[5] See below, statistical appendix, tables 2 and 3.
[6] These calculations are based on the bishops' returns of births and deaths in their respective deaneries. Manuscripts in the statsarkiver of Oslo and Kristiansand.
[7] See below, statistical appendix, tables 5, 6, 7 in the years 1740–5; 1806–10, 1812–16.

68

TABLE 3.13   *Births, deaths and marriages per 1,000 mean population in the diocese of Akershus 1771–6**

	1771	1772	1773	1774	1775	1776
Deaths	21	26	64	29	26	20
Marriages	7	6	6	9	10	9
Births	34	28	22	29	35	32

* Statistical appendix, tables 5, 6 and 7.

in the rate in 1764. This rise was probably a result of more employment opportunities being available as a consequence of the high death rate of 1763 (34 per 1,000). The same explanation also goes for the leap in the crude marriage rate from 6 to 10 per 1,000 between 1773 and 1775. The very high death rate of 1773 (64 per 1,000) undoubtedly caused vacancies on farms and holdings. Land inherited earlier than usual meant marriages could take place earlier than expected. At the same time marriages delayed during the period of distress could now take place.

The behaviour of the birth rate in this period is the most difficult one to explain. The number of births in the Akershus diocese per 1,000 mean population fell by more than a third from 34 to 22 between 1771 and 1773 and then rose by more than half, to 35 per 1,000 in 1775. Part of the explanation lies in the fall in the marriage rate for the newly married are relatively prolific. Kiær discovered from a survey carried out in the 1870s that 50 per cent of the couples married in Norway at that time had a child in the first year of their marriage. He also discovered that a third of all legitimate births in any one year were the product of marriages which had taken place during the previous five years.[1] This high fertility of the recently married is not, however, sufficient to explain all the fall in the birth rate of the population of the Akershus diocese between 1771 and 1773, as the fall in the number of marriages was comparatively small. One assumes that some pregnant women would be counted amongst the dead in 1773 and that the distress of the period would

[1] A. N. Kiær, 'Nogle oplysninger om forholdet mellem ægteskaber og fødsler med særligt hensyn til ægteskabernes stiftelsestid', *Det norske videnskabs-selskabets forhandlinger* (Christiania, 1873), pp. 4, 5, 184.

Population and Society in Norway 1735-1865

give rise to an increase in the number of still-births and miscarriages. But the magnitude of the fall in the birth rate would also suggest that some conscious restraint was being exercised at this time, on births within marriage. Unfortunately, evidence on either contraceptive techniques or abortifaceants in pre-industrial Norway is virtually zero. There is some nineteenth-century evidence that condoms were made from the intestines of sheep and goats[1] and that various brews involving the use of the needles from yew trees, or other evergreens, of ergot, saffron, turpentine, cammomile tea, aloe and cinnamon were concocted to facilitate abortion.[2] How effective or how widespread these practices were is not known.[3]

Some of the smaller fluctuations in the national birth, marriage and death rates may be accounted for by the differential operation

[1] Helge Refsum, 'Eilert Sundt og folkemoralen', *Norsk kultur-historie* (Oslo, 1940), IV, 272.
[2] Personal communication from Helge Refsum, Bergen. Also I. Reichborn-Kjennerud, 'Vår gamle trolldomsmedisin', *Skrifter utgitt av det norske videnskapsakademi*, no. 6 (Oslo, 1927), pp. 179, 184.
[3] The question—'Is there any folk belief on the means to procure an abortion', contained in a questionnaire compiled by I. Reichborn-Kjennerud, Nils Lid and Hjalmar Falk (see their 'Innsamling av Norsk folke-medisin: rettledning og ordliste', *Maal og Minne*, Kristiania, 1921, p. 86) appears to have elicited no response.
There is evidence that prolonged lactation was practised in Sestersdalen to avoid conception (cf. B. J. Hovde, *The Scandinavian countries*, Boston, 1943, II, 759), although other evidence suggests breast feeding was rare in this area at least in the 1860s (cf. Peter M. Holst, 'Helseforholdene i Norge omkring 1880', *Tidsskrift for den norske lægeforening*, Oslo, 1955, p. 13).
The breast feeding of relatively old children was apparently not uncommon in many areas of Norway at the beginning of the present century. Grøn suggests that children were often breastfed until they were two or three years old (cf. Fredrik Grøn, 'Folkemedicin i Sestersdalen', *Maal og Minne*, Kristiania, 1909, p. 79). I. Reichborn-Kjennerud, 'Vaar gamle trolldomsmedisin', *Skrifter utgitt av det norske videnskapsakademi* (Oslo, 1927), p. 27, cites the following examples, taken from a survey carried out in the early 1900s, of the usual period of breast feeding in certain parts of Norway. I do not know how the enquiry was conducted and, therefore, how much reliance can be placed on the figures. In Bamble the usual period of breast feeding was reported to be 1-4 years; in Hegra, 1-2; Hemne, 2-3; Kvinesdal, 1-2; Lenvik, 1-2; Nordfjord, 1-3; Nordfrøya, 2-3; Nordhordland, 1-3; Nordmøre, 1½-3; Setesdal, 4-5, occasionally 12 (sic), Solør, 1-3, occasionally 5 (sic); Sunnhordland, 2-3, occasionally 10 (sic), Sogn, 2-3 and longer periods not exceptional; Sunnmøre, 1-2 occasionally 6 (sic); Tinn, 1-2; Vefsn, 1-3.
Lengthy breast feeding was considered by some Norwegians in the nineteenth century to strengthen children (cf. Sigurd Nergaard, 'Gard og grend. Folkeminner fra Østerdalen', *Norsk Folkeminnelag*, III, Kristiania, 1921). It has also been given as the reason for lower infant mortality rates in mid-nineteenth-century Norway than elsewhere in Europe (see O. J. Broch, *op. cit.* p. 17).

70

The growth of population

of the mechanisms just described, at the regional level. If the region affected had a large population the impact on the national statistics would naturally be greater than if it had a small one. Only when harvests failed generally and the associated epidemics were widespread would the national aggregate fluctuate violently. Fortunately, such nation-wide catastrophes were relatively rare in eighteenth-century Norway and, after 1815, totally absent in the nineteenth. As it happened, they occurred at almost exactly thirty-year intervals and it is to this that we can ascribe the perhaps most notable feature of the Norwegian birth rate in the years 1735–1865, namely its cyclical character.

We have, unfortunately, no reasonably accurate measure of the success or failure of the harvests in eighteenth-century Norway. Such a measure would have, in any case, to be a complex one for we can isolate at least three regional diets, dominated in the first case by fish, in the second by grain (mainly oats and barley) and in the third, by animal products (mainly milk and cheese). A number of the major peaks in the death rate (1741–2, 1748, 1773) occurred in years when the grain harvest failed[1] over large parts of the country and it is noticeable in each that the Akershus diocese, where the diet was based more on grain than elsewhere, suffered particularly badly. Other failures in 1762–3, 1784–5, 1808 and 1812 also made their mark. In the years 1797–1806 the death rate in the diocese of Trondheim reached its highest point in 1803. Imports of grain entering the diocese in that year, at 229,242 tønder were almost three times above the average (84,544 tønder) for the period and almost double those of 1804 (125,262 tønder) ,which had the second highest import. In the Bergen diocese the highest grain imports and the highest death rate of the period coincided in 1804. In Akershus, the highest import figure was recorded in 1804, but this was a year when the death rate was low. However, the second highest import took place in 1801 when the death rate was at its peak for these years.[2]

The state of the grain harvest was obviously not the sole determinant of fluctuations in the death rate. Much depended upon the

[1] For a general outline of the timing of harvest failures see Sverre Steen, *Det norske folks liv og historie gjennem tidene*, VI and VII.
[2] Worm-Müller, *op. cit.* bilag 1.

71

availability of other foods (particularly fish or animal products), on the state of food reserves and on the ability of an area to make good temporary deficiencies by purchases from elsewhere, internally as well as through imports. Much too might depend on whether dysentery and typhus got a foothold or whether climatic conditions or good communications facilitated their advance. Communications by land, for instance, were probably easier within the more populous parts of the Akershus and Trondheim dioceses than they were in either Bergen or Kristiansand. This might well be part of the explanation of the often sharply higher death rates in the two former areas. Once an epidemic of typhus or dysentery began it might continue for several years. In 1808, for instance, both diseases took a hold in the diocese of Akershus, facilitated, it was alleged, by the poor harvest and the return of soldiers and sailors from the front. The diseases were very active throughout 1809 and were still raging violently in parts of the diocese in 1810.[1]

Although there can be no doubt that the pattern of the Norwegian death rate underwent a permanent change with the ending of the Napoleonic wars, we cannot be confident about the reasons for this change. Was the fall in mortality due to the reduction in smallpox deaths and the increased cultivation of potatoes, as contemporaries thought? Or should we stress other factors such as the spread of corn magazines amongst the country parishes.[2] It is possible that improved road transport played a part. Certainly a number of new roads were built in the late eighteenth and early nineteenth centuries. But as late as 1840, Norway had only 3,500 miles of main road and 6,000 miles of parish roads.[3] In any case the roads were used mainly by travellers not freight. Winter was still the season for the carriage of goods,[4] when frozen rivers, and lakes provided a better medium of transport than any man had devised.

Perhaps we too should examine the 1790s more closely, for figures 3 (*a*)–(*e*) suggest that here we have a harbinger of the new

[1] Kraft, *op. cit.* I, 250, 342, 408; III, 40.
[2] O. A. Øverland, *De norske bygdemagasiner* (Kristiania, 1913).
[3] A. Baalsrud, 'Veivesenets og veibygningens utvikling i Norge', *Norsk Geografisk Tidsskrift*, 2 (Oslo, 1928–9), 47–52: Joh. Skougaard, *Det norske veivæsens historie med oversigt over statens veivæsens virksomhed i tidsrummet 1820–1896* (Kristiania, 1899), end map.　　　　[4] O. J. Broch, *op. cit.* p. 166.

pattern of death rates. Any realignment of the argument on to the 1790s would, of course, greatly reduce the possible importance of the potato and might suggest that credit for the return to the older pattern of death rates during the early 1800s (particularly in the Akershus and Trondheim dioceses) goes almost solely to the effects of the Napoleonic wars. The role of war in the eighteenth-century demographic history of Norway should perhaps have received more attention, although the country's position somewhat aside from the main centres of conflict would suggest that war had less of an impact on her population than it had in, for example, Denmark. Aksel Lassen, in his recently published study of Danish population movements, in pointing out that food prices often rose before the onset of epidemics, also notes that the rise was more likely to be a consequence of extraordinary purchases for the armed forces than the result of a bad harvest. He goes on to argue that the greatest epidemics experienced by Denmark (around 1700, 1710–11, 1741–3, 1756, 1763, 1771–3) arose in connection with war for the spread of disease was facilitated as large bodies of people were brought together, usually in insanitary camps, and as the materials of war, particularly food, were gathered from a wide area.[1]

Whatever the ultimate cause of the rapid expansion of population in Norway after 1815 there can be little doubt that the immediate one was the fall in the death rate. The newly independent Norwegian government faced, therefore, a demographic situation not unlike that in many of the currently underdeveloped countries. Not for fifty years did Norway begin to develop a modern industrial sector although the rise in world demand for her traditional exports— timber, fish and shipping—drew increasing numbers of her people away from agriculture. The increased cultivation of potatoes, together with the rapid expansion of population could have hindered, as it appears to have done in Ireland, the growth of labour productivity in agriculture, but it does not appear to have done so.[2] A great deal of new land was brought into cultivation. Between 1820 and 1865 the cultivated area doubled[3] and according to Eilert

---

[1] Aksel Lassen, *op. cit.* pp. 280–3.
[2] Fartein Valen-Sendstad, *Norske landbruks-redskaper, 1800–1850 årene*, De sandvigske samlinger (Lillehammer, 1964), p. 272.   [3] *Ibid.* p. 284.

TABLE 3.14   *Percentage of men and women 0–19, 20–59 and 60 years and over in Norway 1801–65**

	Men						Women					
	1801	1825	1835	1845	1855	1865	1801	1825	1835	1845	1855	1865
0–19	45·0	43·7	46·9	44·8	44·9	47·0	41·0	40·8	43·9	42·3	42·0	44·1
20–59	47·0	47·3	44·7	47·4	46·8	44·8	49·0	48·6	46·0	48·2	48·2	46·1
60–	7·9	8·8	8·2	7·7	8·0	8·1	9·8	10·5	10·0	9·3	9·8	9·7

* Calculated from Johan Vogt, 'En generasjonsstatistikk for det norske folk' *Memorandum fra Oslo universitets sosialøkonomiske institutt*, Oslo, 29 January 1957.

Sundt, the clearing of land was the greatest single occupation.[1] To do this was not easy. Norway received no bonus from a changing age structure, the burden of dependency remaining fairly constant (table 3.14). Yet a Malthusian situation did not develop; the new land was not divided into ever smaller holdings for a peasantry moving ever closer to bare subsistence. Much of it was cleared specifically so that new equipment and new methods of cultivation could be employed,[2] with the result that productivity increased. Until 1865 Norway was able to support a rapidly growing population without a fall in living standards.[3] Beyond that the task proved too great. The growth rate of 1·3 per cent per annum from 1855 to 1865 was followed by one of 0·64 per cent in the decade 1866–75 and of 0·66 per cent in the years 1875–90. By the end of the century only Ireland of all the European countries was losing so large a proportion of her natural increase by emigration as was Norway.[4]

[1] *Folkevennen* (1865), p. 523 cited by H. O. Christophersen, *op. cit.* p. 404.
[2] Fartein Valen-Sendstad, *op. cit.* p. 286.
[3] For evidence on living standards see O. Vig. *op. cit.* pp. 160, 173. Also O. Vig, 'Nogle ord om folketælling m.m.', *Folkevennen*, 4 (Kristiania, 1855), 310–12.
[4] *Norway. Official publication for the Paris exhibition 1900* (Kristiania, 1900), pp. 104–7.

4   *Marriage and fertility*

In the last chapter an attempt was made to show that the rapid growth of population in Norway during the half century after 1815 was largely caused by a fall in the death rate. This fall was a sudden, once and for all change, from a moderately high, by recent standards, and violently fluctuating level before 1815 to a moderately low and surprisingly stable one after that date. Between 1815 and 1865 the mean death rate fell little, nor was there much change in the age specific death rates. The reasons for the fall around the year 1815 and the absence of any subsequent reduction remain somewhat obscure, although vaccination against smallpox and particularly the increase in the food supply following the rapid dissemination of the potato appear to be plausible contributory factors.

When we turn to the birth rate we find no such dramatic development. Although we can associate short-term fluctuations with specific contemporary events, over the period as a whole there is little secular change in its level. The longer swings appear to reflect no more than shifts in the age composition of the population, in so far as one can identify these. A traditional method of allowing for changes in age structure when the data are inadequate is to calculate the ratio of women in the fertile age group to children under the age of five years. Since mortality can be quite heavy amongst the under fives, this measure suffers from the impact of differences in mortality either over time or between different places at the same time. Fortunately, the Norwegian statistics allow us to calculate, from the various censuses taken between 1769 and 1865, the ratio of women aged 21–50 years to live births in the years preceding the censuses. This ratio fluctuates hardly at all—(the range is from 73 to 78)—throughout the period, suggesting that general fertility was stable (table 4.1).

It is possible that the apparent lack of change in general fertility

TABLE 4.1 *Births per 100 women 21-50 at various dates in Norway 1769-1865**

Census	Women 21-50	Births in 5 years preceding census	Births in 5 years preceding census per 100 women 21-50
1769†	147,687	113,336	77
1801	187,294	138,156	74
1825	219,673	170,654	78
1835	232,914	181,363	78
1845	269,074	195,401	73
1855	304,803	234,491	77
1865	340,766	262,738	77

* Population totals 1801–65 from Johan Vogt, 'En generasjonsstatistikk for det norske folk', *Memorandum fra Oslo universitets sosialøkonomiske institutt*, Oslo, 29 January 1957.
† Population total for 1769 calculated from *Norges offisielle statistikk*, **10**, 178 (Oslo, 1949), 31. Birth totals from statistical appendix, table 2.

TABLE 4.2 *Legitimate births per 100 ever married women 15-49 years in Norway in 1769, 1801 and 1865**

Census	Married and widowed women 15-49	Births in 5 years preceding census	Births in 5 years preceding census per 100 ever married women
1769	89,847	109,446	122
1801	116,951	130,006	111
1865	211,160	242,081	115

* Populations as in table 4.1. Totals of legitimate births for 1765–9 and 1796–1800 calculated from *Norges offisielle statistikk*, **10**, 178 (Oslo, 1949), 40–3.

might mask important changes in marital fertility. To see whether or not this is so the number of legitimate births was related to married women (and widows) in the 15–49 age group. Again, a surprising stability is shown over the period as a whole (table 4.2).

The constancy of fertility, both general and marital over the period, appears to reflect corresponding stability in nuptiality.

TABLE 4.3   *Percentage of married or widowed men and women in various age groups in Norway 1801–65**

	Men				Women			
	11–20	21–30	31–40	41–50	11–20	21–30	31–40	41–50
1801	0·2	26·7	77·4	91·3	1·2	35·5	73·3	84·7
1835	0·1	24·4	72·7	86·7	0·6	33·8	73·9	83·6
1845	0·1	22·1	72·3	86·7	0·6	29·9	74·4	84·4
1855	0·1	23·1	73·9	87·9	0·5	31·7	74·4	85·7
1865	0·1	23·3	75·8	89·2	0·2	34·1	74·8	85·5

* *Tabeller vedkommende folkemængdens bevægelse i aarene 1856–65*, N.O.S. Ældre række, C, no. 1 (Christiania, 1868–9), pp. 234–7.

TABLE 4.4   *Mean age of brides and bridegrooms in Norway 1841–65**

	Bridegrooms	Brides
1841–5	30·6	28·2
1846–50	30·4	28·0
1851–5	30·5	28·1
1856–60	30·9	28·1
1861–5	31·0	28·1

* O. J. Broch, *Kongeriget Norge og det norske folk* (Kristiania, 1876), tillæg xvi, 30.

A calculation made by Anders Kiær shows that between 1801 and 1865 the proportion of ever married men declined especially at the younger ages. But there was not very much change and so far as women were concerned, there was virtually no change (table 4.3).

We cannot unfortunately measure the age at marriage in the country as a whole until the 1840s. From then to the 1860s, however, our calculations show that the mean age at marriage of men rises only slightly from 30·6 years in the period 1841–5 to 31 years in the period 1861–5. Corresponding figures for women showed a barely perceptible fall from 28·2 to 28·1 years (table 4.4).

The figures in table 4.4 may reflect a number of influences, particularly any change in the proportion of first to subsequent

TABLE 4.5 *Mean age of brides and bridegrooms (neither of whom had been previously married) in Norway in the years 1841–65**

	Bridegrooms	Brides
1841–5	28·2	26·0
1846–50	28·3	26·2
1851–5	28·6	26·5
1856–60	29·0	26·7
1861–5	29·1	26·6

* O. J. Broch, *Kongeriget Norge og det norske folk* (Kristiania, 1876), tillæg XVI, 30.

TABLE 4.6 *Number of marriages between bachelors and spinsters, bachelors and widows, widowers and spinsters and widowers and widows per 1,000 of all marriages in Norway in the years 1841–65**

	Bachelor–spinsters	Bachelor–widows	Widowers–spinsters	Widowers–widows
1841–5	802	63	103	32
1846–50	829	54	90	27
1851–5	837	49	90	24
1856–60	837	49	91	23
1861–5	835	44	98	23

* O. J. Broch, *Kongeriget Norge og det norske folk* (Kristiania, 1876), tillæg XVII, 31.

marriages and any shift in the age composition of the population. In fact, the mean age at first marriage (i.e. where neither the bridegroom nor the bride had been previously married) showed a rise of almost a year in the case of men (28·2 to 29·1) over the period 1841–5 to 1861–5. The rise in the age at marriage of women, though smaller (26·0 to 26·6) was marked nonetheless (table 4.5). Over this period, however, the number of bachelor/spinster marriages rose at the expense of marriages where at least one partner had been married before (table 4.6).

The change in the mean age at marriage of previously unmarried couples was not, however, as significant as it looks, since virtually all the change is explicable in terms of the shift in the age com-

TABLE 4.7 *Annual number of marriages in Norway of bachelors and spinsters per 100 bachelors and spinsters in the same age groups in the years 1841–65*

| | Of 100 bachelors or spinsters in each age group there married annually | | | | | | | | | |
| | Bachelors | | | | | Spinsters | | | | |
	1841–1845	1846–1850	1851–1855	1856–1860	1861–1865	1841–1845	1846–1850	1851–1855	1856–1860	1861–1865
15–20	0·1	0·1	0·1	0·1	0·1	0·8	0·8	0·8	0·9	0·9
20–25	4·8	4·3	4·2	4·1	4·0	7·5	6·9	6·7	6·8	7·1
25–30	11·7	11·6	11·8	11·5	11·3	10·1	10·2	10·8	10·8	10·2
30–35	11·6	12·2	13·1	13·3	13·5	8·7	9·4	10·4	9·9	9·5
35–40	7·7	7·5	8·6	9·5	9·0	5·3	5·1	5·7	6·1	5·7
40–45	4·7	4·3	4·9	5·9	6·0	3·7	3·4	3·7	4·5	4·4
45–50	2·3	2·2	2·4	2·8	2·8	2·6	2·1	2·1	2·4	2·3

* *Tabeller vedkommende folkemængdens bevægelse i aarene 1856–65*, N.O.S. Ældre række, C, no. 1 (Christiania, 1868–9), p. xxiv.

position of the population towards the higher ages. There was very little change over the period in the number of people marrying at various ages calculated as a proportion of the number of people at risk at those ages (table 4.7).

A priori the level of fertility and nuptiality reflects the economic situation in a society and therefore the stability of both in Norway comes as no surprise. The industrial revolution, however one defines it, had certainly made little impact on the country by 1865.[1] Indeed, until the 1840s, the industrial sector was confined entirely to the sort of undertakings often found in the pre-industrial west: corn mills, saw mills, lime works, distilleries, breweries and shipyards.[2] As the chief source of power was water, rather than steam, production units were both small and scattered. Between 1850 and 1865, the number of industrial workers doubled (table 4.8). Within the metal and machinery trades the number employed in iron

[1] It is reckoned that the agricultural population fell from 83 per cent to 66 per cent of the total population between 1801 and 1865. A. Th. Kiær, 'Det norske folks hovederhverv 1801 samt 1865–1900', *Statsøkonomisk tidsskrift* (Kristiania, 1904), p. 226. It is likely that these figures exaggerate the fall as occupational definitions were more precise in the census of 1865 than in that of 1801.
[2] O. J. Broch, *Kongeriget Norge og det norske folk* (Kristiania, 1876), p. 133.

TABLE 4.8   *Industrial workers in Norway in 1850, 1860 and 1865**

	1850	1860	1865
Timber	4,090	6,130	7,085
Metal and machinery	1,368	1,608	4,999
Textiles	1,481	2,982	3,359
Food and beverages	2,792	2.945	4,072
Clay and stone	1,721	2,498	2,893
Chemicals	92	220	417
Paper, leather and rubber	632	679	914
Lighting and heating	103	200	536
Clothing	—	19	138
Total	12,279	17,281	24,413

* Norges offisielle statistikk, **10**, 178, *Statistiske oversikter for Norge 1948* (Oslo, 1949), table 89.

foundries, machine shops and shipyards making iron ships rose from 1,057 to 4,594. The number employed in textiles rose from 1,481 to 3,359[1] and those of the timber industry group, in saw and planing mills, from 4,090 to 6,997. Despite this impressive rate of growth, however, there were only about 24,000 industrial workers in Norway by 1865: a relatively modest figure by the side of the 113,000 farmers, 113,000 farm servants and 60,000 *husmenn med jord* (crofters).[2]

The Norwegian mining industry employed about 14,000 people in 1865. They and their dependants, numbering some 28,000, made up 2·5 per cent of the country's population.[3] No sustained growth is apparent in any of the various parts of this industry during the first half of the nineteenth century. The iron industry, for instance, produced 10,000 tons of pig iron annually in the years 1841–5, but by 1868–70 it was producing only a little over 5,000 tons per annum.[4] The Kongsberg silver mine and the Røros copper mine also had varying fortunes. At no time was either very important in terms of

[1] Imports of raw cotton rose from 70 tons per annum in the years 1836–40 to 1,800 tons per annum in the years 1856–60. O. J. Broch, *op. cit.* p. 135.
[2] *Ibid.* p. 96, tillæg XXI, p. 36.
[3] *Ibid.* p. 111. Norges offisielle statistikk, X, 178, *Statistiske oversikter for Norge, 1948* (Oslo, 1949), table 89.   [4] O. J. Broch, *op. cit.* p. 108.

its contribution to national employment. Thus, the Norwegian silver mines as a whole provided work for only about 400 men in the late sixties, whilst at the same time about 1,000 men were engaged in mining and smelting copper.[1] Cobalt, nickel, lead and zinc were also mined, but none gave rise to more than small-scale employment. How small can be gauged from the fact that in the years 1866–70 the average number employed in mining and smelting cobalt totalled no more than 58. In mining and refining nickel there were 180 and in mining lead and zinc, 100.[2] In the early 1870s, there was a nickel boom in Norway and it became, for a time, the world's leading supplier. Nevertheless, in 1873 there were only 471 engaged in its production.[3]

Although Norway remained a pre-industrial society until at least the 1860s it would be wrong to suppose that all Norwegians were dependent upon farming. In fact, almost all the rural population in Norway were able to turn to non-agrarian sources of employment and many of them did so. Indeed, it has often been said that there was hardly a single area where farming was the only important source of income, even for farmers themselves.[4]

A. N. Kiær attempted in 1865 to classify all Norwegian parishes according to the dominant occupation in each.[5] Map 1 (p. xiv) is based on this, although it is a classification which Kiær himself was the first to admit was only approximate. The map shows that areas suitable for, and in general dominated by, arable farming were to be found only in the extreme south-east of the country, around the

---

[1] *Ibid.* pp. 107, 108, 110. These works probably gave a considerable amount of part-time employment to farmers and cottars in surrounding districts, particularly with the production and carting of timber. Robert Bremner, *Excursions in Denmark, Norway, Sweden including notices of the state of public opinion in those countries and anecdotes of their courts* (London, 1840), II, 104, remarks that the Kongsberg mines went into decline after 1768, but in 1784 were still working thirty-six shafts and employing 2,500 men. Bremner's statistical information is not always reliable. Elsewhere (*ibid.* II, 79) he notes that 'the lower classes live in the most lawless manner as is well proved by the statistical returns which show that of every 5 children born, one is illegitimate'. This, in fact, is about three times the national rate in the 1830s.
[2] O. J. Broch, *op. cit.* p. 110.   [3] *Ibid.* pp. 109–10.
[4] Ældre række, C, no. 1, *Resultaterne af folketællingen i Norge, 1 Januar, 1866* (Christiania, 1868–9), p. vii; A. Schweigaard, *Norges Statistik,* p. 97: 'Skrider jord-bruget i Norge fremad?', *Morgenbladet,* Christiania, 20 October 1849.
[5] Ældre række, C, no. 1, *Tabeller vedkommende folkemængdens bevægelse i aarene 1856–65* (Christiania, 1868–9), pp. xi–xii.

Population and Society in Norway 1735–1865

Oslofjord, in the south-west and in Trøndelag. The mountainous core of the country was suitable only for the rearing of animals (horses, sheep, cattle and goats) and the subsequent preparation of animal products. Forestry was the major occupation of the people living on the lower slopes of this central mountain area, particularly in the south-east of the country and further north along the Swedish border. The building, manning and provisioning of ships was very important for the communities along the southern coast of Norway. This was particularly true after 1825 when the Norwegian merchant marine began to expand rapidly.[1] The total tonnage of Norwegian shipping actually fell from 148,000 tons in 1815 to 113,000 tons in 1825 but then rose consistently to 706,000 tons (spread over 5,407 ships) in 1865. The number of men employed on Norwegian ships rose from 11,279 in 1835 to 38,066 in 1865.[2] Finally, the inhabitants of the western coastal areas from Rogaland in the south to Finnmark in the north were heavily engaged in fishing, particularly for herring and cod.

However crude this classification, it is enough to dispel any illusion that the Norwegian rural economy was a uniform one. Malthus, as we have seen, seized upon the most obvious and perhaps the most important of these regional divisions and noted its impact on the working of the preventive check. 'On the sea coast where on account of the hopes of an adequate supply of food from fishing, the preventive check did not prevail in the same degree, the people are very poor and wretched; and beyond comparison in a worse state than the peasants in the interior of the country.'[3] This view was reiterated some sixty years later by another traveller, the anonymous author of *My Norske notebook*. The author of this work, who delighted in the pseudonym[4] of A. Lady, remarked that 'the land is

---

[1] Edvard Bull, 'Norway: industrialisation as a factor in economic growth', *Contributions to the first international conference of economic history, Stockholm 1960* (Paris, The Hague, 1960), pp. 266–71.

[2] By 1875 the number of ships had risen to 7,814; the total tonnage to 1,352,000 and the men employed to 60,281. Norges offisielle statistikk, x, 178, *op. cit.* p. 241. At that date the Norwegian merchant marine was the third largest in the world after Britain (5,960,000 tons) and the U.S.A. (2,860,000 tons).

[3] T. R. Malthus, *Essay on the principle of population*, Everyman edition (London, 1914), p. 158.

[4] Only eclipsed by *A long vacation ramble in Norway and Sweden* by X and Y (two unknown quantities), published in Cambridge, 1857.

but too thinly peopled. I mean in the interior. Along the coast the families seem enormous; shoals of little white haired children to be seen in every village.'[1] Daniel Clarke, who, it will be remembered, began the Scandinavian tour with Malthus also commented on the size of families in the coastal areas of Sweden. He observed that on the island of Björkö on the gulf of Bothnia 'the number of children in every family is astonishing: many had twelve, and in some families there were more. When we expressed surprise at this, they said—"Aye, this comes of eating so much fish", an opinion everywhere prevalent among the lower order of people in the maritime parts of Europe whether true or false.'[2] This superabundance of children is still regarded as one of the major demographic characteristics of western Norway (*Vestlandet*) in the nineteenth century.[3]

There is ample statistical justification for the belief that the presence of fish could, at least on occasion, lead to earlier marriage and higher fertility. Consider, for example, the county of Rogaland in the 1840s. At this time herring shoals appeared quite suddenly off the coast of Rogaland in great numbers, and rich catches were made.[4] The deanery of Stavanger, which lies in Rogaland, increased its population by 14 per cent in a matter of ten years 1835–45 through immigration alone; an immigration founded on the fisheries. Only the deaneries of Øst-Finnmark and Oslo showed a higher rate of immigration than this.[5] The rise in the number of marriages from the 1830s to the 1840s was greater in Stavanger and its neighbouring deanery, Karmsund (49 and 51 per cent respectively) than in any other deanery in the country.[6] In one deanery on the other hand, that of Lista in Vest-Agder, a county to the south of Rogaland, there was a fall of 7 per cent in the number of marriages between these two decades. This was the only deanery in the country to record a fall. It was situated in an area that had

[1] A. Lady, *My norske notebook* (London, 1859), p. 7.
[2] Edward Daniel Clarke, *Travels in various countries of Europe, Asia and Africa*, Part III, *Scandinavia* (London, 1819), X, 91–2.
[3] Sverre Steen, *Det gamle samfunn* (Oslo, 1957), p. 33.
[4] Eilert Sundt, *Om giftermaal i Norge* (Christiania, 1855), p. 166.
[5] Eilert Sundt, *Om dødeligheden i Norge* (Christiania, 1855), table 30, pp. 128–9.
[6] Eilert Sundt, *Om giftermaal i Norge*, table 22, p. 165.

6-2

been favoured by vast herring shoals in the 1830s[1] but had lost them, apparently because they were now going to the shores of Rogaland, in the following decade. The 1845 census recorded a higher number of children under the ages of one, five and ten in the county of Rogaland, per 1,000 women 21–50 years of age, than in any other Norwegian county.[2] There was too a higher proportion of brides, though not of bridegrooms, under the age of 25 in Rogaland in both 1841–5 and 1846–50 than in any other Norwegian county, with the exception of Finnmark.[3] In the former period, as many as 61 per cent of the spinster brides marrying bachelor bridegrooms were under 25 years of age in Rogaland. In Nord-Trøndelag, the county with the lowest percentage, the figure was 43.

A similar situation seems to have prevailed in Rogaland and Vest-Agder during the closing years of the Napoleonic wars. The herring shoals had disappeared from its coasts in 1796 but reappeared in 1808.[4] In the years immediately following the return of the herring shoals many people from other areas appear to have migrated to Rogaland, attracted by the fishing and propelled by food shortages in the interior of the country. This was the time when the English were blockading the Norwegian coasts and when a number of grain harvests failed. The population of the rural districts of Rogaland increased, according to the censuses, by as much as 0·9 per cent per annum between 1801 and 1815.[5] With the exception of Vest-Agder, no other county came within reach of this rate of increase. In some

[1] Eilert Sundt, *op. cit.* p. 165; A. Schweigaard, *op. cit.* p. 103; *Beretninger om den økonomiske tilstand m.m. i Norge ved udgangen av aaret 1835 underdanigst afgivne av Rigets amtmænd* (Christiania, 1836), p. 156.

[2] The ratios were 160 under 1 year, 739 under 5 and 1,323 under 10 years per 1,000 women 21–50. Corresponding figures for the country as a whole were 138,651 and 1,183. The county with the lowest ratios, Nord-Trøndelag, had 117, 591 and 1,079 in each of these categories. For the primary data see N.O.S. Ottende række, *Tabeller over folkemængden i Norge den 31te December 1845 samt over de i tidsrummet 1836–1845 ægteviede, fødte og døde* (Christiania, 1847).

[3] The percentage of brides under 25 years of age in Rogaland in the years 1841–5 was 58·4 (in Finnmark, 64·6) and in 1846–50 it was 53·6 (in Finnmark 58·1). Nord-Trøndelag, the county with the lowest percentage of brides under 25 years had respectively 43·3 and 41·9. For primary data see *Folkemengdens bevegelse, pakker 37–63* (riksarkiv, Oslo).

[4] Sverre Steen, *Det gamle samfunn*, pp. 126–7: A. Schweigaard, *op. cit.* pp. 97, 102; O. J. Broch, *op. cit.* p. 112.

[5] N.O.S. Ældre række, C, no. 1, *Tabeller vedkommende folkemængdens bevægelse 1856–65* (Christiania, 1868–9), p. 185.

Marriage and fertility

counties the population actually fell, and the national increase, as measured by the censuses, was only 0·03 per cent per annum.

In 1815 there were in Vest-Agder 416 children under four years of age for every 1,000 women aged 16–47 years. In Rogaland, the number was 400. Elsewhere the numbers were between this and the 267 of Nord-Trøndelag, the county with the lowest ratio.[1] It must be admitted that these calculations are based on figures taken from one of the poorest Norwegian censuses and that the relatively high death rates of the years immediately preceding it might well have affected some areas more than others, thus disrupting this particular measure of fertility more than usual.[2]

Another area of high fertility and relatively early marriage in the first half of the nineteenth century was Norway's most northerly county, Troms and Finnmark. Eilert Sundt's calculations show that part of it, the deanery of Vest-Finnmark, had the highest crude birth and death rate in the country in the years 1831–50. They were respectively 38·9 and 34·1 per 1,000, compared with Sundt's national rates of 31·3 and 20·3 per 1,000.[3] The women of Troms and Finnmark married earlier than the women of any other county in the years 1841–55. As many as 64·6 per cent of the brides in marriages where neither bride nor bridegroom had been married before were under 25 years of age in the years 1841–5. At this date only one other county had more than 55 per cent in this category.[4]

These statistics would appear to corroborate (though far from establish beyond doubt) the non-statistical impressions of Malthus and other observers. But there is strong evidence to suggest that these areas were not typical of Norwegian coastal districts as a whole. The high incidence of early marriage and high fertility in Rogaland and Vest-Agder in certain times reflected what might be termed a *bonanza* situation. The sudden return of the herring shoals meant a sharp rise in the wealth of the area. Many people were able to get employment sufficient to allow them to marry and raise a family earlier than expected, and many no doubt took this opportunity.

[1] Census of Norway, 30 April 1815. Returns from all parishes in manuscript, riksarkiv, Oslo.   [2] Statistical appendix below, table 7.
[3] Eilert Sundt, *Om dødeligheden i Norge*, p. 129.
[4] For primary data see *Folkemengdens bevegelse, pakker 37–63*, riksarkiv, Oslo.

The sudden rise in fertility is significant for it implies that before the arrival of the herring a number of people were positively delaying marriage for economic reasons. This calculated restraint acted in turn as a brake on the birth rate. The demographic experience of Rogaland and Vest-Agder in these years is further evidence that in pre-industrial western Europe the birth rate could be a major variable in determining population trends.

The early marriage and high fertility of Finnmark in the early nineteenth century is, however, only partly explained by the presence of fish. Two factors brought about the nineteenth-century population explosion here, neither of which had been present earlier. The first of these was the potato. Without it the area could hardly have supported its mid-nineteenth-century population. The potato in fact made the area habitable. By the 1870s[1] half of the arable land of this region was under potatoes. Potatoes and fish were the main ingredient of the common man's diet.[2] At the end of the nineteenth century one doctor reported that except on the larger farms, meat was never eaten, nor was there any milk except in the summer. The fish eaten was usually salted.[3]

The second factor contributing to the population rise in Finnmark was the expansion of the population elsewhere in Norway. Before large-scale emigration to the United States began towards the end of the 1860s, many people from the south of Norway moved north. The impact made by this drift to the north was calculated by Sundt. He reckoned that between 1835 and 1845 the population of Vest-Finnmark increased by 15·9 per cent but of this only 2·8 per cent was due to the excess of births over deaths in the area, the rest, 13·1 per cent, coming from immigration. In Øst-Finnmark the overall increase was 21·3 per cent of which as much as 16·8 per cent was the product of immigration. The only other areas showing comparable rates of growth in this period were Oslo and its environs, where nearly five-sixths of the population rise of 31·7 per cent came from immigration, and the area around Stavanger in Rogaland,

[1] For potato acreages see O. J. Broch, *op. cit.* p. 12.
[2] For illustrations of this, Ingrid Semmingsen, *Husmannsminner* (Oslo, 1960), pp. 10, 25, 26.
[3] *Ibid.* p. 10.

Marriage and fertility

where immigration accounted for two-fifths of an increase of 35·1 per cent.[1]

The crude marriage rate in Finnmark in the years 1831–50 was 10·8 per 1,000. The national figure was 7·4, whilst in Gudbrandsdalen, a valley in southern Norway, which experienced some emigration, the rate was only 6·2 per 1,000.[2] Finnmark was, like North America, a colonial area in the early nineteenth century. To it came those who wanted to marry yet could not find the means to do so in the southern part of the country. Those who began a family before getting married were also advised to head north.[3]

Apart from these areas, there is little statistical support for the Malthusian thesis that the preventive check was weaker on the coasts of Norway than in the interior. If we turn to the eighteenth century, we find little difference in the levels of either nuptiality or fertility between coastal areas, where fishing was a major source of income, and completely land-locked areas. Indeed, a somewhat higher proportion of men and women in the younger age groups living in the inland areas were married than was the case on the coast. At the higher ages the opposite was true, although in no age group were the differences large (table 4.9).

The hypothesis that fertility in the sort of society with which we are dealing was closely geared to the proportions married in the fertile age groups, is confirmed by table 4.10. There was little difference in either general or marital fertility between the coastal and inland areas. The fact that the child/woman ratio is higher inland although the birth/woman ratio is not, suggests that mortality at early ages was higher on the coast than in the interior, at least in the years 1762–9. It will be noted, however, that the crude death rate remained at moderate levels during these years with the exception of 1763 (see fig. 1, p. 39). Had the census been taken a decade later, the coastal area may well have shown a higher child/woman ratio than the interior, for the latter would then have reflected the extraordinary mortality of 1773. In that year the crude death rate in the Akershus (inland) diocese reached 64 per 1,000, three times higher than that of the Bergen (coastal) diocese.

[1] Eilert Sundt, *Om dødeligheden i Norge*, table 30, pp. 128–9.
[2] *Ibid.* pp. 128–9.   [3] Eilert Sundt, *Om giftermaal i Norge*, p. 205.

87

TABLE 4.9 *Percentage of married or widowed men and women in various age groups in six coastal deaneries (Sunn-hordland, Nordhordland, Sogn, Sunnfjord, Nordfjord, Sunn-møre) and in six landlocked deaneries (Nedre Romerike, Øvre Romerike, Hedemarken, Gudbrandsdalen, Toten and Valdres, Østerdalen) in 1769**

| | Percentage married or widowed | | | |
| | Men | | Women | |
Age	Coastal area	Inland area	Coastal area	Inland area
16–24	9·1	11·9	11·1	15·0
24–32	49·1	51·1	48·4	52·9
32–40	83·4	78·6	74·8	72·8
40–48	90·5	87·0	82·8	77·6
16–48	51·8	50·9	48·1	49·1

* See below, statistical appendix, table 8.

TABLE 4.10 *Births in 1770 and children aged 0–8 years in 1769 per 1,000 total women and per 1,000 married or widowed women aged 16–48 years in 1769 and living in an inland or a coastal area of Norway**

| | Area | |
	Coastal	Inland
Births in 1770 per 1,000 total women aged 16–48 years in 1769	132	134
Legitimate births in 1770 per 1,000 married/ widowed women aged 16–48 years in 1769	268	259
Children aged 0–8 years per 1,000 total women aged 16–48 years in 1769	832	923
Children aged 0–8 years per 1,000 married/ widowed women aged 16–48 years in 1769	1,729	1,878

* See below, statistical appendix, table 8.

Unfortunately, differences in presentation prevent an exact comparison of the findings of the 1769 census regarding fertility and nuptiality with those of the more accurate census of 1801. Ecclesiastical divisions were used for reporting the results of the 1769 census, whereas civil units were used for those of the 1801 census. We can, however, make a fairly close comparison if we look at the two coastal counties of Hordaland and Sogn and Fjordane on the one hand, and the two land-locked counties of Hedmark and Oppland on the other, since these contain much of the area covered by the deaneries used in tables 4.9 and 4.10. The data presented in tables 4.11 and 4.12 again suggest that there was little or no difference in either the proportions married or in the child/woman ratios of the coastal and the inland areas. Child/woman ratios in table 4.12 do seem to reflect the somewhat lower proportion of married women in the coastal counties, but it will be noted that the ratios for children to married and widowed women are virtually identical for all four counties.

If we move to the 1840s, we are able to calculate median ages at marriage in different parts of Norway. When we look at these in the areas covered in tables 4.9 and 4.10 we find that overall there is little difference between them. On the whole, men and women marry a little earlier in the inland areas than on the coast (table 4.13), which is in line with our earlier findings. However, there was some variation within each area, a point to which we shall return below.

The findings presented in tables 4.9 to 4.13 suggest that Malthus was wrong in supposing fertility and nuptiality to be higher on the coast than inland. Furthermore, over the period as a whole there appears to be little change in these measures, not perhaps unexpected, in view of the relatively unchanging character of Norway's economy. One final measure indicating in a very crude way the stability of the inter-regional fertility patterns in Norway appears in fig. 4. This shows the number of children aged 1–10 years for every 1,000 women aged 21–50 years as recorded in each of the censuses between 1801 and 1865, classified by region. The south-east region (comprising the counties of Østfold, Akershus, Buskerud and Telemark), a farming and lumber area with a sea board, had the highest ratios throughout. It was closely followed, however, by the south midland region, a completely land-locked area (Oppland,

89

TABLE 4.11 *Number of men and women aged 21–30 and 21–50 years married or widowed as percentage of all men and women in these age groups in the counties of Hedmark, Oppland, Hordaland, and Sogn and Fjordane in 1801*

	Total				Total married or widowed				Percentage married or widowed			
	Men		Women		Men		Women		Men		Women	
	21–30	21–50	21–30	21–50	21–30	21–50	21–30	21–50	21–30	21–50	21–30	21–50
Inland counties												
Hedmark	4,015	10,830	4,593	12,234	1,058	6,858	1,553	7,765	26·4	63·3	33·8	63·5
Oppland	4,408	12,199	4,908	13,332	1,191	7,656	1,965	8,805	27·0	62·8	40·0	66·0
Coastal counties												
Hordaland	4,357	11,117	4,908	12,680	1,177	6,924	1,584	7,523	27·0	62·3	32·3	59·3
Sogn and Fjordane	3,872	9,815	4,252	11,078	880	5,786	1,187	6,182	22·7	59·0	27·9	55·8

* N.O.S. Ældre række, C, no. 1. *Tabeller vedkommende folketellingerne i Norge i aarene 1801 og 1825* (Christiania, 1874).

TABLE 4.12   *Children 0–10 years per 1,000 total women and per 1,000 married or widowed women aged 21–50 years in the counties of Hedmark, Oppland, Hordaland and Sogn and Fjordane in 1801**

	Children 0–10 years	Women 21–50 years	Married or widowed women 21–50 years	Children 0–10 years per 1,000 Total women	Children 0–10 years per 1,000 Married or widowed women
Inland counties					
Hedmark	15,489	12,234	7,765	1,266	1,995
Oppland	17,270	13,332	8,805	1,295	1,961
Coastal counties					
Hordaland	14,706	12,680	7,523	1,160	1,955
Sogn and Fjordane	12,317	11,078	6,182	1,112	1,992

* N.O.S. Ældre række, C, no. 1. *Tabeller vedkommende folketællingerne i Norge i aarene 1801 og 1825* (Christiania, 1874).

TABLE 4.13   *Median age at first marriage in coastal and inland deaneries of Norway in the years 1846–50**

	Bachelors (years)	Spinsters (years)
Coastal deaneries		
Sunnhordland	27·8	25·6
Nordhordland	27·2	25·7
Sogn	28·0	26·2
Sunnfjord	27·5	25·4
Nordfjord	27·7	26·6
Sunnmøre	27·7	26·1
Inland deaneries		
Nedre Romerike	27·2	25·5
Øvre Romerike	26·9	25·5
Hedemarken	26·8	25·9
Gudbrandsdalen	27·4	25·0
Toten and Valdres	27·0	25·1
Østerdalen	28·7	25·7

* See below, statistical appendix, table 9.

Hedmark) also dominated by arable, pastoral and lumber interests. The south-western area (Vestfold, Aust-Agder and Vest-Agder) had a somewhat greater orientation towards shipping and here fertility was generally somewhat lower than in either of the foregoing areas although in 1845 it equalled that in the south-east and was slightly above that of the south midland region. This exception

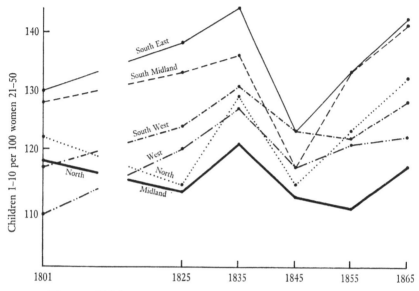

Fig. 4. Children aged 1–10 per 100 women aged 21–50 in different parts of Norway at the censuses of 1801, 1825, 1835, 1845, 1855 and 1865.*

* Statistical appendix, table 30.

may be a reflection of the considerable, if shortlived, development of a fishing industry in the 1830s off the Lista coast. The fishing areas of western Norway (Rogaland, Hordaland, Sogn and Fjordane, Møre and Romsdal) had still lower fertility. It was particularly low around 1800, which could reflect a downturn in fishing activity about that time. The lowest fertility of all is seen to be in the north midland area (Sør-Trøndelag and Nord-Trøndelag), an area with fishing off the coast and arable and pastoral farming in inland areas. Finally, the northern region (Nordland, Troms and Finnmark) had lower than average fertility until the 1850s, though the extreme northerly subdivisions of this region usually had above average fertility. To sum up: fertility in Norway was highest in the south midland and south-eastern areas, lowest in the western coastal counties (Vestlandet) and the north midlands (Trøndelag), with the south-west and the extreme north falling somewhere in between. (It should be noted that the fluctuation in fertility over time as indicated by fig. 4 is very probably a reflection of changes in the age composition of the female population.)

Figure 4 appears to show only modest differences in fertility between the various parts of Norway, although the crudity of the measure should be recognised. Differences in infant and child mortality for instance, could well reduce the gap between the apparent fertility of the western and south midland regions. For infant mortality in the 1830s was very considerably higher in the coastal areas of the west than in landlocked areas of the east (table 4.14).

One should not, therefore, make too much of the apparent regional differences in fertility. On the other hand, it would be equally wrong to ignore them, for they are our only check on the validity of non-quantitative speculation. At the least, they corroborate earlier evidence of the incorrectness of Malthus's observations regarding the level of fertility in inland and coastal areas.

We can note in conclusion that this is not the only discrepancy between what one might expect *a priori* and what is revealed by the statistical data, such as they are if we look, for instance, at the age at marriage data (statistical appendix, table 9). We discover that for the 1841–55 period, contrary to general expectations, the areas where men married at a relatively early age were not always those where women did so. That is to say, men married later in some areas than others, but a corresponding difference is not observable in the age at marriage of their wives (table 4.15). Thus the median age at first marriage of men in Hedemarken was 26·6 years in 1841–5; of women, 25·5. In neighbouring Gudbrandsdalen, however, men married later (median age 27·4 years) but the women on the whole earlier (median age 24·8 years) than in Hedemarken. Similar contrasts are observed in the west between Hardanger and Voss, and Søndre Sunnmøre.

TABLE 4.14 *Deaths under 1 year of age per 1,000 births occurring in the same year, in some inland and coastal areas of Norway, 1832–8**

	Births	Deaths under age 1 year	Deaths under age 1 year per 1,000 live births
Inland deaneries			
Nedre Romerike	4,690	517	110·2
Øvre Romerike	11,989	1,295	108·0
Hedemarken	5,647	686	121·5
Gudbrandsdalen	8,129	979	120·4
Toten and Valdres	8,636	840	97·3
Østerdalen	3,687	373	101·2
Coastal deaneries			
Nordhordland	6,383	1,223	191·6
Sunnhordland	6,397	1,037	162·1
Ytre Sogn	2,859	508	177·7
Sunnfjord	4,432	833	188·0
Nordfjord	3,300	618	187·3
Søndre Sunnmøre	2,506	445	177·6

* *Folkemengdens bevegelse pakker*, riksarkiv, Oslo.

TABLE 4.15 *Median age at first marriage (bachelors–spinsters) in certain Norwegian deaneries in the years 1841–55**

Deanery	Male median age			Female median age		
	1841–1845	1846–1850	1851–1855	1841–1845	1846–1850	1851–1855
Hedemarken	26·6	26·8	27·3	25·5	25·9	26·5
Gudbrandsdalen	27·4	27·4	27·9	24·8	25·0	26·1
Hardanger and Voss	28·7	28·4	28·8	24·8	25·2	25·5
Søndre Sunnmøre	27·5	27·7	28·0	26·5	26·1	26·7

* See below, statistical appendix, table 9.

We can now summarise the findings of this chapter. First, age specific fertility and nuptiality in Norway appears to have changed very little over the period 1769-1865. Second, this lack of change is associated with a relatively slight change in the occupational pattern of the country. Third, although Norway experienced no industrial revolution in this period, there were significant variations in occupation between different parts of the country—the most important (or at least the most apparent) of these differences being between the arable, pastoral, lumber areas of the east and the fishing areas of the west and north. Fourth, contrary to the opinions of Malthus and other commentators, fertility and nuptiality was not generally higher in the coastal areas than in land-locked areas. Often, indeed, inland areas had higher fertility and nuptiality and an earlier age at marriage than coastal areas, although by the 1840s the earliest age at marriage in the country was in an area many of whose inhabitants were occupied in fishing (Vest-Finnmark). It was probably also the fortuitous arrival of large shoals of fish which, on occasion, raised human fertility temporarily in the coastal areas of Rogaland during the 1840s. Fifth, over the period as a whole, fertility differentials between different parts of the country remained relatively constant. Sixth, it is not possible to associate directly differences in occupational structure with differences in fertility via age at marriage since one of the intervening links—the age at marriage of women—is not positively correlated with the age at marriage of men. Here is perhaps one of the more striking pieces of information to emerge from the Norwegian statistical material and one that will be examined further in the next chapter.

5 *The social structure of fertility*

In the previous chapter we went behind the national aggregates to see if there were regional differences in nuptiality and fertility in eighteenth and nineteenth-century Norway. What emerged was not altogether expected. The often-assumed links between supposed employment opportunities and fertility, and between the age at marriage of men and women were not corroborated by the available statistical evidence. To understand the significance of these findings we need to delve deeper into the inner workings of Norwegian society. To reduce this operation to manageable proportions three relatively small areas have been chosen for detailed analysis. Each has been selected with a view to pointing up the central character-istics of one of the main regional economies. The first, a fishing community, consists of a small group of islands off the west coast; the second, a high mountain valley, lying in the centre of southern Norway, was dominated by timber and pastoral interests, and the third was an arable area in the lowlands along the eastern shores of Lake Mjøsa (map 1).

The parish of Herøy, the first of these three areas, consists of the island of Herøy, some smaller islands and a portion of the mainland. The entire parish lies in Sunnmøre in the county of Møre and Romsdal. The coasts of Sunnmøre were more renowned than any other in southern Norway for their fishing opportunities and, within Sunnmøre, Herøy was particularly famous.[1] The possibilities for farming were limited, much of the land consisting of bare rock or stony soil and clearing it demanded enormous effort. There were also numerous springs which necessitated extensive drainage opera-tions. The climate did nothing to encourage the farmer. The summers were wet and relatively cold, whilst fog often prevented the crops from ripening and storms in the latter part of the summer

---

[1] Jens Kraft, *Topographisk-statistik beskrivelse over kongeriget Norge*, 5 (Christiania, 1832), 63, 82.

sometimes beat down growing plants. There was little pasture and little wood. All wood for building purposes had to be imported and only three or four farms had sufficient fuel for their own needs, even at the beginning of the nineteenth century. In these circumstances it is hardly surprising that the inhabitants of Herøy turned to the sea for the greater part of their livelihood and it was only when this failed that they turned to agriculture.[1]

This lack of interest in agriculture resulted in the persistence of inefficient methods and out-of-date equipment. All seed was sown in the spring although winter sowing would have been more productive because the winters were mild. As late as the 1830s there was no rotation of crops.[2] Agriculture was made still more difficult by the system of land holding. Known as *fellesskapet*, this was similar in many ways to the English open field system. The land was divided into tiny holdings, one man's fields being intermingled with those of his neighbour's. To each holding was attached a complex of private and common rights. The system existed in other parts of Norway throughout much of the nineteenth century, but nowhere was it as dominant as in Møre and Romsdal.[3] Here it was fostered by the existence of a possible income from fishing[4] and within agriculture a spade–rake culture, which made smallholdings tolerable.

If Herøy is not untypical of many communities to be found along the western coast of Norway from Rogaland to Finnmark, Hallingdal is representative of many of the valleys which cut into the central massif of Norway. The rivers and streams draining it flow into the Oslofjord. As with Herøy, the physical environment did not hold much promise for the arable farmer.[5] The winters are long and bitter, the summers short, though in the lower reaches of the valley quite warm. There is little cultivable land and what there is often lies on steeply sloping ground. Only in the lower parts of the valley is there sufficient good, flat land suitable for the finer grain crops

[1] *Ibid.* pp. 69–72, 77–9.   [2] *Ibid.* p. 72.
[3] The enclosure commission (*utskiftningskommisjon*) in 1856 found that whereas in Østfold only 0·3 per cent of the farms were unenclosed and in Telemark only 3·3 per cent, the percentage in Rogaland was 52·4, in Sogn and Fjordane 71·8, in Hordaland 86·7 and in Møre and Romsdal 89·6. See W. Keilhau, *Det norske folks liv og historie gjennem tidene*, **8** (Oslo, 1929), 38.
[4] Hans Strøm, *Physisk og œconomisk beskrivelse over fogderiet Søndmøre* (Sorøe, 1762), p. 569.   [5] Jens Kraft, *op. cit.* **2**, 296.

and here the grain was sometimes injured by summer drought.[1] Higher up the valley, patches of potentially fertile land had to be laboriously cleared of stones before they could be cultivated.[2] Because of the long winters the growing period was short in much of the valley. Snow often lay on the ground until June and ashes were strewn to melt it.[3] As it was customary to begin ploughing in May, irrespective of whether spring was late or not, the snow sometimes had to be gathered into heaps with the ploughman wending his way between them.[4] Autumn frosts were also a great menace. Agricultural methods were primitive and remained so for much of the nineteenth century.[5] Ploughs, for instance, were only tipped with iron and most farm implements were made of wood.[6] There was no rotation of crops. Once a fertile piece of land had been discovered some grain would be grown on it for six to eight years. It would then be allowed to lie fallow.[7]

It is hardly surprising that, in view of these conditions, farming should be neglected in Hallingdal when less heart-breaking occupations were available. In the upper reaches of the valley men turned to the rearing of and trading in cattle, sheep and goats and to the preparation of such animal products as butter, meat, tallow and skins.[8] The further one progressed up the valley the greater the number of cattle relative to the amount of arable land. In the 1830s there was one cow for every 0·75 acre of arable land in the parish of Nes, which occupied the lower part of the valley, whereas in Ål, at the head of the valley, there was one cow for every 0·25 acre of arable land.[9] A slightly above average sized farm in Hol (at that

[1] Jens Kraft, *op. cit.* p. 298.
[2] For what this could entail in terms of one man's efforts can be gathered from an interview with an 80-year-old farmer from Hol—a parish at the upper end of the valley—who reckoned that he had in his lifetime removed 40,000 cart loads of stones from his land. *Dagbladet*, 20 May 1959. For a similar story see Lars Reinton, *Folk og fortid i Hol: frå 1815 til våre dagar* (Oslo, 1943), II, 82.
[3] Jens Kraft, *op. cit.* 2, 299.   [4] Lars Reinton, *op. cit.* p. 58.
[5] Note the complaints on this score from the county governor (*amtmann*) of Buskerud in 1846–50. *Beretning om kongeriget Norges økonomiske tilstand i aarene 1846–50, Buskeruds amt* (Christiania, 1853), pp. 1 ff.
[6] Lars Reinton, *op. cit.* p. 154.   [7] Jens Kraft, *op. cit.* 2, 55.
[8] *Ibid.* p. 303.
[9] Norges Officielle Statistik. Ældre række, C, no. 2, *Beretning om kongeriget Norges økonomiske tilstand i aarene 1856–60, Buskeruds amt* (Christiania, 1863), p. 3.

time part of the parish of Ål) in 1866 consisted of seven acres of arable or artificial meadow with good soil, 30 acres of good hay-producing land and an unspecified quantity of rough pasture. In an average year 22 bushels of barley and 20 bushels of potatoes were sown and 110 bushels of barley and 100 bushels of potatoes were harvested. The little over 200 tons of hay that was gathered helped to feed two horses, 17 cows, two oxen and 33 sheep.[1] A great deal of fertile land was required to produce hay for winter fodder, vast amounts being required.[2] The average cow was said to consume as much as 1,400 lb of hay each winter.[3] Thus, in the areas where cattle rearing was most widespread, there were almost 100 acres of meadow for every single acre of land under crops.[4]

Men turned to forestry in the lower regions of Hallingdal for the land here was well wooded. Even at the beginning of the 1860s, after many years of cutting, forests still covered as much as 62 per cent of the land area of Nes. In the parish of Gol, which occupied the central part of the valley, the percentage was down to 18. In Ål at the head of the valley, only 8 per cent of the land was wooded and as a result of the decline in the supply of timber, turf was used for fuel.[5]

The third area chosen for close analysis comprises two rich arable parishes, Nes and Ringsaker, on the banks of Lake Mjøsa. This was the granary of Norway.[6] No other region in the country could surpass its corn production figures.[7] Some idea of the richness of the area can be gathered from the fact that the average farm tax assessment was one of the highest in the country and double that of Hallingdal.[8] The landscape was such as many tourists hardly

[1] Lars Reinton, *op. cit.* p. 52.
[2] N.O.S. Ældre række, C, no. 2, *Beretning om kongeriget Norges økonomiske tilstand i aarene 1851–55* (Christiania, 1858), p. 60.
[3] *Ibid.* p. 60.
[4] *Ibid.*
[5] N.O.S. Ældre række, C, no. 1, *Beretning om kongeriget Norges økonomiske tilstand i aarene 1861–65 Buskeruds amt* (Christiania, 1867–9), pp. 7–8.
[6] Jens Kraft, *op. cit.* 1, 625–6.
[7] S. Skappel, *Hedemarkens Amt 1814–1914* (Kristiania, 1914), p. 29.
[8] Jens Kraft, *op. cit.* table facing 1, 622 and 11, 296. According to calculations made from there the average assessment in Hallingdal at the beginning of the nineteenth century was 0·44 skpd. whilst in the two Hedemarken parishes at the same time it was 1·05 skpd.

expected to find in Norway. Malthus, travelling through country near Nes and Ringsaker in the summer of 1799, remarked that

the principal road from Christiania to Drontheim[1] leads for nearly 180 English miles through a continued valley...by the side of a very fine river, which in one part stretches out into the extensive Lake Miosen. I am inclined to believe that there is not any river in all Europe, the course of which affords such a constant succession of beautiful and romantic scenery. It goes under different names in different parts. The verdure in the Norway valleys is peculiarly soft, the foliage of the trees luxuriant, and in summer no traces appear of a northern climate.[2]

Malthus was not the only traveller to praise the beauty of this area. Capell Brooke writing in 1820 observed that

through the whole valley of Gudbrandsdalen,[3] the stranger will be perfectly astonished no less at the magnificence of the scenery than at the rich aspects of the country on all sides. If he previously figures to himself Norway as consisting only of an assemblage of barren rocks and mountains, how surprised he will be to meet with abundant signs of labour, industry and plenty. In every direction the small farms of the peasants catch the eye, showing a degree of comfort rarely to be met with in other countries. If their mountains be deemed barren providence has amply made them amends in the great fertility of the valleys arising as well from the shelter afforded them as from the depths of the soil.[4]

The German traveller, Leopold von Buch, visited Nes and Ringsaker in 1806–8 and wrote equally enthusiastically about them.

In the *prestegjelden*[5] where agriculture alone is carried on in Nes, for example, there are 1,344 inhabitants to the geographical square mile... this is unheard of in Norway[6]...the lands and buildings of every description in Ringsaker proclaimed the existence of fertility. I was in fact lost for a few moments in astonishment when a winding of the road

---

[1] The German name for Trondheim.
[2] T. R. Malthus, *Essay on the principle of population*, Everyman edition (London, 1914), p. 165, note 4.
[3] This valley opens out into Lake Mjøsa.
[4] A. de Capell Brooke, *Travels through Sweden, Norway and Finmark to the North Cape in the summer of 1820* (London, 1823), p. 104.
[5] Parish.
[6] Not really. The writer—or his English translator—must have been confusing English and Norwegian miles. Today the latter is 10 km. Before 1870 it was 11 km.

brought us immediately opposite the great and beautiful stone church of Ringsaker, situated in the middle of several farm houses, which both in size and elegance bore testimony to the prosperity of their owners.[1]

Nes had very little infertile soil and being close to Lake Mjøsa the climate was much more moderate than it was only a few miles inland. Ringsaker too had a good soil and a similar climate although in neither regard was it so well favoured as Nes. At the beginning of the nineteenth century, agricultural methods here were as good as the best in Norway, which meant that they were far superior to those of most areas. Corn yields were high in both parishes. In Nes, taking all types of grain together, they were never less than six-fold and sometimes rose as high as ten- and twelve-fold in the 1820s. Despite dense populations, both Nes and Ringsaker were able to sell large quantities of corn to other parishes. One reason advanced for the high standard of agricultural practice in Nes and Ringsaker and in neighbouring parishes was that the major alternative occupations which attracted people away from agriculture in other areas, in particular forestry and fishing, were little in evidence.[2]

Were these sharp differences in the economic conditions of the three areas reflected in their population development? We have already noted the observation by Malthus that 'on the sea coast on account of the hopes of an adequate supply of food from fishing, the preventive check did not prevail in the same degree...(as) in the interior of the country'.[3] We might then have expected to find in Herøy earlier marriage, higher birth rates and—if Malthus is correct in suggesting that the coastal populations were 'beyond comparison in a worse state than peasants in the interior of the country'[4] because of the supposed weakness of the preventive check—higher death rates than in either Hallingdal or the Hedemarken parishes of Nes and Ringsaker. (For the sake of brevity, these last two parishes will in future be referred to as Hedemarken.)

[1] Leopold von Buch, *Travels through Norway and Lapland during the years 1806, 1807 and 1808*, translated from the German by John Black (London, 1813), p. 80. One of the farms mentioned by von Buch could well have been that of the vicar of Ringsaker. About 1806 it produced 1,600–2,000 bushels of grain annually according to N.I.C. Hofman Gevel Bloch, *Reiseiagttagelser eller udtog af en dagbog holden paa en reise fra Throndhjem til Christiania i aaret 1806* (Kjøbenhavn, 1808), p. 37.
[2] Jens Kraft, *op. cit.* 1, 624–9.
[3] T. R. Malthus, *op. cit.* p. 158.   [4] *Ibid.*

Again, following Malthus, we might expect later marriage, lower fertility and, because of this, lower mortality in Hallingdal than in the other two areas, for Hallingdal depended on the products of its forests and upon its cattle, sheep and goats. The valley as a whole was not self-sufficient in corn.[1] To preserve both the forests and the meadows in areas such as this, Malthus pointed out that it was necessary to limit settlement.[2] If farms were subdivided and crofts created, the woods would have to provide more fuel and building materials. To prevent this, timber merchants, entering into contracts with farmers for the purchase of wood, insisted that no more people should be allowed to use them than were doing so at the time the contract was signed. Similarly, as we noted earlier, the farmers dependent on their animals realised that to settle more people on the fertile land in the valleys would curtail the amount that could be devoted to the production of hay. This would mean cutting down flocks, a sacrifice as wounding to the pride of the farmer as to his pocket. It would mean, too, that the rich summer pastures which they held on the mountain tops would be under-utilised, causing them to lose some of the incomes they had previously enjoyed from the products of these pastures.[3]

The statistical evidence of fertility, mortality and nuptiality, however, fails to confirm the Malthusian argument. In Herøy, in 1801, for instance, there were only 359 children under five years of age for every 1,000 women aged 15–49 years, as against 625 in Hallingdal and 496 in Hedemarken (table 5.1). Marital fertility in the three areas shows (table 5.2) parallel differences. It might be argued that this was an atypical situation, true only of one year at the beginning of the nineteenth century. Alternatively, it might be argued that different levels of mortality amongst the under fives distorted the ratios. It is possible to check the latter by calculating the number of deaths of children under five years of age per 1,000 births, during the years 1816–65 (table 5.3) and the deaths of children under one year per 1,000 births in the years 1832–65 (table 5.4). These indicate that mortality was higher in these age groups in Herøy than in either

---

[1] *Beretninger om den økonomiske tilstand m.m. i Norge ved udgangen af aaret 1835 . . .*
Buskeruds amt (Christiania, 1836), p. 54.
[2] T. R. Malthus, *op. cit.* pp. 161–2.   [3] *Ibid.*

TABLE 5.1 *Children under 5 per 1,000 women 15–49 in Herøy, Hallingdal and Hedemarken 1801**

	Children under 5	Women 15–49	Number of children under 5 per 1,000 women 15–49
Herøy	231	643	359
Hallingdal	1,381	2,211	625
Hedemarken	1,177	2,371	496

* Calculated from the original returns of the 1801 census in the parishes of Herøy (Sunnmøre), Nes and Ål (Hallingdal), Nes and Ringsaker (Hedemarken).

TABLE 5.2 *Children under 5 per 1,000 married and widowed women 15–49 in Herøy, Hallingdal and Hedemarken 1801**

	Children under 5	Married and widowed women 15–49	Number of children under 5 per 1,000 married and widowed women 15–49
Herøy	231	335	689
Hallingdal	1,381	1,168	1,182
Hedemarken	1,177	1,273	925

* Calculated from the same source as table 5.1 above.

TABLE 5.3 *Deaths under age 5 years per 1,000 live births in Herøy, Hallingdal and Hedemarken 1816–65**

Period	Deaths under age 5 years per 1,000 live births		
	Herøy	Hallingdal	Hedemarken
1816–25	255·5	145·2	181·6
1826–35	242·5	185·1	179·8
1836–45	211·0	179·3	160·2
1846–55	199·2	134·7	134·6
1856–65	197·1	139·2	156·0
1816–65	218·7	158·0	161·5

* Statistical appendix, table 10.

TABLE 5.4   *Deaths under age 1 year per 1,000 live births in Herøy, Hallingdal and Hedemarken 1832–65**

Period	Deaths under age 1 year per 1,000 live births		
	Herøy	Hallingdal	Hedemarken
1832–45	175·7	124·5	99·8
1846–55	114·5	92·8	74·1
1856–65	108·6	82·0	83·8
1832–65	134·2	105·2	86·4

* Statistical appendix, table 11.

TABLE 5.5   *Annual average live births around the years 1835, 1845 and 1855 per 1,000 women 21–50 years at those dates in Herøy, Hallingdal and Hedemarken**

	Annual average births per 1,000 women 21–50		
	1835 and 1836	1844–6	1854 and 1856
Herøy	127	139	138
Hallingdal	217	186	207
Hedemarken	155	147	182

* Statistical appendix, table 12.

Hedemarken or Hallingdal but the difference was not such as to destroy the conclusions we have drawn from table 5.1. Furthermore, the differences in fertility suggested by table 5.1 are confirmed when we calculate the annual average number of births in years immediately adjacent to the census years 1835, 1845 and 1855 per 1,000 women of 21–50 years recorded at those censuses. In doing this, we eliminate the impact of mortality on our fertility ratios. We find, for example, that in 1835 (table 5.5) there were 127 births per 1,000 women aged 21–50 in Herøy but in Hallingdal there were 217 and in Hedemarken 155. A similar difference emerges (table 5.5) if we look at the position around the census years of 1845 and 1855. In view of these differences in fertility, we might expect to find that women married earliest in Hallingdal and latest in Herøy. We would expect to find that the proportion of married women,

TABLE 5.6 *Percentage of female population 21–30 and 21–50 years of age, married or widowed, in Herøy, Hallingdal and Hedemarken in 1801**

	Total women		Total married/ widowed women		Percentage married/ widowed women	
	21–30	21–50	21–30	21–50	21–30	21–50
Herøy	173	553	43	333	24·9	60·2
Hallingdal	701	1,790	291	1,159	41·5	64·7
Hedemarken	724	2,007	224	1,268	30·9	63·1

* Calculated from enumerators' returns of 1801 census in parishes of Herøy (Sunnmøre), Nes and Ål (Hallingdal), Nes and Ringsaker (Hedemarken) in riksarkiv, Oslo.

especially in the younger age groups, would be higher in Hallingdal than in Herøy. Again, unfortunately we can test the hypothesis at only a few points in time. It is encouraging to find, therefore, that the different indices support each other. For instance, in 1801 only 24·9 per cent of the women of Herøy aged 21–30 years were either married or widowed, in Hallingdal the corresponding figure was 41·5 per cent (table 5.6). Again, of the spinsters marrying bachelors, 36·9 per cent were brides before they were 25 years of age in Herøy in the years 1839–65 compared with 52·1 per cent in Hallingdal.[1]

When we turn to the male age at marriage and nuptiality statistics, we discover a rather different pattern from the female one. For male nuptiality was higher in Herøy than in Hallingdal in 1801. Some 33·8 per cent of the men of 21–30 years of age in Herøy were either widowed or married as against 22·1 per cent in Hallingdal (table 5.7). As for age at marriage, there was little difference between the two areas in the years 1839–65. Of the bachelors marrying spinsters 22·4 per cent were under 25 years of age in Herøy, whilst in Hallingdal the proportion was 24·3 per cent. In Hedemarken, however, men married much earlier. Here, as many as 35·3 per cent of bachelor bridegrooms were under 25 years of age at this time.[2]

In trying to explain these differences we derive a great deal from

[1] Statistical appendix, table 13.   [2] Statistical appendix, table 14.

TABLE 5.7 *Percentage of male population 21–30 and 21–50 years of age, married or widowed, in Herøy, Hallingdal and Hedemarken in 1801**

	Total 21–30	Men 21–50	Total married/ widowed men		Percentage married/ widowed men	
			21–30	21–50	21–30	21–50
Herøy	163	452	55	317	33·8	70·1
Hallingdal	661	1,769	146	1,023	22·1	57·9
Hedemarken	605	1,683	182	1,141	30·1	67·9

* Source as table 5.6 above.

the enumerators' returns for the census of 1801. By studying how households and families were constructed it is possible to discover at least some of the factors which led to the differences in age at marriage, in nuptiality and in fertility outlined above.

In 1801 the combined populations of the three areas was 21,387. Of these as many as 98 per cent lived in households headed by persons described either as crofters or farmers. Apart from a few people described as schoolmasters, soldiers, smiths or other craftsmen, most of the remaining 2 per cent lived in the households of government and church officials. If we confine our attention to the households of farmers and crofters only, we find that in Herøy almost 80 per cent of households were headed by farmers, whilst at the other end of the scale in Hedemarken, only 40 per cent of households belonged to farmers. In Hallingdal just over 46 per cent of the households were headed by farmers (table 5.8). These proportions suggest that at least in this regard the three areas were representative of the districts in which they lay; for there were relatively few crofters in the western counties of Hordaland, Sogn and Fjordane, and Møre and Romsdal at this time as compared with Hedmark, Oppland, Buskerud and Akershus in the east (table 5.9).

As a rule the farm households in Hallingdal and Hedemarken were larger than those in Herøy. The average households in Hedemarken and Hallingdal had between seven and eight members, compared

TABLE 5.8 *Distribution of population between the house-holds of farmers and crofters in Herøy, Hallingdal and Hedemarken in 1801**

	Farmers			Crofters		
	Herøy	Hallingdal	Hede-marken	Herøy	Hallingdal	Hede-marken
No. of households	365	722	651	95	830	1,000
Inhabitants	1,967	5,300	5,025	287	3,985	4,381
Percentage of households	79·4	46·5	39·5	20·6	53·5	60·5
Percentage of inhabitants	87·3	57·1	53·4	12·7	42·9	46·6
Inhabitants per household	5·4	7·3	7·7	3·0	4·8	4·4

* Source as table 5.6 above.

TABLE 5.9 *Male population in selected occupations aged 21–50 years as percentage of all male population in the rural districts of some Norwegian counties in 1801**

		Cottars				Day	
County	Farmers	with land	without land	Craftsmen	Servants	labourers	Total
Akershus	31·0	29·0	4·0	5·1	17·2	5·2	91·5
Hedmark	35·7	32·1	2·8	6·3	13·7	3·4	94·0
Oppland	32·7	35·4	2·4	5·4	13·2	4·3	93·4
Buskerud	35·2	26·5	5·5	4·6	10·6	7·7	90·1
Hordaland	61·5	9·1	4·9	0·3	16·6	2·8	95·2
Sogn and Fjordane	52·4	9·6	5·5	0·6	24·1	1·7	93·9
Møre and Romsdal	51·8	10·8	3·4	1·2	24·7	2·0	93·9

* Statistical appendix, table 15.

TABLE 5.10 *Percentage distribution of farmer and crofter households by number of inhabitants in Herøy, Hallingdal and Hedemarken in 1801**

Inhabitants per household	Farm households			Crofter households		
	Herøy (%)	Hallingdal (%)	Hede-marken (%)	Herøy (%)	Hallingdal (%)	Hede-marken (%)
1	0	0	0·3	2·1	0·1	0
2	3·6	2·2	2·5	41·1	9·6	13·3
3	9·9	2·6	5·4	30·5	17·6	20·8
4	19·2	8·7	8·0	15·8	18·8	23·9
5	23·8	11·2	9·7	5·3	21·7	19·0
6	17·5	13·9	13·1	2·1	14·2	12·1
7	15·1	16·2	12·7	2·1	10·5	5·6
8	5·5	15·4	13·8	0	3·6	3·0
9	3·6	10·5	8·4	1·1	2·3	1·4
10+	1·9	19·3	26·1	0	1·6	0·9
	100·0	100·0	100·0	100·0	100·0	100·0

* Statistical appendix, table 16.

with just over five in Herøy. These mean figures conceal, however, an important feature of the distribution of population amongst the farmer households—its concentration in households that were of above average size. For example, in Hedemarken there were 651 farmer households which between them held 5,025 people, an average of 7·7 per household. Over 50 per cent (2,552) of these people lived in 34·5 per cent (225) of the households, each of which had nine or more members (table 5.10). The unconscious bias of anecdotal evidence on farm household size can be attributed to this skewed distribution. Since the *majority of people* lived in the *minority of large households* that were of above-average size, the chance of meeting, listening to and recording the experiences of someone who had lived in this minority of large households would be considerably greater than that of meeting a member of one of the many small households. In Hedemarken there were four times as many households with only two members as there were with fifteen (45 as against 12). But 180 people lived in the twelve 15-

TABLE 5.11 *Marital status of farmers and crofters in Herøy, Hallingdal and Hedemarken in 1801**

	Farmers			Crofters		
	Herøy	Hallingdal	Hede-marken	Herøy	Hallingdal	Hede-marken
Single						
Men	1·9	3·9	2·5	1·0	1·7	0·4
Women	—	—	—	—	—	0·2
Married†						
I i	57·5	71·2	74·1	52·6	78·9	80·9
I ii	14·0	7·8	9·0	7·4	3·6	3·6
I iii	1·9	0·7	0·8	—	0·2	0·2
I iv	0·3	—	—	1·1	—	—
II i	14·5	7·9	7·1	15·8	6·1	7·7
II ii	1·4	0·7	1·2	5·3	1·1	1·5
II iii	0·5	0·1	—	1·1	—	0·1
III i	1·9	0·6	0·3	1·1	0·5	0·9
III ii	0·5	—	0·3	2·1	—	0·3
IV i	0·3	—	0·2	—	—	0·3
IV ii	—	—	0·2	—	—	—
Percentage married	92·8	89·0	93·2	86·5	90·4	95·5
Widowed						
Widowers	3·3	3·6	1·2	5·3	3·3	1·1
Widows	1·9	2·5	2·8	7·4	3·5	2·4
Not classified	—	1·1	0·3	—	1·1	0·4
	100·0	100·0	100·0	100·0	100·0	100·0

* Statistical appendix, table 17.

† Numerals show marital history of the marriage partners. Hence a woman in her third marriage is entered here as iii, whilst a man in his second appears as II.

member households, twice as many as in the forty-five two-member ones. These figures suggest that anecdotal evidence based on the reminiscences of members of these larger units leads us to exaggerate the average size of households. The same principle applies to the numbers of servants, children and lodgers.

At the head of most of the farm households was a married man. In Hedemarken and Herøy 93 per cent of the farmers were married men and in Hallingdal 89 per cent. These aggregates conceal an interesting difference between the married farmers in Herøy and those in Hallingdal and Hedemarken. For 18·6 per cent of the Herøy farmers were married to women who had been married at least once before their current marriage. The percentage of Hallingdal farmers in this position was only half this figure (9·3) and of those in Hedemarken, 11·5. In none of the areas did an unmarried woman head a farm household (table 5.11).

The median age of all farmers was lowest in Herøy where it was 40 years and highest in Hedemarken at 46 years. In Hallingdal it was 44 years.[1] There were no farmers under 23 years of age in either Herøy or Hedemarken and only three in Hallingdal, two of whom were unmarried. At the other end of the scale there were relatively few farmers over 60 years of age. This was partly because of the high death rates operating at this age and partly, in Hallingdal and Hedemarken, though not it seems in Herøy, because of the *livøre* or *føderåd* system.[2] This was an arrangement whereby the heir to a farm agreed to give the farmer an annual allowance in exchange for his handing over control. In both Hallingdal and Hedemarken there were more than twice as many people over 60 years of age drawing these allowances as there were active farmers. The system does not appear to have operated in quite the same way in Herøy.

The median age of farmers' wives was 43 years in Herøy, 42 in Hedemarken and 40 in Hallingdal. Herøy thus recorded the lowest median age for farmers and the highest for farmers' wives. One contributory reason for this was the greater proportion of marriages taking place between bachelors and widows in Herøy than in either Hedemarken or Hallingdal. In the years 1827–65 as many as 11·3 per cent of marriages in Herøy were between bachelors and widows as against 4·1 per cent in Hedemarken and 6·3 per cent in Hallingdal. As a rule, such a marriage meant that the bridegroom was younger than the bride.

Farmers and their wives made up 36 per cent of the membership of the households in Herøy, 26 per cent in Hallingdal and 25 per cent in Hedemarken. The remaining members of farmer households

[1] Statistical appendix, table 18.
[2] Sverre Steen, *Det norske folks liv og historie gjennem tidene* (Oslo, 1932), **6**, 318 for a brief description of the system.

TABLE 5.12 *Marriages between bachelors and widows as a percentage of all marriages in Herøy, Hallingdal and Hedemarken from 1827 to 1865**

	Bachelor–widow marriages as a percentage of all marriages		
Period	Herøy (%)	Hallingdal (%)	Hedemarken (%)
1827–35	14·1	5·9	6·4
1836–45	10·2	8·2	4·7
1846–55	9·8	5·5	2·8
1856–65	11·8	3·9	3·0
1827–65	11·3	6·3	4·1

* Statistical appendix, table 19.

can be divided into four groups. The first consists of the farmer's children, the second of other relatives either direct or acquired through marriage, the third of farm servants (*tjenestefolk*), who received most of their wages in kind, and the fourth of lodgers, who were not related to the head of the household or to his wife but who may have been working for him.

The first of these groups, the children, was the biggest. In Herøy 35 per cent of the membership of farmer households was made up of children. In Hallingdal the proportion was 42 per cent and in Hedemarken 35 per cent. The average number of children on each farm in Herøy was 1·9, in Hedemarken 2·7 and in Hallingdal 3·2. Of the farmers in Herøy, 68·5 per cent had two or fewer children living with them, in Hedemarken 49·2 per cent were in this position and in Hallingdal 40·2. A large number of children in any one household was then relatively rare. Only 2·7 per cent of the farmers in Herøy had six or more children living with them although the percentage was higher in the other areas: 7·5 in Hedemarken, 15·5 in Hallingdal (table 5.13).

The number of children living with their parents depended upon the birth, death and migration rates operating on the particular farm. Since the fertility of young women is usually higher than that of old, we would expect fewer children in Herøy than in Hedemarken as

TABLE 5.13 *Percentage distribution of farm and crofter households by number of children of household heads in Herøy, Hallingdal and Hedemarken in 1801**

Children per household	Farm households			Croft households		
	Herøy (%)	Hallingdal (%)	Hede-marken (%)	Herøy (%)	Hallingdal (%)	Hede-marken (%)
0	24·7	13·7	14·3	53·7	21·4	22·6
1	21·1	11·4	16·3	27·4	23·0	27·5
2	22·7	15·1	18·6	11·6	18·9	20·6
3	14·2	17·6	16·7	5·3	18·8	15·8
4	10·4	13·7	16·4	2·1	9·5	9·4
5	4·1	13·0	10·1	—	5·8	2·7
6+	2·7	15·5	7·5	—	2·5	1·4
	100·0	100·0	100·0	100·0	100·0	100·0

* Statistical appendix, table 20.

TABLE 5.14 *Children under 5 years per 1,000 farmers' wives and widows 15–49 years in Herøy, Hallingdal and Hedemarken in 1801**

	Children	Wives and widows	Children per 1,000 wives and widows
Herøy	209	254	822
Hallingdal	678	513	1,322
Hedemarken	443	460	963

* Source as table 5.6 above.

farmers' wives were on average younger in the latter. For the same reason we would expect fewer younger children per farmer's wife in Hedemarken than in Hallingdal. Our expectations are borne out by the 1801 census (table 5.14). According to this there were 822 children under five years of age for every thousand farmers' wives or widows in Herøy as compared with 963 in Hedemarken and 1,322 in Hallingdal.

As a rough indication of the rate at which farmer's children left home we might compare the number of children over twenty years of age with those aged eleven to twenty years. Hedemarken, the district with the largest and richest farms, appears in this calculation to have kept its children on the farm longer than elsewhere. Herøy let them go earlier than either of the other two areas. Thus, there were 456 children aged twenty years or more living on the farms of their parents in Hedemarken for every 1,000 of their brothers and sisters aged 11–20 years. In Herøy this was true of only 263 children whereas in Hallingdal the number was 377. Except in the case of Herøy, sons appear to have stayed at home longer than daughters, although in both Herøy and Hedemarken the difference between the proportion of boys and girls at home was slight. Differential death rates between the two sexes might well have produced this. In Hallingdal, however, the difference is quite marked. There we find in the farm households as many as 434 sons aged twenty years and over for every 1,000 aged 11–20 years, as compared with 312 daughters (table 5.15). The figures give support to some literary evidence which suggests that young women often left Hallingdal in the winter months to work as servants on the lowland farms or in towns like Drammen and Oslo.[1] If the 1801 census had been taken in July instead of February we may have found more farmers' daughters at home. That women rather than men should migrate from Hallingdal in the winter may reflect the bigger demand for female servants at this time of year as well as a greater reluctance on the part of men to go into domestic service.[2]

The second largest group of dependants in farm households were the servants (*tjenestefolk*). The average number per 100 farmers was 87 in Herøy, 80 in Hallingdal and 142 in Hedemarken.[3] The relatively

---

[1] Lars Reinton, *op. cit.* p. 39; Ola Langslet, *Nes herred i Hallingdal* (Drammen, 1914), p. 39.

[2] A common complaint in eighteenth-century Norway was that both men and women preferred to work as day-labourers than as servants on a yearly contract. The government tried to rectify this situation by decree. For an example of such an order see that of Nicolaus Christian Spiesmacher, *foged* (sheriff) of Aker and Follo, published in the *Norske intelligenz-seddeler*, 21 May 1766. See also Hans Strøm, *op. cit.* I, 565–6; Peter Holm, 'Forsøg til en beskrivelse over Lister og Mandals amter', *Topographisk Journal for Norge* (Christiania, 1793–4), 2, 8, 56; Oscar Albert Johnsen, *Norges bønder. Utsyn over den norske bondestands historie* (2nd ed. Oslo, 1936), p. 304.

[3] Statistical appendix, table 22.

TABLE 5.15 *Farmers' children over 20 years per 1,000 aged 11–20 years living with their parents in Herøy, Hallingdal and Hedemarken in 1801**

Area	Sons	Daughters	All children
Herøy	252	273	263
Hallingdal	434	312	377
Hedemarken	461	450	456

* Statistical appendix, table 21.

large number of servants in Herøy may come as a surprise in view of what has been said about the limited opportunities for farming in that area. It should be remembered, however, that the sea in the west of Norway demanded as much labour as the land in the eastern part of the country. Many servants both male and female spent much of their time on the fishing grounds. Sometimes this was alongside their own masters in his boat with his tackle, but as Eilert Sundt has pointed out, a servant could well be sent to work in a fishing boat belonging to another man. What he earned, however, would go direct to his master.[1] One should also remember that even a small farmer might employ a servant or two in the period when his own children were too small to be of much assistance.

Many farmers had no *tjenestefolk* (table 5.16): 61 per cent of those in Hallingdal, 49 per cent in Hedemarken and 44 per cent in Herøy. Very few farmers had large numbers of servants. Under 2 per cent had more than three servants in Herøy, although in Hedemarken 15 per cent were in this position and in Hallingdal 4 per cent.

Most servants were in their late teens or early twenties. In Herøy 61 per cent were between 16 and 30 years of age, in Hallingdal 71 per cent and in Hedemarken 73 per cent. Female servants outnumbered male in all three areas, especially in Hedemarken, where 66 per cent of the servants were women. In Hallingdal 60 per cent of the servants were women and in Herøy 57 per cent. Female servants were somewhat older than male servants, even though in Hallingdal and Hedemarken they appear to have been recruited at

[1] Eilert Sundt, *Fiskeriets bedrift* (Christiania, 1862), p. 10.

TABLE 5.16 *Percentage distribution of farmer and crofter households by number of servants (tjenestefolk) in Herøy, Hallingdal and Hedemarken in 1801**

	Farm households			Croft households		
Servants per household	Herøy (%)	Hallingdal (%)	Hedemarken (%)	Herøy (%)	Hallingdal (%)	Hedemarken (%)
0	43·8	60·5	49·0	91·6	95·4	97·5
1	34·0	17·6	14·9	7·4	3·7	2·0
2	16·2	11·4	13·4	1·0	0·6	0·2
3	4·4	6·1	7·8	—	0·2	0·1
4	0·8	2·6	6·9	—	—	—
5+	0·8	1·8	8·0	—	—	0·1
	100·0	100·0	100·0	100·0	100·0	100·0

* Statistical appendix, table 22.

earlier ages than the men. The median age of male servants in Herøy, Hallingdal and Hedemarken was 21, 21 and 22 years respectively. The corresponding figures for women were 23, 22 and 23. Almost all servants were unmarried. Malthus was right in this respect. Out of 232 male servants in Hallingdal, only two were married and none were widowers. In the same area only one woman servant was married and three were widows. In Hedemarken twelve male servants were married and two were widowed out of a servant body of 303. The corresponding figure for the 590 women servants were six married and 14 widowed. Only in Herøy was the proportion of married servants higher. Eleven of the 136 male servants were married and one was a widower. Of the 181 female servants six were married and five were widowed.[1]

The lodgers, making up the last two groups, can be divided into those who were and those who were not related to the farmer or his wife. In many cases such a differentiation would make little difference to the nature of their work or to their position in the household. Nor is the division likely to be a very accurate one. It is most probable that in a number of cases the enumerators failed to specify

[1] Statistical appendix, table 18.

TABLE 5.17   *Percentage distribution of farmer and crofter households by number of relatives of the household head or his wife, other than children in Herøy, Hallingdal and Hedemarken in 1801**

Relations per household	Farm households			Croft households		
	Herøy (%)	Hallingdal (%)	Hede-marken (%)	Herøy (%)	Hallingdal (%)	Hede-marken (%)
0	74·0	65·9	50·7	93·7	87·8	86·0
1	16·2	15·0	21·2	5·3	8·1	8·9
2	5·8	10·4	17·2	1·0	3·0	4·2
3	1·9	5·0	5·8	—	0·7	0·6
4	1·9	2·1	2·2	—	0·4	0·3
5+	0·3	1·7	2·9	—	—	—
	100·0	100·0	100·0	100·0	100·0	100·0

* Statistical appendix, table 23.

that a man or woman was a relative of the farmer or of his wife when this was in fact the case.

Many farmers had no relatives living with them other than their wives and children. This was the position with 74 per cent of the farmers in Herøy, 66 per cent in Hallingdal and 51 per cent in Hedemarken. Few farmers had more than one or two relatives living with them. In Hedemarken only 11 per cent had three or more relatives in their households, whilst in Hallingdal 9 per cent and in Herøy 4 per cent were in this category (table 5.17). In Herøy the average number of relatives per 100 farmers was 42, in Hallingdal 69 and in Hedemarken 99. Many of these relatives were old people, often drawing an allowance from the farmer in whose household they lived. In a majority of these cases they were the parents of the farmer or of his wife. Sometimes however, they were brothers, sisters, uncles or aunts with some claim on the farm as part of their inheritance. In Hallingdal, over half the relatives were said to be in this position. Out of a group of 272, there were only eight single men and eight single women. The rest of the group was made up of 62 married men and 64 married women, 46 widowers and 84 widows. The striking excess of widows over widowers reflects partly the lower rates of mortality amongst women and partly perhaps the greater success attending the efforts of an heir in persuading a widowed mother as opposed to a widowed father to retire and give up the farm. Of the relatives who were not described as *livøre* as many as 89 per cent were unmarried. A similar pattern emerges from the Hedemarken census. Here, 59 per cent of the relatives were classified as *livøre* amongst whom were 111 married men, 118 married women, 43 widowers and 104 widows. Amongst the relatives who were not *livøre*, 85 per cent were unmarried.[1] The situation in Herøy was, however, different from that in either Hallingdal or Hedemarken; for here none were described as *livøre*. The parents of some farmers were, however, described as *husmenn*. In Herøy two-thirds of the farmers' relatives were unmarried, and amongst the twenty-four widowed persons only two were widowers.

In Hallingdal and Hedemarken we find the *livøre* concentrated in the higher age groups, whilst the other relatives were more evenly distributed. Thus, in Hallingdal 75 per cent of the *livøre* were over 60 years of age whilst in Hedemarken the proportion was 73 per cent.[2]

Many farmers had no unrelated lodgers living with them, and the proportion of this category of farmer in Herøy was as high as 80 per cent, whereas in Hedemarken and Hallingdal it was 56 per cent in each case. Few had more than one or two. Only 5 per cent of farms in Hedemarken had three or more unrelated lodgers and this was true also of Hallingdal. In Herøy only 2 per cent were in this category (table 5.18).

It emerges from this analysis of part of the 1801 census that the relatively small nucleated household of father, mother and two or three children was much more common amongst Norwegian farmers than one might expect. Almost all farmers (90 per cent) in the areas studied were married, between 75 per cent (in Herøy) and 85 per cent (Hallingdal and Hedemarken) had at least one child living with them at the time of the census, whilst 40–50 per cent had between two and four children. There were, it is true, a considerable number of servants and lodgers, but these were distributed unevenly. Many

[1] Statistical appendix, table 18.   [2] *Ibid.*

TABLE 5.18 *Percentage distribution of farmer and crofter households by number of lodgers who were unrelated to the household head or his wife in Herøy, Hallingdal and Hedemarken in 1801**

Lodgers per household	Farm households			Croft households		
	Herøy (%)	Hallingdal (%)	Hede-marken (%)	Herøy (%)	Hallingdal (%)	Hede-marken (%)
0	80·3	56·2	56·5	84·2	65·8	74·5
1	13·7	25·5	28·0	10·5	17·6	15·2
2	4·1	10·5	10·4	4·2	8·6	7·0
3	1·6	4·4	3·4	—	4·5	1·8
4	0·3	2·2	0·9	—	2·3	0·7
5+	—	1·1	0·8	1·0	1·3	0·8
	100·0	100·0	100·0	100·0	100·0	100·0

* Statistical appendix, table 24.

farmers, for instance, had no servants whatsoever although a small minority had a large number.

If we take all the farm households together we find that servants and lodgers constituted between 30 and 40 per cent of the total membership, although many contained none of either category. Nevertheless, these groups were the ones which differentiated the farm households from those belonging to the crofters. Even when, as in Herøy, the average farm household was little bigger than that of the crofter in the east of the country, the major structural difference between them was that in the former servants made up 16 per cent of the membership, whilst in the latter they made up only about one per cent.

There were many more crofter than farmer households in both Hallingdal and Hedemarken. In Herøy the opposite was the case, there being only twenty-six crofters for every 100 farmers compared with 115 in Hallingdal and 154 in Hedemarken (table 5.8). As in the case of the farmers, the overwhelming majority of crofters were married men, there being no significant difference in this respect between the three areas—86 per cent in Herøy, 90 per cent in Hallingdal and 95 per cent in Hedemarken (table 5.11). As farmers only allowed men to occupy crofts in order to avail themselves of the labour that the crofter and his family could provide there was little point in giving crofts to inveterate bachelors. Thus, only 1·0 per cent of the crofters in Herøy were unmarried men; in Hedemarken the percentage was as little as 0·4; in Hallingdal it was 1·7. Widowed crofters were more common. In Hallingdal, 3·3 per cent of the crofts were held by widowers. In Hedemarken the corresponding figure was 1·1 per cent and in Herøy 5·3 per cent (table 5.11).

At the beginning of the nineteenth century it was not unusual for widows of crofters to retain the crofts of their deceased husbands subject to their not re-marrying.[1] As the pressure of population on the land rose during the first half of the nineteenth century this rather benevolent system declined.[2] Instead, the custom of granting crofts on a yearly lease spread. In 1801, however, a number of widows are seen to be holding crofts. In Hallingdal 3·5 per cent of the crofters were widows, in Hedemarken 2·4 per cent and in Herøy as many as 7·4 per cent (table 5.11). In Herøy, however, some of these crofters were specifically described in the 1801 census as the parents of farmers. Elsewhere, therefore, they would probably have been classified as *livøre*.

Most of the crofters in Hallingdal and Hedemarken were in their first marriage (82·7 per cent of those in Hallingdal, 84·7 per cent in Hedemarken). In Herøy on the other hand, only 61·1 per cent of the crofters were in their first marriage. This, together with the fact that their median age was 56 years, against 47 in Hallingdal and 45 in Hedemarken, lends further support to the hypothesis that the crofters of Herøy in 1801 were not fulfilling the same roles as their namesakes in the other two areas.

The median age of the crofters in Hallingdal was three years above that of the farmers, 47 as against 44. In Hedemarken however, the reverse was the case. There the median age of crofters was 45 and that of farmers 46 years.[3] The explanation of these differences lies no doubt within a complex of factors including variations in the

---

[1] This ban was to protect the farmer against the possibility of getting an unsuitable crofter. See Thomas Stang, *Den norske husmandsklasses tilstand* (Christiania, 1851), p. 80. [2] *Ibid.* p. 27; Lars Reinton, *op. cit.* pp. 66–7.
[3] Statistical appendix, table 18.

system of recruitment to and retirement from farms and crofts. Social cleavages also played their part. In Hedemarken the farms were bigger than in Hallingdal and the farmers richer and more conscious of the social distance between themselves and their crofters. There was relatively little social intercourse between them.[1] The economic function of a crofter—his labour—appeared all important. In Hallingdal, however, the division between the two groups was less obvious. Sometimes crofters were drawn only recently from within the farmer's own family. Indeed, one occasionally comes across the brother of a farmer described in the census of 1801 as having a piece of land which he 'uses as a crofter' (*bruker jord som husmann*).[2] In the west, in Herøy for example, there were relatively few crofters in 1801 and many of those who were described as such would have been known as *livøre* in the east of the country. When the number of crofters increased in the early nineteenth century they were necessarily drawn from amongst the farm holding community.[3] Because the system was of relatively recent origin in the west and because the farms were much smaller than those in the east, the social division between the crofter and the farmer was comparatively narrow.[4] In the eastern part of the country however, the division between the two widened.[5]

This difference in the degree of class exclusiveness might contain the explanation of why in an area like Hedemarken, a crofter was more likely to lose his croft when he became too old to fulfil his labour services than he was in an area like Hallingdal or Herøy. Thus in 1801 some 17 per cent of the crofters in Hallingdal were 60 years of age or over as compared with 13 per cent in Hedemarken.[6]

1 Andreas Holmsen, 'Landowners and tenants in Norway', *Scandinavian Economic History Review*, 6, 2 (1958), 128; R. Frimannslund, address to the *Historisk klubb*, Oslo 8, March 1955 (mimeographed) on the *gårds- og grannesamfunns* project being carrried out by Instituttet for sammenlignende kulturforskning, Oslo.
2 Census of 1801. Enumerators' return no. 63, for Ål parish, Hol Sogn. Eilert Sundt, *Om ædrueligheds-tilstanden i Norge* (Christiania, 1859), p. 90 notes that in the 1850s it was common for the younger sons of a farmer to take a croft on their eldest brother's farm.
3 Ingrid Semmingsen, *Husmannsminner* (Oslo, 1960), pp. 97–8.
4 A. Holmsun, *op. cit.* p. 128; R. Frimannslund, *op. cit.* p. 8; Sundt, *op. cit.* pp. 90, 107.
5 J. C. Lous, *Om Husmandsvæsenet* (Christiania, 1851), pp. 72–3.
6 The census of 1875 revealed that the mean age of crofters in Norway was 50–51 years. Only 5 per cent were under 30 years of age; 22 per cent were under 40 and 34 per cent

In both areas, largely because of the *livøre* system, the proportion of farmers over 60 was only about 10 per cent. The lower average age of the Hedemarken crofters may also have been brought about by earlier recruitment. One would expect access to crofts to be quicker in a rich, expanding economy like Hedemarken partly because more labour would be required in such an economy and partly because the circulation of existing crofts would be faster (because of the compulsory retirement of aged crofters) than it would be in an area like Hallingdal. In Hallingdal, an unprogressive economy delayed the entry to crofts and the close personal ties existing between farmers and crofters delayed the latter's departure from them. Support for this argument comes from the nuptiality and age at marriage statistics. In 1801 in Hedemarken 30 per cent of the men aged 21–30 years were married or widowed as compared with only 22 per cent in Hallingdal. Turning to age at marriage, we find that 35 per cent of the men in Hedemarken who contracted first marriages between 1839 and 1865 were under 25 years of age as against 24 per cent of their counterparts in Hallingdal.[1]

Crofters and their wives made up 60 per cent of the membership of households headed by crofters in Herøy, 40 per cent of those in Hallingdal and about 45 per cent of those in Hedemarken. In each case this was a higher proportion than made up the corresponding group in the farmers' households. Of the remaining groups (children, servants, other relatives and unrelated lodgers) only the children approach a sizeable total. We would not, of course, expect to find that crofters had a lot of servants although we might have expected to see a somewhat higher proportion of the household membership being made up of relatives other than children. Presumably, because many crofters were allowed to keep their crofts until they died, and because a *livøre* system was not practicable, there were not many elderly relatives in crofter households. Widows predominate among those we find.

Children accounted for just over 40 per cent of the membership

were under 45. At the other end of the scale, 37 per cent were over 55 years of age. J. N. Mohn, *Statistiske meddelelser om husmandsklassens betydning i samfundet og husmændenes økonomiske stilling* (Kristiania, 1880), p. 21.
[1] Statistical appendix, table 13.

TABLE 5.19 *Crofter children over 20 years of age per 1,000 aged 11–20 living with their parents in Hallingdal and Hedemarken in 1801**

	Sons	Daughters	All children
Hallingdal	310	288	300
Hedemarken	266	194	236

* Statistical appendix, table 21. Herøy excluded because of small numbers of children.

of the crofter households in both Hallingdal and Hedemarken. In Herøy they provided only 25 per cent: an understandably low proportion in the light of our presumptions about the function of crofts there and of the age composition of the crofters and their wives. In all areas the crofters, their wives and children made up between 80 and 85 per cent of the membership of the household. The average number of children per 100 crofts was 70 in Herøy, 200 in Hallingdal and 170 in Hedemarken. In Herøy 93 per cent of the crofters had two or fewer children living with them at the time of the census. The corresponding percentage in Hallingdal was about 63 and in Hedemarken 71 (table 5.13).[1]

As the children of the crofters provided a large share of the servant population, few moving directly from the croft in which they were born to the one in which they might expect to die, we might predict that they would usually leave home earlier than did the farmer's children since many of the latter did not go into service. Our prediction is borne out by the findings of the 1801 census (table 5.19).

The number of young children in a crofter's home was primarily dependent upon the fertility of himself and his wife. So far all statistics in the study have suggested that marital fertility was a function of the age of the wife. When we find, therefore, that the median age of the crofters' wives in Hedemarken was 45 years, as against 42 for farmers' wives, we would expect farmers to have more

[1] These figures are interesting in the light of the allegation made in the late 1840s that many crofters had to support 10–12 children, an unlikely figure it would seem, notwithstanding the drop in mortality that occurred in the meantime. For the allegation see 'Menigmands ven om M. Thranes arbeiderforeninger', *Morgenbladet* (Christiania, 13 November 1849).

TABLE 5.20   *Children under 5 years per 1,000 crofters'*
wives and widows 15–49 years in Hallingdal and Hede-
*marken in 1801**

	Children	Wives and widows	Children per 1,000 wives and widows
Hallingdal	545	548	994
Hedemarken	599	680	881

* Source as table 5.6 above.

children than crofters. We would also expect this to happen in
Hallingdal where the median age of crofters' wives was 45 years as
against 40 years for that of farmers'.[1] Herøy was again something
of an exception, though the pattern remains, the corresponding ages
being 51 and 43 years. In Hallingdal the difference in fertility
between farmers and crofters was quite marked. In 1801 there were
1,322 children aged 0–4 years for every 1,000 farmers' wives and
widows (table 5.14) aged 15–49 years as against 994 crofters'
children (table 5.20).

In Hedemarken the difference between the fertility of the farmers'
and crofters' wives was less marked. This is not surprising since the
difference between the median age of the two was less than in
Hallingdal. In Hedemarken there were 963 farmers' children 0–4
years of age for every 1,000 farmers' wives between 15–49 years,
whilst the corresponding number of crofters' children was 881
(tables 5.14 and 5.20).

One anomaly remains to be explained. Fertility was, assuming
the data to be accurate, higher amongst the crofters of Hallingdal
than amongst those of Hedemarken, even though the median age of
crofters' wives in Hallingdal, at 45, was one year above that of the
crofters' wives in Hedemarken. However, when we calculate the
median age of those crofters' wives who were in the fertile age group,

[1] W. Stys, 'The influence of economic conditions on the fertility of peasant women',
Population Studies, **11**, 2 (1957), 136, 139 notes that in Poland the richer peasant
girls marry earlier than the poorer and the 'richer peasants have much larger families
than those who are poor'.

15–49 years, we find the Hallingdal wives were one year younger than their counterparts in Hedemarken—37 as against 38 years.[1]

Before trying to explain these different fertility rates in terms of the social mechanisms revealed by the census of 1801, we need to take a closer look at the age differences between the farmers and the crofters and their respective wives. In Hedemarken, we discovered that the median age of the farmers was 46 years and that of the crofters 45. Although crofters were thus one year younger than the farmers, the median age of crofters' wives at 44 years was two years greater than that of the farmers' wives at 42. In Hallingdal, too, the age gap between the farmers and their wives was greater than that separating the crofters from theirs.

This marital age gap is similar to the one discovered by Eilert Sundt when he made a survey of age at marriage amongst the property-owning classes (chiefly farmers) and the propertyless (chiefly crofters). To obtain the necessary statistics Sundt asked all the priests in the two dioceses of Akershus and Kristiansand to tell him at what ages people had married in their parishes in the years 1851 and 1852.[2] He also asked for the previous marital status of the bride and bridegroom and the occupation of the bridegroom as well as the social origins of the bride. Sundt found that in both dioceses the mean age at first marriage of the farmers was 29·5 and of their brides 26·0 years. The mean age at marriage of the crofters was 27·25 and of their brides 26·75.[3] Thus crofters married earlier than farmers but their brides were, on average, older than those of the farmers'. There was, therefore, a greater age gap between the farmers and their wives than there was between the crofters and theirs.

This marital age pattern—revealed both by the 1801 census and by Sundt's enquiry—is an unexpected one. So much so that it would appear necessary to probe a little more deeply into it. This has been done by looking at the situation in other parts of the country and by adopting a somewhat different measure. Data relating to some 7,000 married couples have been abstracted from the enumerators' returns for the census of 1801. These couples have been classified by region, occupation of husband (whether farmer or crofter),

---

[1] Statistical appendix, table 18.
[2] Eilert Sundt, *Om giftermaal i Norge* (Christiania, 1855), pp. 183, 185.
[3] *Ibid.* table 30, p. 197.

number of times either of the partners married, and by the age gap separating husbands from their wives.

The sample was drawn from five different parts of Norway. Two of the areas, Hallingdal and Hedemarken, are identical with the ones already discussed. A third, here called Sunnmøre, is made up of Herøy and some adjacent parishes.[1] A fourth, here called Ryfylke, consists of a group of parishes on the coast of Rogaland.[2] This was an area of small farms whose inhabitants, like those of Herøy, were dependent upon the sea for a living. The fifth area is part of the valley of Østerdalen in the extreme east of the country.[3] Like Hallingdal, it had a harsh climate and its inhabitants were mostly engaged in lumbering and pastoral activities.[4] A certain amount of government-sponsored colonisation was tried here in the late eighteenth century.[5]

In order to reduce the complexity of the description, only three age gaps will be discussed. The first where at least 5 years separated the ages of husband and wife, the second where the gap was one of at least 10 years and the third where it reached 15 years or more. Taking all the marriages in all the five areas together, it appears that in 11 per cent the gap was 15 years or more. In over 27 per cent it was 10 years or more and in 57 per cent it was 5 or more. Interesting differences, however, are hidden by these aggregates. In Ryfylke and Sunnmøre, for instance, the proportion of marriages where the age gap was above 10 or 15 years was greater than elsewhere. On the other hand, in Østerdalen it was well below the average. Thus, in only 7 per cent of the Østerdalen marriages was the age gap 15 years or more whereas both in Ryfylke and Sunnmøre it was so in 14 per cent of the marriages. Hallingdal and Hedemarken occupied an intermediate position with 11·2 and 9·8 per cent respectively (table 5.21).

---

[1] Vanylven, Ullstein (less Hareid).
[2] Torvastad, Avaldsnes, Skjold, Nedstrand, Vikedal, Skudenes.
[3] Elverum, Amot, Trysil, Tynset, Tolga.
[4] S. Skappel, *Hedemarkens amt, 1814–1914* (Kristiania, 1914), pp. 29, 44. Also according to Skappel the area was more dependent upon imports of grain than any other in southern Norway.
[5] For an unsuccessful attempt in the mid-eighteenth century, Nils Collin, 'Nogle reisebemerkninger nedskrevne 1757', *Norsk Historisk Tidsskrift*, 4 (Kristiania, 1877), 503–11.

TABLE 5.21   *Age gap separating farmers and crofters from their respective wives in parts of Norway in 1801**

	Age gap (years)					
	0	1–4	5–9	10–14	15+	All marriages
Sunnmøre	6·0	36·5	25·6	17·6	14·2	100·0
Ryfylke	6·0	35·4	26·9	17·6	14·2	100·0
Hallingdal	4·5	34·4	30·8	19·1	11·2	100·0
Hedemarken	5·8	37·7	31·9	14·7	9·8	100·0
Østerdalen	7·2	40·6	30·4	15·2	6·7	100·0
All areas	5·9	37·0	29·5	16·7	10·9	100·0

* Statistical appendix, table 25.

When the above marriages are broken down into those where the husbands were older than their wives and those where the wives were older than their husbands we discover a somewhat more involved situation (table 5.22). Taking all the five areas together we find that the husband was 5 or more years older than his wife in 38 per cent of the marriages; in 19 per cent the opposite was true. In 18 per cent of all marriages, the husband was 10 or more years older than his wife; in 9 per cent the wife was that much older than her husband. Finally, in 7 per cent of all marriages the husbands were 15 or more years older than their wives; in 4 per cent of all marriages the wives were 15 or more years older than their husbands. Excluding Hallingdal, we find that the other four areas did not differ very much from the general average in so far as the proportion of marriages where husbands were older than their wives was concerned. Thus, the proportion of marriages where the husband was 15 or more years older than his wife varied from 5 to 8 per cent. Where the corresponding gap was one of 10 years or more the range was 16–19 per cent and where it was 5 years or more the range was 29–38 per cent. In Hallingdal, however, the proportion was higher in each category, being 9 per cent (15 years or more), 23 per cent (10 years or more), and 46 per cent (5 years or more) (table 5.22).

TABLE 5.22 *Age gap separating farmers and crofters from their respective wives in parts of Norway in 1801 classified according to whether wife or husband the elder partner**

		Age gap (years)							
		1–4		5–9		10–14		15+	
		Husband	Wife	Husband	Wife	Husband	Wife	Husband	Wife
	Same age	older		older		older		older		Total
Sunnmøre	6·0	17·8	18·7	12·0	13·6	9·4	8·2	7·1	7·1	100·0
Ryfylke	6·0	20·6	14·8	17·1	9·8	11·1	6·5	8·2	6·0	100·0
Hallingdal	4·5	21·3	13·1	22·9	7·9	14·9	4·2	8·5	2·7	100·0
Hedemarken	5·8	19·6	18·1	19·7	12·2	9·3	5·4	6·8	3·0	100·0
Østerdalen	7·2	25·4	15·2	22·0	8·4	10·9	4·3	5·0	1·7	100·0
All areas	5·9	21·3	15·7	19·4	10·1	11·2	5·5	7·1	3·8	100·0

* Statistical appendix, table 26.

Differences between the eastern and western areas emerge when we calculate the percentage of marriages in which the wife was older than her husband. The contrast was greatest between Sunnmøre and Østerdalen. In Sunnmøre wives were 5 or more years older than their husbands in 29 per cent of all marriages. This was so in only 14 per cent of the Østerdalen marriages. In marriages where the wives were 15 years or more older than their husbands the corresponding percentages were 7 per cent (Sunnmøre) and 2 per cent (Østerdalen). In Hallingdal the position was exactly the same as in Østerdalen (table 5.22).

These figures mask two potentially significant variables; namely the proportion of first to subsequent marriages and secondly the ratio of crofters to farmers. For every 1,000 married farmers there were in Ryfylke 582 married crofters; in Sunnmøre only 212, in Hallingdal 1,171, in Hedemarken 1,590 and in Østerdalen 668 (table 5.23). The highest proportion of second marriages amongst both farmers and crofters was in Sunnmøre and Ryfylke. Neither partner had been previously married in 70 per cent of the farmers' marriages in Ryfylke and in 66 per cent in Sunnmøre. The corresponding figures for Hallingdal, Hedemarken and Østerdalen were 80 per cent, 80 per cent and 82 per cent respectively. Amongst the

TABLE 5.23 *Marital status of farmers and crofters in Sunnmøre, Ryfylke, Hallingdal, Hedemarken and Østerdalen in 1801**

Marital status†	Ryfylke	Farmers Sunnmøre	Hallingdal	Hedemarken	Østerdalen
I i	69·9	66·2	80·1	79·5	82·2
I ii	12·8	13·0	8·7	9·7	8·3
I iii	0·9	1·8	0·8	0·8	0·1
I iv	0·1	0·2	—	—	—
II i	12·5	13·7	8·9	7·7	7·9
II ii	1·9	1·5	0·8	1·3	0·8
II iii	0·2	0·3	0·2	—	—
III i	1·1	2·3	0·6	0·3	0·4
III ii	0·3	0·3	—	0·3	0·1
III iii	0·1	0·2	—	—	—
III iv	—	0·2	—	—	—
IV i	0·2	0·2	—	0·2	0·1
IV ii	—	0·2	—	0·2	—
	100·0	100·0	100·0	100·0	100·0
No. of marriages	1,087	648	642	601	969
		Crofters			
I i	75·1	59·9	87·2	84·7	88·6
I ii	5·9	8·8	4·0	3·7	3·9
I iii	0·3	—	0·3	0·2	—
I iv	0·2	0·7	—	—	—
II i	10·0	20·4	6·8	8·1	6·3
II ii	3·5	5·1	1·2	1·6	0·5
II iii	0·3	2·2	—	0·2	0·2
III i	3·3	1·5	0·5	0·9	0·6
III ii	0·8	1·5	—	0·3	—
IV i	0·2	—	—	0·3	—
IV ii	0·3	—	—	—	—
V iii	0·2	—	—	—	—
	100·0	100·0	100·0	100·0	100·0
No. of marriages	631	137	751	955	647

* Statistical appendix, table 27.
† Numerals specify marital history of couples. Hence a woman in her third marriage is entered as iii; a man in his second appears as II.

crofter marriages in Ryfylke, 75 per cent were between never-marrieds and in Sunnmøre this was the case with 60 per cent. The other three areas were very much alike: 87 per cent in Hallingdal, 85 per cent in Hedemarken and 89 per cent in Østerdalen (table 5.23).

A significant feature of the above statistics is that in the areas where a high proportion of farmers were in their first marriages this was true also of the crofters. Conversely, when a relatively low proportion of farmers were in their first marriages this too was true of the crofters. Analyses of the age gap separating the farmers and crofters from their respective wives (after first excluding marriages where either one or both partners had been married before) reveals some striking variations. The first and most obvious of these is that crofters were more frequently married to women who were some years their senior than was the case with farmers. In Hedemarken, for example, 24 per cent of the crofters were married to women who were more than 5 years their senior and 9 per cent were married to women who were more than 10 years their senior. In the same area the corresponding figures for farmers was 9 per cent and 2 per cent. Secondly, in Sunnmøre and Ryfylke it was as common for crofters' wives to be older than their husbands as it was for crofters to be older than their wives. Thus in Ryfylke 27 per cent of the crofters were 5 or more years older than their wives, 12 per cent were 10 or more years older and 3 per cent 15 or more years older. Crofter's wives, on the other hand, were older than their husbands by 5 years or more in 25 per cent of the marriages, by 10 years or more in 12 per cent and by 15 years or more in 4 per cent.

A third feature of interest is that in some areas the marital age patterns of farmers and crofters were similar, in others very different. Thus, in Sunnmøre it was quite common for farmers in their first marriage to choose as their brides women who were older than they were, sometimes very much older. To a lesser degree this was also the position in Ryfylke. It was much less common however in Hedemarken and Østerdalen and one might almost say it was rare in Hallingdal. For in Hallingdal only 17 per cent of farmers' wives were older than their husbands and of these 11 per cent were less than 5 years older. As for crofters, we find that in Sunnmøre very many wives were older than their husbands. This was also true, to a lesser extent, of Ryfylke and Hedemarken. It was much less common in Østerdalen and Hallingdal. We might press the statistics further and suggest that in Ryfylke and Sunnmøre the marital age pattern associated with crofters in the eastern part of the country (the tendency for wives to be older than their husbands) was also characteristic of many farmers' marriages. In Hallingdal and Østerdalen on the other hand, the marital age pattern we have associated with farmers (a tendency for wives to be younger than their husbands) is also noticeable amongst the crofters. In Hedemarken the marital age pattern of most farmers is more markedly different from that of the crofters than in any other area. If we take all the areas together, we find that one in five of the crofters' wives were 5 or more years older than their husbands as compared with one in ten of the farmers' wives. The two extreme cases are the crofters' wives in Sunnmøre and the farmers' wives in Hallingdal. One in three of the former were 5 or more years older than their husbands, compared with one in sixteen of the latter. And whereas one in six of the crofters' wives in Sunnmøre were 10 or more years older than their husbands and one in twenty-five were 15 years or more older: the corresponding ratios amongst the farmers' wives of Hallingdal were one in 62 and one in 250 (tables 5.24 and 5.25).

If we could explain these marital age patterns we would be near the root cause of the differences in fertility noted earlier in this chapter. Here we desperately need the literary evidence which would give us 'that psychological insight into individual lives'[1] without which any explanation must remain tenuous. Fortunately, we have the evidence collected by Eilert Sundt on this point and the next chapter will be devoted to presenting this.

Before turning to this however, it would be appropriate to draw together the points made in this chapter relevant to such a discussion. Our examination of family and household structure in several areas in Norway at the beginning of the nineteenth century has revealed

---

[1] George Clark, *War and society in the seventeenth century* (Cambridge, 1958), p. 99, writes—'we have to rely in most countries on social history of the impressionist kind: we still need surveys and statistics. This is far more so when we go down to the bottom of the scale and here because of the poverty of our literary sources, we are further from having any *psychological insight into individual lives*' (my italics).

TABLE 5.24 *Age gap separating farmers from their wives, where neither partner previously married, in parts of Norway in 1801, classified according to whether wife or husband the elder partner*

	Age gap (years)							
	1–4		5–9		10–14		15 +	
	Husband older	Wife	Husband older	Wife	Husband older	Wife	Husband older	Wife
Sunnmøre	21·4	24·0	13·1	15·4	8·4	6·5	1·6	1·4
Ryfylke	27·4	16·4	20·9	8·8	11·3	3·4	4·3	1·3
Hallingdal	22·2	10·7	30·4	4·7	17·9	1·2	7·0	0·4
Hedemarken	23·0	13·2	26·6	7·1	14·2	1·9	6·5	0·4
Østerdalen	27·5	14·9	25·3	6·8	11·5	1·8	3·4	0·4
All areas	24·9	15·6	23·5	8·2	12·6	2·8	4·5	0·8

	Total marriages			
	Husband older	Wife older	Same age	
Sunnmøre	44·5	47·3	8·2	100·0
Ryfylke	63·9	29·9	6·2	100·0
Hallingdal	77·5	17·0	5·5	100·0
Hedemarken	70·3	22·6	7·1	100·0
Østerdalen	67·7	23·9	8·4	100·0
All areas	65·5	27·4	7·1	100·0

* Statistical appendix, table 28.

that the majority of the population in these areas lived in households that were headed either by a married farmer or a married crofter. Second, the farmer household was generally larger than that of the crofter, containing more children, servants, lodgers and relatives. This however, was not invariably the case; farmers in the western area, Herøy, having households only slightly bigger than the crofters in Hallingdal. Third, farmers appear to have had more children than crofters mainly because while they themselves married later than did crofters, their wives were on the whole younger than those of crofters. Thus the farmer was usually several years older than his wife, while the crofter, on the other hand, was either only slightly older than his wife or—not infrequently—younger than her. This

TABLE 5.25 *Age gap separating crofters from their wives, where neither partner previously married, in parts of Norway in 1801, classified according to whether wife or husband the elder partner**

	Age gap (years)							
	1–4		5–9		10–14		15 +	
	Husband older	Wife	Husband older	Wife	Husband older	Wife	Husband older	Wife
Sunnmøre	20·7	14·6	11·0	14·6	9·8	13·4	6·1	3·7
Ryfylke	20·9	18·4	15·4	13·3	8·9	8·0	3·0	3·8
Hallingdal	24·9	15·7	21·1	9·9	12·7	4·9	4·4	2·1
Hedemarken	19·5	23·9	17·7	14·7	5·9	6·1	3·3	2·8
Østerdalen	27·2	16·2	20·4	10·5	8·9	5·6	3·7	0·5
All areas	22·9	18·8	18·5	12·3	8·9	6·2	3·7	2·4

	Total marriages			
	Husband older	Wife older	Same age	
Sunnmøre	47·6	46·3	6·1	100·0
Ryfylke	48·2	43·5	8·3	100·0
Hallingdal	63·1	32·6	4·3	100·0
Hedemarken	46·4	47·5	6·1	100·0
Østerdalen	60·2	32·8	7·0	100·0
All areas	54·0	39·7	6·3	100·0

* Statistical appendix, table 29.

pattern varied somewhat from district to district. In some areas the division between crofters and farmers was very marked as in Hedemarken. In others, for instance, Sunnmøre and Ryfylke, considerable numbers of farmers married women some years their senior. Elsewhere, in Hallingdal and Østerdalen, the farmer pattern (wives usually younger than their husbands) appears to have been that of many crofters' marriages too. What lies behind these differences is obviously crucial to our understanding of the mechanism of nuptiality and, in turn, of the level of fertility in pre-industrial Norway. That such differences exist at all indicates that treating the pre-industrial west, especially in demographic matters, as an homogeneous unit almost certainly leads to gross misinterpretation.

6 *The determinants of marital age patterns*

Eilert Sundt, in many of his writings, was concerned with sexual relations in Norway. Apart from *On marriage in Norway*, he published three volumes each entitled *On morality in Norway*.[1] These were replete with statistical analyses and case studies. Sundt is therefore a major source for our examination of marriage and fertility. The fact that his investigations took place towards the end of the period covered by the present study and might, therefore, be misleading about earlier conditions, is fortunately not a major drawback. First, Sundt had a very strong historical sense and was always at pains to discover whether a phenomenon was of recent origin. Second, as we have seen, both fertility and nuptiality appear to have been remarkably steady over the period as a whole and the economic and social conditions, in terms of which we would normally explain these phenomena, also appear to have been comparatively stable.

Sundt, it will be recalled, was consciously addressing a lay audience and a relatively uneducated one at that: the farmers, cottars, fishermen and other ordinary members of Norwegian society. His writing often takes an anecdotal form and—as he admits quite openly—he frequently combined in the one story experiences from several sources. Thus we get neither the clinical analysis nor the precise language that we expect in a modern sociological work. But the 'folksy' character of the extracts from Sundt's work which appear below should not be taken as the product of a naïve mind, for Sundt was not a man to make glib generalisations or gloss over the difficulties of his subject.

Sundt suggests that the sons of most Norwegian farmers could not think of marriage until they had a farm of their own. They were

[1] *Om sædeligheds-tilstanden i Norge* (Christiania, 1857); *Fortsatte bidrag angaaende sædeligheds-tilstanden i Norge* (Christiania, 1864); *Om sædeligheds-tilstanden i Norge. Tredie Beretning* (Christiania, 1866).

prepared to wait to inherit one, to save in order to buy one, or to court another farmer's daughter who at marriage would either bring a farm with her or a dowry with which one might be purchased. Often, of course, the farmer's son would acquire land by a combination of all these means. Generally, he would look for a wife amongst the daughters of neighbouring farmers. A majority of farmers' sons did in fact marry farmers' daughters, according to Sundt's survey. The proportions varied quite widely from one part of the country to another, but over the country as a whole 76 per cent of the propertied classes—largely farmers according to Sundt—married women from their own class. The remaining 24 per cent married women from the lower, propertyless class—largely the daughters of crofters. In parts of the west and south-west the proportion of bridegrooms from the propertied class marrying women from the the same class fell to around 70 per cent, while in the extreme north of the country it fell to 60 per cent (table 6.1).

The daughters of farmers were naturally much sought after and the bigger their 'expectations', the bigger the crowd of suitors. As the 'expectations' of most of the girls would be widely known long before they reached a marriageable age,[1] marriage negotiations might begin early and continue over a number of years. Sometimes, if a suitable marriage could be arranged, the son of a farmer would wait many years till the girl reached marriageable age or came into an inheritance.

The farmer's son constantly goes with the thought of a good match in mind and with great diligence seeks to find and win a girl whose inheritance or dowry can help him to pay for a farm: as soon as a wealthy man's daughter is grown up she is such a good match and she is certain to see many suitors; but since the good matches are always few as against the many who seek them, a majority of the latter must year after year see their hopes disappointed. Often then it is an elderly bachelor and a fairly young girl who are at last united.[2]

It has happened not once but many times that a boy who, perhaps, at 27 years of age was in a position to establish a family, has waited until he became 37, and for the heartless reason that by that time a certain rich

[1] This was because in Norway the proportion of an inheritance going to a particular son or daughter was fixed by law, and as it usually consisted of land and stock the amount could be estimated fairly easily.
[2] Eilert Sundt. *Om giftermaal i Norge* (Christiania, 1855). p. 211.

TABLE 6.1 *Percentage of inter and intra-class marriages in different parts of Norway in 1855 and 1856. Class I are the propertied, mostly farmers. Class II the propertyless, mostly crofters**

Deanery groups†	Bridegrooms of class I with brides of			Bridegrooms of class II with brides of		
	Class I	Class II	Sum	Class I	Class II	Sum
1	82	18	100	14	86	100
2	81	19	100	8	92	100
3	78	22	100	13	87	100
4	80	20	100	10	90	100
5	79	21	100	24	76	100
6	70	30	100	40	60	100
7	81	19	100	27	73	100
8	72	28	100	30	70	100
9	80	20	100	14	86	100
10	81	19	100	30	70	100
11	73	27	100	23	77	100
12	82	18	100	14	86	100
13	78	22	100	16	84	100
14	60	40	100	24	76	100
15	63	37	100	14	86	100
Total	76	24	100	18	82	100

* Eilert Sundt, *Forsatte Bidrag angaaende Sædeligheds-Tilstanden i Norge* (Christiania, 1864), pp. 14–15, 31–2.

† Sundt grouped the deaneries as follows: (1) Nedre, Mellem, Vestre and Østre Borgesyssel, Nedre Romerike. (2) Øvre Romerike, Soløer and Odalen, Østerdalen, Hedemarken, Gudbrandsdalen. (3) Toten, Valdres, Hadeland Ringerike and Hallingdal, Kongsberg. (4) Drammen, Nordre and Søndre Jarlsberg, Larvik, Bamble, Nedre Telemark. (5) Øvre Telemark Østenfjeldske and Vestenfjeldske, Østre and Vestre Nedenæs, Råbygdelaget. (6) Mandal, Lister, Dalerne. (7) Jæren, Stavanger, Karmsund, Ryfylke. (8) Hardanger and Voss, Sunnhordland, Nordhordland. (9) Ytre and Indre Sogn. (10) Sunnfjord, Nordfjord, Søndre and Nordre Sunnmøre. (11) Romsdal, Nordmøre, Fosen. (12) Søndre and Nordre Dalerne. (13) Søndre and Nordre Innherad, Namdalen. (14) Søndre and Nordre Helgeland, Søndre and Nordre Salten, Lofoten, Vesterålen. (15) Tromsø, Vest and Øst Finnmark. NOTE. Sundt omitted the 'major' urban concentration in the Bergen and Trondheim diocesan deaneries.

farmer's daughter would have reached a marriageable age and that he would by then have won the father's consent to carry to his house both the girl and the fortune.[1]

There was, of course, in all areas factors likely to disturb this pattern. One of the most important was the frequency with which bachelors married widows, the latter often being older than their second or subsequent husbands. One observer writing from the west coast of Norway in the late eighteenth century alleged that few widows who held land managed to bury their husbands before suitors made themselves known, if not directly then through intermediaries.[2] Sundt repeats the 'well known' story from the Bergen diocese of a person who, whilst paying court to a widow at the funeral feast of her late husband, learned from her that she had already promised herself to the carpenter who had come to take the measurements for his coffin![3] The frequency with which bachelors married widows varied considerably from one part of the country to another. Table 5.23 shows that in our sample of parishes from the 1801 census 14 per cent of the farmers in the Ryfylke parishes were married to widows, whilst in Sunnmøre 15 per cent were in this category. In Hallingdal 10 per cent of the farmers were married to widows, in Hedemarken 10·5 per cent and in Østerdalen 9 per cent. (See also statistical appendix, table 31.) This variation in part reflected the landholding system. In areas where the land was owned by the occupier the 'åsete' right usually prevailed. Under this the eldest son (or in the absence of sons, the eldest daughter), had the right to the farm on the death of his parents. If his father should die and his mother remarry, her second husband would lose the farm on her death. Where the farmers were but tenants—as many were in western Norway even as late as the mid-nineteenth century—this obstacle to the re-marriage of widows did not exist and it was precisely in such areas that bachelor–widow marriages were most frequent.[4]

[1] Eilert Sundt, *Om giftermaal i Norge*, p. 213.
[2] Eilert Sundt, *Om sædeligheds-tilstanden i Norge. Tredie beretning*, p. 44.
[3] *Ibid.* p. 45.
[4] Eilert Sundt, 'Harham: et exempel fra fiskeri-distrikterne', *Folkevennen*, **8** (Kristiania, 1859), 34.

The custom of *heimbytte*—literally 'home exchange'—also influenced the marital age pattern. According to this, a man in one family would bind himself to a woman in another on condition that a man from the latter's family would marry a woman from his. The arrangements were made by parents who saw it as an opportunity to get two of their children established on a piece of land. If the agreement was made whilst the prospective couples were still children and something happened to prevent the marriages from taking place (apart from the death of one of the partners) the party breaking the agreement was expected to compensate the other.[1]

Sundt mentions several instances of this kind of dual marriage that had come to his notice.

In one case it was a brother and sister who exchanged homes in that the eldest sons on two farms took each others sisters. There had been talk of this for a long time so that the young people were used to regarding each other as engaged even in their childhood days. They were very respectable families on both sides and both the young couples lived in the most happy and loving association.

In another case an as yet young man told me that he desired his father's agreement to marry someone and that he got this on condition that the brother of the girl he had chosen would marry his sister. The boy asked the brother and fortunately he showed himself willing to be a party to the arrangement. Both bridegrooms were heirs to farms and I presume that as the property was about the same on both sides each got an equally large dowry with his bride and that neither side lost. One will gather just how completely the matter has been systematised when one learns what 'home exchange money' means.

If, in the last mentioned instance, the brother approached by the boy to marry his sister had declined, then the latter boy might still have got his father's permission to marry so long as he had indemnified his own sister by paying her, for example 100 spd. For whilst originally she had had the prospect of being married to a 'farm' as a result of a 'home exchange', she would enjoy an equally good prospect when it became known that she would bring her husband such a considerable dowry as 100 spd. is here regarded.[2]

Sometimes marriages were arranged and took place before it was possible to provide the couple with a farm. To counteract the obvious drawbacks of such a marriage—strained relations between

[1] *Ibid.* p. 47.   [2] *Ibid.* pp. 47–8.

the older and younger couples, children born before the parents were able to support them—the newly engaged or newly married couple would be separated, the husband being sent to work as a servant on one farm, his wife going to another. Should a child be born before the separation took place it would be reared by one or other of the grandparents. As a result it was possible to find in some farm households two distinct cohorts of children, the eldest born before the parents separated, the youngest after they had come together in a more permanent relationship.[1]

Sundt, discussing variations on this practice, noted that boys and girls travelled down the coast from the villages of Sunnfjord to Bergen to take employment as servants.

Often a boy and girl would return to the village, marry and then travel back to Bergen to work again as servants, Sometime afterwards the wife would come back again, bear a child, put it out to nurse and return to the town. Many years might well elapse before such a couple had earned enough that they might return together and consider buying or leasing a small farm. Thus it could happen that a father saw his child for the first time as, perhaps, a ten year old boy.[2]

This kind of arranged marriage is well known in other societies and has frequently been the subject of comment. Less commonly, however, is there discussion of the sort of arrangements which led to the marital age pattern frequently to be found amongst the Norwegian cottars—wives older than their husbands. Sundt examined this problem too in some detail in his work *On marriage in Norway*. His mode of treatment here and his style are typical of much of his writing and these, together with the inherent interest of the passage warrant the extensive quotation which follows.

The well to do farmer's 18 year old daughter appears in the eyes of all the boys in the parish as a grown girl; for her inheritance will not be greater than it is then and what she is bound to lack in domestic experience will come with the years. But it is not so with the 18 year old cottar's daughter. She perhaps is newly come into service on the farm. Not only that, she is continually learning that like nearly all cottar children she is very backward in womanly pursuits (a mistress finds that even the every-day cloth spun by the girl is so uneven and either too loose or too tight that an

<hr/>

[1] Eilert Sundt, *op. cit.* pp. 62–3.   [2] *Ibid.* p. 64.

138

arrangement must be made with the dairywoman so she can be released from the dairy for a whole day to learn how to warp a loom). What is more, the 23 year old boy who works on a neighbouring farm does not invite her to accompany him to the dance in the cottar's living room on a Sunday since she is so young. However, it is not taken amiss if she comes uninvited to the party just to look at the jollification; and it is possible that he, for the sake of neighbourliness dances a single dance with her; but she is not one of the girls he sets his cap at (to the extent of spending 12 *skilling* for coffee and honey cake), she is not the one whom he takes great pains to accompany home at night—this night wandering which is for so many the beginning of familiarity and love, later developed by regular nightly visits, Saturday visits, in which the young people become 'acquainted' (i.e. acquainted is about the same as being engaged). The 23 year old boy who has adult pay and performs a grown mans' work also considers himself full grown: the 18 year old girl on the other hand is for him still only an adolescent. And he is perhaps so well brought up that he knows that it is not right for a grown up boy to approach a girl in that intimate way, with night visits, etc. First of all she has not yet sufficient understanding to act on her own account and her parents, being a long way away are even less able to advise her. And secondly, honest fellow servants and other people at the farm (for example, the trusted cottar who has the task of waking the sleeping girls in the morning) would fairly certainly reproach him if he 'slept' with the girl. who, since she is so young, it could not be his intention to marry. For it is something which has a firm hold here in this circle of society that a good boy who thinks about marrying must seek a capable, 'working person', and therefore stick to an older one who has got some education and some practice in womanly pursuits.

Such is a woman's position in this circle of society. The superior spirit and personal charm she might possess do not command a high price: dowry and inheritance there cannot be much to speak of. But the servant boy has thoughts about the time when he will get a place and it is of the most obvious importance to him to obtain a woman who can be a capable housewife and a cook and milkmaid as well. If he must clear himself a holding she must be able to help him move the logs his axe has fashioned while the food sack hangs on the nearest pine branch and the child sleeps by its side. She must take a part in building the house and in collecting its contents.

A young boy who has not more than the few dollars he has saved from his servant's pay marries a girl about his own age or a little older who has been so long in service and used her pay so well that she, in addition to good wearing apparel and bed linen, owns two pots, a baking pan and a couple of candlesticks and perhaps at most a cow running with her master's herd. We see here a match of the type that is so very common amongst the working people in the countryside. Many perhaps, will find it reasonable to suppose that he chooses her in particular because he knows that she has this small fortune; that he takes her for the sake of the pots and other valuables. But such an explanation is almost certainly incorrect. The servant boy or the cottar's son who knows that the work of himself and his wife must be his livelihood, is hardly tempted as much as is the farmer's son to make his choice on such a basis. The farmer's son can hardly imagine any way of earning a living other than getting the money to buy a farm. On the other hand, it is quite believable—and a good indication of the praiseworthy understanding in this class of society—that the boys sets great price on those useful things that have been collected, on the grounds that they are for him an infallible proof of the girls' thrift and activity of mind—housewifely qualities which he, as a result of his entire position in life must necessarily consider very highly.

One ought not to imagine that in the exercise of his intelligence the young man necessarily smothered that lively feeling and natural inclination which ought to be present in the choice of a bride. But the calculus goes so far at times and perhaps not so occasionally, that we fast lose sight of that cheerful hope of life which should spur on youth and guide manhood. Once or twice I have, on a visit to a cottar's family, conceived a certain suspicion and have then asked directly:

'Tell me Nils, how was it possible that such an active boy as you could go out and take such an old person as a wife? She looks to me to be a capable person but she is so much older than you.' The answer has sounded thus:

'I thought that when I took such an old woman the crowd of young ones would not be so great for it is difficult for one who is in small circumstances to feed so many.'

Once there was a particularly unpleasant circumstance and when I had received the same answer almost in the same words, I added somewhat reluctantly:

'I think you've got a greater flock than any man should have.' But, unabashed, the man continued:

'Yes, but the three young ones she had with her when we married don't hurt me at all, for the father of the one is a farmer and of the other two a tailor, who are in good positions so there is no difficulty with the payments each year.' Those who are so quick to censure the youth of the working class for their recklessness with regard to marriage and their domestic affairs might ponder what can well be the element in the position of the working class that calls for such an unnatural way of thinking and such a way of life.

That it so often happens in the working class that a younger boy marries an older girl can in many cases be caused more by a particular circumstance on the part of the girl. It is possible that it is an older girl who courts a younger boy.

When the thing is put so straightforwardly it will seem highly offensive and unnatural for those of my readers who may not be aware of the particular rural conditions that I have in mind. But it is difficult to judge a single feature of lower-class life when one does not know the whole, and in order to be able to give a comprehensive explanation of this particular matter I must enter into a little detail here.

On a dark and nasty autumn evening, a Saturday evening, Per a young servant boy stands outside the kitchen window of a farm and stares in through the dark panes. The cold weather doesn't trouble him much for he is young and besides he feels a strange new warmth in his breast each time the fire in the chimney flares up and he catches a glimpse of Ann, the fine servant girl who sits by the spinning wheel, between some other womenfolk. Patiently Per waits for an hour until Ann on some errand or other comes out of the farmhouse. Now he must take a grip on himself and with as little clumsiness as possible make use of this brief minute. So perhaps he himself does the errand and as he does so takes the opportunity to ask her if she will be with him at the dance tomorrow. It is fairly certain that Ann understands what he is about and declines the invitation. But she is also inventive and knows how to give him such an acceptable reason that he cannot take her refusal ill and it is likely that he goes away with greater hope than when he came. Next Saturday he also gets into conversation with her and it is possible that now he notices more clearly that his visits are not disagreeable to her. It is fairly certain, therefore, that he is on the spot a third time and if she accepts the little cotton handkerchief he has got for her and with a handshake thanks him for it, he pays no heed to the snow and the storm on the way home. The fourth Saturday evening he deliberately arranges matters so that he comes to the farm after the people there have gone to bed, and almost as strongly as his heart beats in his breast, he beats on the window pane. He doesn't need to make much noise for in all probability Ann, expecting this to happen, has lain awake until now. She comes out and at this late evening hour when all other eyes are closed she sits a long time and talks with him in the woodshed. They talk about whether or not there is a possibility at this time for people like them to get a holding or some other reasonable livelihood. The fifth evening he has more heart 'Oh let me go in with you Ann' and whilst a couple of girls and a boy snore around them in the room, the two sit on a bench and carry on a whispered conversation. The sixth evening—there must be no interruption in Per's Saturday visits as Ann might then think he is on the wing somewhere else—the sixth evening Ann is, by chance, very tired after one or two heavy jobs during the day. She lies down on the bed and allows him to sit on the edge of it. No doubt Ann is not alone in bed, little Mari lies together with her. But luckily Ann has her place on the outer edge. The seventh evening Per sits once again for a time on the edge of the bed—but then he kicks off his shoes, throws off his jacket and after a weak and short opposition on the part of Ann lies by her side, flings his arms about her neck, repeats all his good promises, gets her consent, and falls asleep. Ann takes care that he is on his feet and away again before any of the people of the house are up. But now Per and Ann are 'acquainted' (engaged), and these nightly visits will be repeated each Saturday. When they are secretly engaged, it is possible that on occasion another suitor slips into Ann before Per, but I think Ann, as a fine girl will know how to get him to the door ('No, we can't chat any longer, I'm going to be up early tomorrow. I tell you Hans, get on your way'). No doubt the situation cannot be kept secret very long but it is a point of honour for fellow servants not to disclose this kind of secret and when it is found that they believe in one another and that she does not receive other boys and that he does not visit other girls, none of their acquaintances will criticise them in the slightest. For this is the custom of the country in many of our rural districts and the only way by which young people of the servant class can become 'acquainted' and in many cases it is conducted in all modesty and faithfulness. This night courtship is naturally always extremely dangerous for flesh and blood. But it is a mistake to assume that all the girls who take to their lovers in this way are girls without modesty. In all classes where night courtship has its home there are rules for it which maintain a certain strictness in the ideas of how a modest girl must behave. Indeed, it is something which often occurs that a girl hands in her notice purely on the grounds that she cannot allow herself to be known to serve together with a girl who has gone against the prevailing rules and so acquired a bad reputation in the servant class.

But—to come back to the matter which I began with—as I have up to now depicted the situation of Per and Ann it looks as if it was Per who took the first step, but it could very well have been Ann, and this same Ann could still very well be a modest girl both in her own estimation and in that of others. I myself believe Ann to be a steady and understanding girl, who has long recognised that lifelong misfortune awaits the woman who embarks upon marriage with an unsteady boy. Ann has probably had offers from several boys but prudently refused them all and thought that she would do better to work and collect some property for herself so that she could at least live her life in her own way. But slowly the years go by. It happens that she begins to dread the thought of the burdens of a lifetime in service and the pain of a lonely old age and probably by now she has turned the suitors away from her. But a capable working person as she is has something boyish and masculine in her nature and it may well happen, therefore, that she, without being ashamed of herself, sets herself at some young simple hearted person as Per—(an older boy, whom I dare say would rule both himself and her pleases her not so much).

If she has, moreover, by long and faithful service, won the esteem of her master and with it the hope of getting a good croft from him if it should happen that she marries, then upon reflection she makes her decision and with as much delicacy as is needed, does small services for Per and shows him other acts of attention. This arouses tender thoughts on his part; with girlish bashfulness he seeks her out that first Saturday evening, each time subsequently getting the new courage needed to affect a victory —a victory that was easier than he thought. But she will constantly stand by the honest boy whom she herself cares about.

And if we could visit them some years after on their holding, we would certainly find that they live well together—although no doubt in a particular way. I picture him as a toiler, after performing well his day's work he comes in tired and weary in the evening, eats his porridge and lies down to sleep, content that now he has done what he should do. But it is his wife's will that prevails in the house. The difficulty of bringing up the children rests on her. It is her diligence and thrifty skill that keeps the cow in such good condition on such poor fodder, that ensures the corn bin is never empty in spite of the poor harvest, that sees there is always a little meat left in the house from the last year's killing until the butchering season in the autumn, and that every second year provides Per with a fine new suit to go to Church in even though he has only two winter fed rams. And as a result of this Ann trusts people will not say about her that she is mean towards her husband and Per cannot do anything but admit it. 'It is for the best that Ann rules.'

What I have told about Per and Ann is not an actual story but in the presentation I have chosen to use I have joined together a great number of the experiences that I have had in moving amongst the people regarding the habits and ways of thought of the working class. And what I specially would have emphasised for the benefit of the people of the more cultivated classes is that remarkably great freedom which is found in the girl's relationship with the boy. One can anticipate, what experience also establishes, that when there is such great freedom it more frequently happens that the less modest girl over-steps the known borders of what is decent which, as we have said, is also firmly fixed there. I refer to a case such as a girl, who at a young and unsettled age, loses her honour and as a result gives herself up to a more and more wanton life, with the abominable plan that since the father of her first child deceived her, then probably the second or the third child's father will in turn be caught by her and become her husband. It is just the girl who has lost her character and become despised who has a double reason to dread lonely old age and she probably feels, therefore, that she has a kind of right to seek a bread winner. I believe that many could verify that such cases are not unknown and when the depraved girl gets her plan through then certainly one will often find that it is an inexperienced young boy she has caught in her net. But each time that occurs it contributes to producing the condition that our statistics have shown, namely that so often in the working class it is young boys and older girls who marry.[1]

This tale contains the essential features of the courtship which led to many cottars being younger than their wives. One could elaborate on each and every aspect of it. In this story Ann appears to have shared a room with her fellow servants within the house. In many parts of the country, however, servants traditionally slept in byres,[2] often in enormous bunk-beds each holding three or four people.[3] Sundt delicately conveys the sex play, usually stopping short of intercourse, which took place at the Saturday meetings of servants from different farms. He observes that the rules of this play were strict and that servants conscious of their reputations were loath to be associated with those who broke them. Elsewhere Sundt notes that the rules varied from village to village.

Evening came and they were to go to bed together—that was in order. The girl already lies on the bed but fully dressed and the boy throws off his jacket and kicks off his shoes, no more. In this he followed the custom of his village. But unfortunately this was not the custom of the village to which the girl belonged.

'If you're taking off your jacket you'll be taking off your trousers' she screamed, and shot out of the room.[4]

The relative freedom accorded to both sexes to meet in this way, particularly in the cottar class probably helped render tolerable the

[1] Eilert Sundt, *Om giftermaal i Norge*, pp. 214–23.
[2] Eilert Sundt, *Om sædeligheds-tilstanden i Norge* (Christiania, 1857), table 3, p. 47.
[3] *Ibid.* p. 38.   [4] *Ibid.* p. 62.

long time most couples had to wait before being able to get married. For courtships of the kind described in the story of Per and Ann could well continue for many years. Sundt examines one which lasted nine.[1] Undoubtedly, however, there was much pre-marital intercourse and Sundt collected material from all over Norway to illustrate the amount. In some areas a majority of women marrying cottars were pregnant at marriage but this was not true of every part. Sundt shows that in general the amount of illegitimacy was high where male and female servants were lodged together in out-houses and byres as was the number of pre-marital conceptions. In other areas where the servants were lodged separately or where attempts were made to control the 'night wanderings' and 'night courtship', the incidence of both illegitimacy and pre-marital con-ceptions was low (tables 6.2 and 6.3).

The importance of the economic role of women in Norwegian rural society is another feature of Sundt's story. Women did far more of the outside work on Norwegian farms and crofts than in many other parts of western Europe. This followed from the nature of Norwegian agriculture. For their husbands, if they were cottars might spend most of the working day on their landlord's farms: if farmers themselves they could well be away from home for several months each year either fishing off the Lofoten Islands or working in the forests. It is hardly surprising, therefore, that, as was often recognised, 'the material progress of a family depended as much upon the wife as upon the husband'.[2] The sort of work women did—with virtually no mechanical aids—included spreading manure on the fields, clearing them of leaves and twigs in the spring and harrowing them after they had been ploughed. All the operations involved in haymaking and harvesting might fall to them as well as the dairy work.[3] In this sort of situation one can well understand why the choice of a marriage partner was somewhat more than a matter for the heart.

What light do these explanations of the farmer and cottar marital age patterns throw on the regional variation noted earlier? There we

[1] *Ibid.* p. 68.
[2] Eilert Sundt, 'Bygde-skikke', *Folkevennen,* **7** (Kristiania, 1858), 232.
[3] *Ibid.* pp. 226-7, 230.

TABLE 6.2 *Number of illegitimate births for every 100 legitimate births and for every 100 marriages occurring from 1846 to 1855 in different parts of Norway**

Deanery groups†	Illegitimate births for every 100		Ranking on basis of	
	(a) Legitimate births	(b) Marriages	(a)	(b)
1	8·7	33·9	8	8
2	15·9	61·8	13	13
3	7·9	32·5	7	7
4	6·0	23·1	6	6
5	3·4	14·9	2	2
6	2·2	10·4	1	1
7	4·3	19·6	4	5
8	4·1	15·6	3	3
9	14·2	57·9	12	12
10	4·6	16·8	5	4
11	20·1	70·2	15	15
12	18·7	65·0	14	14
13	12·4	42·3	10	10
14	14·1	51·7	11	11
15	10·6	40·0	9	9

* Eilert Sundt, *Fortsatte bidrag angaaende sædeligheds-tilstanden i Norge* (Christiania, 1864), p. 27.
† For grouping of deaneries see note to table 6.1.

observed that in Hedemarken there was a marked tendency for farmers to be older than their wives and for cottars to be younger than theirs. Elsewhere, however, the population as a whole appeared to lean towards either the farmer or the cottar pattern. Thus in Sunnmøre and to a lesser extent in Ryfylke the marital age pattern of both farmers and cottars appear to approximate to the Hedemarken cottar model whereas in Hallingdal and Østerdalen the Hedemarken farmer model is evident amongst both groups.

A part of the explanation for these deviations might well lie in the life-cycles of the cottars and farmers in the different areas. In the west we have seen that in 1801 there were large numbers of servants, but few cottars in relation to the number of farmers. In the eastern areas there were both large numbers of servants, and of course

TABLE 6.3 *Number of married couples in Class I (proper-tied) and Class II (propertyless) who had children before marriage, within 4 months and between 4 and 8 months of marriage per 100 of all couples married in 1855–6 in different parts of Norway* *

Of 100 married couples the following had children

	Class I				Class II			
Deanery groups†	Before marriage	Within 4 months after marriage	From 4–8 months after marriage	Total	Before marriage	Within 4 months after marriage	From 4–8 months after marriage	Total
1	5	17	10	32	11	23	12	46
2	9	20	12	41	24	25	16	65
3	6	20	15	41	13	25	13	51
4	3	17	11	31	10	25	11	46
4	2	10	11	23	6	21	13	40
6	1	9	12	22	3	12	11	26
7	5	18	9	32	8	30	13	51
8	3	14	13	30	9	26	11	46
9	10	22	13	45	18	23	10	51
10	5	12	13	30	14	23	10	47
11	14	17	13	44	30	15	11	56
12	13	12	6	31	25	14	8	47
13	9	18	14	41	15	25	11	51
14	17	13	13	43	30	14	12	56
15	12	9	9	30	26	9	10	45

* Eilert Sundt, *Fortsatte bidrag angaaende sædeligheds-tilstanden i Norge* (Christiania, 1864), p. 44.
† For grouping of deaneries see note to table 6.1.

cottars, relative to farmers.[1] In Herøy for instance, there were 87 servants for every 100 farmers in 1801 but only 26 cottars, and a number of the latter were in reality retired farmers. In Hallingdal, on the other hand, there were 80 servants for every 100 farmers but as many as 115 cottars, while in Hedemarken there were both more servants and more cottars—138 and 154 respectively—for every 100 farmers.[2] Thus in Herøy and, our evidence suggests, in much of the rest of western Norway, the farm servants were overwhelmingly

[1] Table 5.9 and statistical appendix, table 15.
[2] Statistical appendix, table 18.

the sons and daughters of farmers. As there were no cottars they could be nothing else. In Hedemarken, however, there were so many cottars that we can assume that they provided a large proportion of the servant body.

These conclusions are born out by the rate at which the farmers' children left home in the two areas. The farmers of Hedemarken had almost twice as many of their children over 20 (relative to those aged 11–20) living with them as did the farmers of Herøy (table 5.15). Indeed, in Hedemarken even the proportion of cottars' sons over 20 living with their parents was slightly higher than the proportion of farmers' sons living with their parents in Herøy (table 5.19). We might infer from this that the son, and to a lesser extent the daughter, of a farmer in the west of Norway had an occupational life cycle not dissimilar from the son and daughter of a cottar in the east. Both would become servants at some time during their teens and in all likelihood would find their marriage partner amongst their servant acquaintances, in a manner perhaps not dissimilar from that described by Sundt in the story of Per and Ann. Further, the very considerable number of men in this area who married widows would help to, as it were, legitimise the marriage of the young bachelor to the old spinster. The parallel between the farmer of the west and the cottar of the east is heightened when we note that many of the farms in western Norway were little bigger than the crofts in the east so that the farmer in the west might well have looked for much the same qualities in his wife as did the cottar in the east.[1]

The explanation for the tendency of the Hallingdal population to display the farmer marital age pattern probably lies along similar lines. The number of farmers and cottars was much more evenly balanced in Hallingdal than in either Herøy or Hedemarken. The number of servants relative to both was lower by a considerable margin than in Hedemarken but only slightly lower than in Herøy. Farms were smaller than in Hedemarken but not as small as in Herøy and one can assume from this and from the fact that farmers' children in Hallingdal left home at an earlier age than did those of Hedemarken, though not as early as those in Herøy (table 5.15),

[1] O. Vig, 'Om landalmuens næringsdrift og levemaade', *Folkevennen*, 1 (Kristiania 1852), 167–8.

that a good number became servants. Some might move from the servants' quarters to a farm of their own; some would go to a croft. But in neither case did they need share the ideal regarding marriage partners held by those of their fellow servants who were the children of cottars. More likely, indeed, they tried to retain the pattern of life of their brothers or sisters or cousins who had not gone into service, as did the farmer's brother entered in the census as one 'who held land as a *husmann*' instead of under the more usual title of '*husmann* with land',[1] suggesting the recent acquisition of a new status and the possible carry-over to it of earlier habits.

One can then, as yet, move only part of the way towards elucidating the variations in marital age patterns, in nuptiality and fertility revealed by the statistics. The matter is a complex one and with the advent of industrialisation becomes even more so as the variables increase. Were the marital age patterns of the countryside carried into the towns, or did changing employment opportunities produce new patterns? As yet we cannot say, but our study of the marital patterns of rural Norway before industrialisation suggests that we would be wise not to make *a priori* assertions.

[1] See above, p. 120.

7 *Conclusion*

This study is part of an international discussion which, in recent years, has concentrated the attention of demographic historians on the processes of population growth in western Europe during the eighteenth and nineteenth centuries. The debate has ranged ever more widely as new questions have been asked, new concepts incorporated and new regions examined. In recent years much of the discussion has turned on the quality of the statistical and non-statistical material available for analysis. All too late, perhaps, population historians have realised that too many of their 'bricks' lacked 'straw'.

Our examination of the statistical sources has substantially borne out the traditional view that Scandinavia has been better served than most areas, and for a longer period, by her administrators. Their efforts have made these countries something of a Mecca for demographic historians. One might imagine the difficulties of carrying through a registration system or taking a census would be insuperable in a country as extensive as Norway, greater in area than the United Kingdom and the Irish Republic combined, stretching over 1,000 miles from north to south, dissected by fjords, and with movement further impeded by a mountainous terrain and a harsh climate. On the whole, however, the evidence of the vital statistics and census returns support each other, suggesting a high degree of diligence and skill on the part of the clergy of the Norwegian state church who were responsible for their collection. The clergy were aided by the co-operation and homogeneity of the public—nonconformity was not a problem—and by the efficiency and continued interest of the central administration. Fortunately too, they were spared the rapid growth of urban areas which bedevilled English vital registration in the late eighteenth and early nineteenth centuries.

Conclusion

The population statistics of Norway in the years 1735–1865 are not, of course, without faults. Attention has been drawn to a number of these and no doubt others await exposure. Ironically, one of the most widely publicised Norwegian population statistics (because of the prominence given it by the key United Nations' publication, *The determinants and consequences of population trends*),[1] is shown to have been inaccurate. A clerical error pushed up the crude death rate in 1742 from about 50 to over 70 per 1,000. The inclusion of the Icelandic births and deaths in the Norwegian totals for 1761–9 is another error not previously noted.

When we turn to the non-statistical, often anecdotal, evidence of Norwegian population conditions we often find it to be inaccurate. This we would expect from our findings in other societies *pace* K. H. Connell, who has argued that 'it is seldom wise for the historian to dispute what seemed commonsense to contemporaries'.[2] This belief in the comments of what have been described as 'observant'[3] or 'well-informed'[4] contemporaries also has the support of H. J. Habakkuk and T. H. Marshall. Much, of course, hinges on the terms 'observant' and 'well-informed', but as few commentators had adequate quantitative backing for their observations, our evidence suggests we should approach them with considerable caution.[5] The examination of Malthus's writings on Norway, for example, reveals the shortcomings of this kind of evidence. No one could fault Malthus on enthusiasm or intelligence, but the nature of the task he set himself in Norway was quite obviously beyond him.

[1] United Nations Population Division, *The determinants and consequences of population trends* (New York, 1953), p. 51. Cited most recently in Ralph Thomlinson, *Population dynamics. Causes and consequences of world demographic change* (New York, 1965), p. 79.
[2] K. H. Connell, 'Some unsettled problems in English and Irish population history, 1750–1845', *Irish Historical Studies*, 7 (1951), 229.
[3] H. J. Habakkuk, 'English population in the eighteenth century', *Economic History Review*, 2nd ser. 6 (1953), 118.
[4] T. H. Marshall, 'The population problem during the industrial revolution', *Economic Journal (Economic History Series)*, 4 (1929), 429.
[5] Perhaps demographic historians should take a leaf out of the new economic historian's book. See Robert William Fogel, *Railroads and American economic growth: essays in econometric history* (Baltimore, 1964), p. 245—'Authoritative opinions of the past, on most quantitative matters which concern economic historians, are crude approximations derived from poor data on the basis of inadequate statistical tools. They should not be accepted without statistical verification unless the absence of data makes verification impossible.'

Population and Society in Norway 1735–1865

Inevitably his writing was biased by the nature of his social contacts, the course of his itinerary, his preoccupations, and his willingness to generalise from one or two observations or circumscribed statistical material. Eilert Sundt was by contrast very conscious of the danger involved in speculating on the basis of individual experience. At the time he wrote his book on marriage, for instance, educated Norwegian opinion was unanimous in condemning reckless improvident marriages said to be entered into by the poor at an early age.[1] 'It is shocking to behold so frequently', wrote Dean Bødtker in the influential *Morgenbladet* 'young people of 18–20 years marrying without the least thought for the future.'[2] His views were widely acclaimed. Early marriage the consensus of opinion had it, was a growing menace. Yet the statistical evidence belies the contemporary opinion. Marriage could hardly be called early and was in fact getting somewhat later at the time Bødtker and his fellow Norwegians wrote.[3] At the time less than 1 per cent of bridegrooms and 6 per cent of brides were under 20 years of age. Ironically, in Bødtker's own deanery (Darlerne in the Trondheim diocese) marriage was later than in almost any other part of rural Norway.[4]

This preoccupation with the supposed earliness of marriage amongst the lower classes was not, of course, confined to Norway. If we look at the writings of contemporaries in early nineteenth-century Ireland we find them virtually unanimous that entry into marriage occurred at a very early age. 'There is no dispute', writes Connell, 'in contemporary comment that early marriage was an outstanding feature of Irish social life.'[5] The most comprehensive study of contemporary opinion on the matter was carried out by the Poor Inquiry Commission which reported in 1835.[6] The commis-

[1] Eilert Sundt, *Om giftermaal i Norge*, pp. 4–6; Dean Bødtker, 'Om letsindige ægteskaber blandt landalmuen', *Morgenbladet*, 20 December 1850; G. P. Blom, *Indberetning om en reise i udlandet til undersøgelse af fattigvæsenet og dets lovgivning* (Drammen, 1844), pp. 24, 70–1; D. Valstad, 'Et blik paa fattigvæsenet', *Morgenbladet*, 19 July 1852; Anon. 'Hvilke forføinger kan og bør statsstyrelsen træffe for at indskrænke udgifterne til fattigvæsenet?', *Morgenbladet*, 25 August 1858; Anon. 'Om fattiges giftermaal', *Morgenbladet*, 13 March 1853.
[2] Bødtker, *loc. cit.*
[3] Statistical appendix, table 9.   [4] *Ibid.*
[5] K. H. Connell, *The population of Ireland 1750–1845* (Oxford, 1950), p. 51.
[6] *Report of the poor inquiry commission, reports from commissioners*, Parliamentary papers (London, 1836).

152

sion held hearings throughout the country which were attended by witnesses from all walks of life. They included farmers, tradesmen, labourers, landed gentry and clergy, both Protestant and Catholic. Many were asked what they considered to be the 'usual age of marriage of labourers' in their locality. From the mass of evidence the commission made a summary which took the following form: 'The Galway labourers usually marry from eighteen to twenty-one; in Leitrim from sixteen to twenty-two; and in Mayo and Sligo usually under twenty-two years of age. In the County of Dublin at twenty-six; in Kilkenny at from twenty to twenty-five; in Kings County at from seventeen to twenty...'[1] and so on.

When we penetrate behind the summary to seek out the underlying evidence we discover how insubstantial it often was: how frequently it took an anecdotal form and how rarely it was the product of an even remotely systematic quantitative exercise. Take, for instance, the evidence of the Reverend Mr Ryan, a Catholic parish priest from County Tipperary.

A lad about 20 who had nothing in the world came to be married. I remonstrated with him on account of his poverty but he said that he only got £3 a year and that he had to spend all that in washing, and mending clothes and so he would get a wife to do these things for him; he could not be poorer and when he had children he would be no worse off.[2]

The observation of two labourers (Davenport and Davison) from County Down took an even more bizarre form.

Labourers usually marry from 16 or 18 to 20 or thereabouts—*Davenport*. When asked did he remember any case of this early marriage? He did not remember one, but *Davison* stated that he himself married at 20 and also that his son had done so the other day.[3]

As mentioned earlier, the report of the Poor Inquiry (Ireland) Commission was published in 1836. The evidence upon which it was based was collected during the previous two or three years. Up to this time there had been no systematic statistical enquiry into age at marriage in Ireland. This was remedied, however, in 1841 when the commissioners responsible for the census of that year calculated the age at marriage of people who had married during the 1830s.

[1] *Ibid.* appendix H. Part ii, parl. papers (1836), xxxiv, 669.
[2] *Ibid.* xxxi, 60.　　　　　　[3] *Ibid.*

Some striking differences in the male age at marriage emerge when we compare the statistics compiled by the census commissioners and the literary evidence collected by the Poor Inquiry Commission only a few years earlier. The summary of the latter's evidence from four of the five counties of Connaught (Galway, Leitrim, Mayo and Sligo) suggests that during the early 1830s the median age at marriage was no later than 19 years. Yet the evidence of the 1841 census suggests that at no time in the 1830s could it have been under 25 years.[1]

Since there is no reason to believe that the census caused the age of marriage to appear later than it actually was—quite the contrary, it was probably biased in the opposite direction—the marked difference between its findings and those of the Poor Inquiry Commission must cause grave concern. Hitherto our interpretation of Irish demographic history in the late eighteenth and early nineteenth centuries has been based on the impressionistic observations of contemporaries, who, convinced that marriage occurred at an exceptionally early age in Ireland, were at no loss to explain it. That the explanations were both numerous and ingenious does nothing, of course, to compensate for the fact that the phenomenon they appeared to explain existed mainly in the imagination.

This Irish illustration is a particularly notable example of the weaknesses of much past and present comment on population conditions. It indicates how careful one must be to assess the reliability of all sources of information. It is for this reason that considerable emphasis in this study has been placed on the evaluation of the sources—literary and statistical—of Norwegian demographic history. Eternal vigilance is essential. The evidence of an acute observer might well contain as big a flaw, the result, perhaps, of bad luck, as that of the most casual traveller. For instance one investigator in

[1] The ages at marriage in the Poor inquiry report were supposedly for *labourers* only, as Connell noted when citing from the report in *The population of Ireland 1750–1845*, pp. 51–2. In his 'Peasant marriage in Ireland: its structure and development since the Famine', *Economic History Review*, 2nd ser. **14** (1962), 520, he substitutes *men* for *labourers*. Professor Connell tells me, however, that his view of the nature of Irish peasant society in the 1830s, leads him to believe that there would be little difference between the age at marriage of the male population generally and of the labourers in particular. For further discussion see my 'Marriage and population growth in Ireland, 1750–1845', *Economic History Review*, 2nd ser. **16** (1963), 301–13.

order to measure the prevalence of the psoriatic itch crossed Norway from east to west, travelling for the most part through Hallingdal and Sogn, examining the members of households along his route. He found the disease to be present in *all* the thirty-seven households he examined and concluded that it was widespread in the country as a whole. Some years later an examination was made of a sample of army recruits drawn from the entire country. The results showed that the highest incidence of the disease just happened to be in Hallingdal and the Sognfjord district![1] Again when we note the comment of the author of *My norske notebook* that the interior of Norway was sparsely populated but that on the coast the families were 'enormous; shoals of little white haired children to be seen in every village',[2] we do not imply the observation was inaccurate—so far as it went. But it should be remembered that nucleated settlements were more common on the coast than in the interior, and that in the tourist season most of the populations of the interior, particularly the children, were scattered across the mountain pastures often miles from the usual tourist routes.

When we turn from the more methodological to the more substantive findings of this study, we find they conflict with a number of those of other workers in other societies. Talbot Griffith argued in *The population problems of the age of Malthus* that the rise of England's population began in the second half of the eighteenth century and was primarily the product of a relatively gradual fall in the death rate.[3] J. T. Krause, on the other hand, has undermined the statistical basis of this argument and suggested that the death rate probably remained stationary during the period of most rapid population growth and may even have risen in the closing years of the eighteenth century. For Krause the birth rate was accordingly the main variable.[4] K. H. Connell also considers a rise in the birth rate to have been the most important cause of the rise in Ireland's population during the years 1780–1840. This rise in the birth rate has been ascribed by Connell to a substantial fall in the age at marriage of

[1] Eilert Sundt, *Om skabklaaens udbredelse* (Christiania, 1867), p. 16.
[2] Cited above, p. 83.
[3] G. Talbot Griffith, *Population problems of the age of Malthus* (Cambridge, 1926), *passim*.
[4] J. T. Krause, 'Some neglected factors in the English industrial revolution', *Journal of Economic History*, **19** (1959), 529–31.

both men and women, although the factors likely to bring this about would appear to have had their primary impact on the age at marriage of men. Thus Connell argues that in Ireland the willingness of the landlords to multiply the number of small tenancies and the acceptance by the peasants of the potato as their sole means of subsistence (without which these smallholdings would have been insufficient to maintain a family), gave easy access to land at an early age.[1] In England, according to Krause, the industrial revolution widened the field of economic opportunity, allowing men to marry earlier, while in the districts not immediately affected, the Speenhamland system of poor relief acted as a direct incentive to early marriage and the creation of a large family. The enclosure of several million acres also increased rural employment.[2]

None of these explanations appears to fit the rise of Norway's population, a rise that was high by the standards of its own past and by that of European contemporaries. The growth of population, maintained at about 1·3 per cent per annum for half a century, began suddenly in Norway at the end of the Napoleonic wars. This rate was three times that of the immediately preceding twenty years and two to three times as fast as that of the period 1735–1815, and it occurred throughout all parts of the country. In the short term it was brought about by both a rise in the birth rate and a fall in the death rate, but it was the latter that was the important factor over the half century. Before 1815 the death rate fluctuated sharply, sometimes rising to 50 per 1,000 and rarely falling below 20. After 1815 it rose above 20 per 1,000 in only eight years and in five of these it did not reach 21. On the other hand, it never fell below 16 per 1,000.

The explanation of this fall in mortality remains almost as obscure as in other countries. Evidence presented here suggests that vaccination against smallpox and the rapid dissemination of the potato may have been the most important causes of falling mortality. This conclusion receives some support from the fact that the south-western areas in which both were first introduced displayed falling death

[1] K. H. Connell, *The population of Ireland 1750–1845, passim.* I have argued against this interpretation in 'Marriage and population growth in Ireland, 1750–1845', *Economic History Review,* 2nd ser. **16** (December 1963), 301–13.
[2] J. T. Krause, *op. cit.* p. 530.

rates somewhat earlier than did other parts of the country. Whether or not the potato played this precise role, its importance in Norwegian agriculture can hardly be overestimated. It was the major innovation of the first quarter of the nineteenth century and was undoubtedly a significant contributor to the 70 per cent increase in labour productivity in agriculture which took place between *c.* 1800 and 1835.

The ending of the demographic crises of the eighteenth century, during which mortality rose to high levels (i.e. crude death rates of 30–50 per 1,000), also helped to stabilise the birth and marriage rates, since both tended to fall when the death rate rose. This movement of births and marriages suggests that the cause of the high mortality in the crisis years was a harvest failure, whether on land or at sea, or some other economic disaster. Had the mortality risen in response to some non-economic change, such as the advance of an independently operating epidemic of typhus, smallpox or dysentery there would have been less reason for marriages or births to have been reduced, except of course in so far as the victims of the epidemic contributed to either. One might expect, on the contrary, that births and marriages would rise as inheritances and jobs appeared sooner than expected.

Fertility appears not to have changed much over the years 1735–1865. Changes in the age composition of the population brought about by high mortality and low fertility in the 1740s, 1770s and 1800s resulted in 'long swings', roughly thirty years in duration, in the crude birth rate. This movement did not, however, change over the period as a whole and birth rates remained remarkably steady through the course of each swing. In keeping with this, both levels of nuptiality and, where it can be measured, the age at marriage, remained stable. It was this stability which combined with the fall in mortality to produce the increased rate of population growth after 1815.

This pattern of population growth appears then to be very similar to that experienced by many underdeveloped countries in recent years. But there was one very important difference. Neither the birth nor the death rates were, on average, as high as those of many underdeveloped countries—in the recent past as far as the death rate is concerned, or at the present time in the case of the birth rate. For example the crude birth and death rates of India are estimated to have averaged respectively 47 and 40 per 1,000 over the years 1881–1941.[1] The difference between the vital rates of pre-industrial Norway and parts of the pre-industrial world in the present century is not, however, quite so marked in the case of the death rate; for in both societies this could rise to horrendous levels, though it did so much less frequently in Norway than in say early twentieth-century India. The main reason for the generally lower level of mortality in Norway was the lower level of fertility. Birth rates were never much over 30 per 1,000 and were quick to respond to changing economic circumstances, The main mechanism of this change was the age at marriage. As this appears to be the most fundamental difference between the demographic behaviour of much of the currently under-developed world and the pre-industrial west, considerable attention has been paid to the factors bearing upon it in Norway.

Marriage over Norway as a whole appears to have taken place in the late twenties so far as concerns men and in the mid-twenties for women. There were variations between one part of the country and another but *pace* Malthus and other observers, the age at marriage was not uniformly higher in areas dominated by fishing than it was in inland areas. On occasion, however, the fortuitous arrival of large herring shoals could cause somewhat earlier marriage and higher fertility. There was plenty of room for shifts both in age at marriage and fertility. Only about half the women in the fertile age group were married, although considerable pre-marital intercourse and conception occurred. The extent of pre-marital intercourse and conception naturally reduces the value of the age at marriage as a guide to differences in marital fertility and should obviously be borne in mind when international comparisons are being made.

The links between age at marriage and occupational opportunities appear to be strong although more complicated than is normally supposed. As a society which drew the bulk of its livelihood from exploiting the land and the sea, Norway appears as a country of

[1] D. V. Glass and E. Grebenik, 'World population, 1800–1950', in H. J. Habakkuk and M. Postan (eds.), *The Cambridge economic history of Europe* (Cambridge, 1965), VI, 84.

often part-time farmers and farm labourers. The latter worked either as unmarried servants living in the household of a farmer or, when married, held a smallholding in exchange for the work they performed for him. The marital age patterns of the farmer and his cottars appear on occasion to be strikingly different: the former tended to marry late but to choose a young woman for his bride, the latter married somewhat earlier, but usually chose a woman who was as old as himself and not infrequently older. Thus, one of the standard assumptions—that the later a man married the older his wife—underlying the current discussion of population change in late eighteenth and early nineteenth-century England, appears not to apply to pre-industrial Norway.[1] The reasons for this difference are not easy to follow, but seem to be mainly explicable in terms of the different economic and social desiderata of the two occupations. In some areas the social division between the farmers and cottars was very marked and this was reflected in the sharpness of the difference between the two marital age patterns. Elsewhere the two groups were economically and socially closer together, or the one was small in size relative to the other. Here the patterns tended to merge, in some areas approximating more closely to the cottar model, in others to that of the farmer.

A detailed breakdown of the social structure of certain areas, made possible by the fullness of the 1801 census, enables us to analyse the composition of farmer and cottar households, and thus approach an understanding of the factors bringing about this divergence or convergence in the pattern of marriage in different areas. It has also enabled us to dispel some of the notions as to household size and composition put forward by contemporary observers, notably Malthus. Households, both of farmers and cottars were much smaller than the recorded opinions of contemporaries would lead us to suppose. There were fewer children and fewer servants living in than is commonly thought and children did not leave home to go into service as early as is traditionally believed. There was also very considerable variety in the composition of households, not

[1] The Norwegian cottar pattern of marriage has recently been discovered in late seventeenth- and early eighteenth-century Devonshire. E. A. Wrigley, 'Family limitation in pre-industrial England', *Economic History Review*, 2nd ser. **19** (London), April 1966, 87.

only between different occupational groups but between different areas.

This study carries the story of Norwegian population developments from the time at which it is possible to measure them with reasonable accuracy up to the threshold of the country's industrialisation. Demographically that process does not appear to have had a major impact, at least in its early years. What evidence we have, and this is to be presented elsewhere, suggests that the pre-industrial patterns of age at marriage identified in this study were carried over into the industrial era. Fertility changed relatively little and when it eventually did so moved to the lower levels associated with a modern industrial society. Nor did mortality undergo any profound change until the twentieth century. The only novelty of the last four decades of the nineteenth century, from a demographic point of view, was the heavy emigration, particularly to the United States.

APPENDIXES
BIBLIOGRAPHY
INDEX

1 *Statistical appendix*

SOURCE MATERIAL FOR TABLES 1-7

Materialien zur statistik der Dänischen staaten (3 vols; Flensburg and Leipzig, 1786); J. P. G. Catteau-Calleville, *Tableau statistique des états danois* (3 vols; Paris, 1802); *Norges Officielle Statistik* (subsequently abbreviated to N.O.S.), Fjerde række, *Tabell over ægteviede, fødte og døde i Norge for aarene 1801 til 1835 inclusive* (Christiania, 1839); N.O.S., Ottende række, *Tabeller over folkemængden i Norge den 31te December 1845 samt over de i tidsrummet 1836–45 ægteviede, fødte og døde* (Christiania, 1847); N.O.S., Sextende række, *Tabeller over folkemængden i Norge den 31te December 1855 samt over de i tidsrummet 1846–55 ægteviede, fødte og døde* (Christiania, 1857); N.O.S., Ældre række, C, no. 1, *Tabeller vedkommende folkemængdens bevægelse i aarene 1856–65* (Christiania, 1868-9); manuscript copy of the 1769 population census of Norway in the library of the statistisk sentralbyrå, Oslo: bishops' archives for diocesan lists of births, marriages and deaths from 1735 to 1800 in the statsarkiv of Oslo, Kristiansand and Bergen. I was put on to these lists by Fru Sølvi Sogner of the Norsk lokalhistorisk institutt, Mogens Thorsensgt. 13, Oslo. I am also grateful to her for having the lists sent to the riksarkiv, Oslo and for providing me with a number of diocesan totals (see below) which she had constructed from the deans' and priests' lists on the occasions when there were gaps in those provided by the bishops.

I have also used three other manuscripts, each of which gives totals of births and deaths for the various dioceses. They appear to be based on material in the *Oeconomie og Commerce Collegium* or the *Danske Cancelli* in Copenhagen. One in the Danske rigsarkiv (catalogue no. Rtk. 352.27 tabelvæsen og statistik) is entitled 'Tabel over fødte og døde i Danmark og Norge, Slesvig og Holstein, Oldenborg og Delmenhorst 1735–75', another in the library of the statistisk sentralbyrå, Oslo (in Folkemengdens bevegelse, pakke 2) is marked 'General tabel over døde og fødde i Danmark, Norge og Holstein etc. fra 1735 til 1755 begge inclusive' and bears the note 'denne Tabel har jeg inddraget af de specielle lister som jeg forefandt i Oeconomie og Commerce Collegio' (signed) C. Anker. The third manuscript is in the statsarkiv, Oslo (in Bispearkivene.

Population and Society in Norway 1735–1865

Ministerielle forretninger. Innberetninger. Rekke 1. Box 6. Biskopene 1733–1814) and is entitled 'General-tabelle over fødde og døde udi Danmark og Norge fra anno 1743 til anno 1756 begge inclusive'. The original of this is said to be in the *Danske Cancelli*, skab 11, pakke 53. Curiosa.

TABLE 1   *Mid-year populations in the dioceses of Norway 1735–1865*

Year	Akershus	Kristiansand	Bergen	Trondheim	Norway
1735	261,925	94,865	109,232	150,087	616,109
1736	265,181	95,640	110,210	151,166	622,197
1737	267,172	96,443	110,889	152,482	626,986
1738	267,910	97,330	111,534	153,479	630,253
1739	269,398	98,326	112,277	154,163	634,164
1740	270,846	99,286	112,776	154,861	637,769
1741	269,721	97,783	111,773	155,227	634,504
1742	262,737	95,091	110,384	153,595	621,807
1743	256,785	94,632	110,463	151,499	613,379
1744	257,740	95,534	111,194	151,205	615,673
1745	261,161	96,764	112,365	152,127	622,417
1746	264,617	97,868	113,867	153,023	629,375
1747	267,355	98,741	115,382	153,388	634,866
1748	268,041	99,392	116,612	153,508	637,553
1749	268,855	99,462	116,812	153,914	639,043
1750	271,199	99,913	116,446	154,422	641,980
1751	273,246	101,151	116,831	154,610	645,838
1752	275,672	102,313	117,751	155,169	650,905
1753	278,858	103,237	118,839	156,156	657,090
1754	281,978	104,185	120,165	157,992	664,320
1755	284,080	105,102	121,364	159,999	670,545
1756	286,272	106,129	122,632	161,049	676,082
1757	289,313	107,498	124,117	162,168	683,096
1758	293,006	108,468	124,992	163,723	690,189
1759	295,825	108,629	125,631	164,940	695,025
1760	298,673	109,263	126,642	166,215	700,793
1761	302,673	110,347	127,734	167,520	708,274
1762	306,272	111,070	128,793	169,019	715,154
1763	307,710	110,521	128,852	169,754	716,837
1764	308,258	109,770	128,873	170,278	717,179
1765	309,899	110,198	129,158	170,937	720,192

TABLE 1 (*cont.*)

Year	Akershus	Kristiansand	Bergen	Trondheim	Norway
1766	311,246	110,929	129,260	170,834	722,269
1767	313,756	112,013	130,078	171,009	726,856
1768	317,173	113,059	131,120	171,808	733,160
1769	320,051	113,939	132,126	173,064	739,180
1770	322,135	115,072	133,328	174,648	745,183
1771	324,662	115,937	133,823	176,389	750,811
1772	326,859	116,220	133,410	177,346	753,835
1773	320,247	115,741	133,234	175,591	744,813
1774	313,197	115,248	133,724	174,178	736,347
1775	314,306	115,826	134,853	175,620	740,605
1776	317,354	116,849	135,858	177,214	747,275
1777	320,720	117,936	136,714	178,670	754,040
1778	324,684	119,034	137,893	180,057	761,668
1779	328,226	119,817	138,571	180,391	767,005
1780	330,362	120,611	138,988	180,786	770,747
1781	332,869	121,740	140,048	182,185	776,842
1782	335,627	122,814	140,993	183,999	783,433
1783	336,757	123,337	141,260	185,767	787,121
1784	337,483	123,775	141,661	187,225	790,144
1785	337,347	123,858	141,847	187,273	790,325
1786	337,162	123,988	141,995	187,245	790,390
1787	338,776	124,694	142,667	188,578	794,715
1788	339,853	125,195	143,349	190,021	798,418
1789	339,319	125,342	144,051	190,917	799,629
1790	340,315	125,490	144,882	191,979	802,666
1791	343,605	125,951	145,878	194,043	809,477
1792	347,186	126,470	146,576	196,682	816,914
1793	351,161	127,185	147,446	199,570	825,362
1794	355,651	128,160	148,689	202,303	834,803
1795	360,001	129,129	149,762	204,566	843,458
1796	363,346	130,131	150,961	206,610	851,048
1797	367,080	131,292	151,832	208,732	858,936
1798	371,314	132,376	152,277	210,804	866,771
1799	375,658	133,219	152,761	213,641	875,279
1800	378,305	133,645	153,284	216,265	881,499
1801	377,052	134,044	154,097	217,758	882,951
1802	375,307	135,010	154,634	218,333	883,284

TABLE I (*cont.*)

Year	Akershus	Kristiansand	Bergen	Trondheim	Norway
1803	376,643	136,243	154,437	217,779	885,102
1804	379,534	137,098	154,315	216,813	887,760
1805	382,839	137,897	155,026	216,959	892,721
1806	386,520	138,999	156,130	218,544	900,193
1807	389,697	140,110	157,015	219,912	906,734
1808	390,216	141,142	158,148	220,324	909,830
1809	382,157	141,828	159,041	220,503	903,529
1810	374,602	141,997	159,316	220,564	896,479
1811	375,412	142,240	159,413	219,501	896,566
1812	378,945	143,275	159,705	218,407	900,332
1813	380,109	144,371	160,152	216,948	901,580
1814	379,520	145,338	160,451	214,690	899,999
1815	382,612	146,760	160,934	214,471	904,777
1816	388,945	148,537	162,098	216,853	916,433
1817	396,038	150,649	163,988	220,016	930,691
1818	401,635	152,685	166,109	222,832	943,261
1819	405,882	154,655	168,569	225,657	954,763
1820	410,686	157,077	171,153	228,791	967,707
1821	417,562	159,312	173,245	231,712	981,831
1822	425,086	161,068	175,125	234,416	995,695
1823	432,680	163,249	177,351	237,466	1,010,746
1824	439,981	165,643	179,805	240,850	1,026,279
1825	447,470	168,208	182,277	244,475	1,042,430
1826	455,907	171,266	184,844	248,156	1,060,173
1827	463,622	174,249	187,213	251,674	1,076,758
1828	470,190	176,813	189,379	255,039	1,091,421
1829	476,788	179,361	191,891	258,382	1,106,422
1830	483,438	181,679	194,489	262,116	1,121,722
1831	489,162	183,667	196,332	266,300	1,135,461
1832	494,213	186,103	198,202	270,171	1,148,689
1833	498,471	189,043	200,582	273,488	1,161,584
1834	502,754	191,536	202,617	276,442	1,173,349
1835	508,836	193,824	204,912	279,309	1,186,881
1836	515,339	196,298	207,086	282,335	1,201,058
1837	520,508	198,472	208,218	285,018	1,212,216
1838	524,823	200,939	209,548	287,254	1,222,564
1839	527,382	203,399	211,362	289,270	1,231,413
1840	530,213	205,535	213,076	291,310	1,240,134

TABLE I (*cont.*)

Year	Akershus	Kristiansand	Bergen	Trondheim	Norway
1841	535,458	207,905	215,157	294,818	1,253,338
1842	541,700	210,387	217,359	299,958	1,269,404
1843	548,394	213,099	219,233	304,749	1,285,475
1844	555,326	215,889	221,192	309,371	1,301,778
1845	563,007	218,760	223,170	314,337	1,319,274
1846	570,879	221,241	225,051	319,021	1,336,192
1847	576,814	223,257	226,878	323,105	1,350,054
1848	581,722	225,522	227,967	326,200	1,361,411
1849	588,622	228,181	228,654	329,698	1,375,155
1850	596,958	231,376	230,150	333,650	1,392,134
1851	605,061	234,039	232,413	337,604	1,409,117
1852	612,274	236,045	234,591	341,927	1,424,837
1853	618,739	238,098	236,806	346,256	1,439,899
1854	627,532	240,550	239,489	351,329	1,458,900
1855	638,119	243,190	241,896	356,879	1,480,084
1856	648,945	244,690	244,880	362,132	1,500,647
1857	659,806	247,316	246,741	367,077	1,520,940
1858	671,565	250,365	249,190	372,049	1,543,169
1859	684,634	253,975	252,596	378,010	1,569,215
1860	697,304	257,709	256,041	384,108	1,595,162
1861	706,797	259,718	257,101	388,711	1,612,327
1862	714,180	261,002	257,534	392,631	1,625,347
1863	723,690	264,012	260,002	397,351	1,645,055
1864	734,025	267,026	262,694	403,358	1,667,103
1865	744,691	270,055	265,658	409,392	1,689,796

TABLE I

Certain assumptions were made before the calculation was begun of mid-year populations for each of the years 1735–1865. The first of these was that the 1801 census totals were correct. The census was taken on 1 February of that year but it was assumed, for simplicity's sake, that it had been taken on 31 December 1800. Second, for the reasons given in the text, I have assumed the census of 1769 to be deficient, particularly so in the diocese of Trondheim. Of an assumed national under-enumeration of *c.* 19,000, I have allotted *c.* 6,500 to Akershus, 1,400 to Kristiansand, 2,300 to Bergen and 9,000 to Trondheim. This implies a loss by emigra-

*Annual gains (+) and losses (−) of population to and from
the dioceses and the kingdom of Norway, 1735–1865*

Year	Akershus	Kristiansand	Bergen	Trondheim	Norway
1735–49	—	—	—	—	—
1750–9	− 100	—	—	+ 100	—
1760–9	− 200	− 100	− 100	+ 150	− 250
1770–80	− 250	− 200	− 200	+ 250	− 400
1781–90	− 350	− 300	− 300	+ 350	− 600
1791–1800	− 400	− 400	− 400	+ 400	− 800
1801	− 400	− 260	− 280	—	− 940
1802–14	− 400	− 260	− 280	+ 20	− 920
1815	− 400	− 268	− 322	+ 20	− 970
1816	− 108	—	—	+ 200	+ 92
1817–25	− 80	—	—	+ 200	+ 120
1826–9	− 180	—	+ 34	+ 460	+ 314
1830	− 180	—	+ 38	+ 460	+ 318
1831–4	− 180	− 28	—	+ 500	+ 292
1835	− 262	− 32	—	+ 554	+ 260
1836–7	− 200	− 50	− 120	+ 600	+ 230
1838	− 200	− 50	− 120	+ 693	+ 323
1839–40	− 200	− 50	− 120	+ 1,000	+ 630
1841–4	− 400	− 400	− 300	+ 1,200	+ 100
1845	− 400	− 432	− 312	+ 800	− 344
1846	− 587	− 600	− 460	+ 500	− 1,147
1847–50	− 1,460	− 600	− 460	+ 500	− 2,020
1851	− 1,880	− 1,460	− 900	+ 309	− 3,931
1852–4	− 1,880	− 1,460	− 900	+ 150	− 4,090
1855	− 1,914	− 1,460	− 928	+ 150	− 4,152
1856	− 600	− 500	− 800	+ 150	− 1,750
1857	− 1,500	− 1,400	− 2,000	+ 100	− 4,800
1858	− 600	− 500	− 800	+ 100	− 1,800
1859	− 300	− 200	− 400	+ 100	− 800
1860	− 300	− 200	− 400	+ 100	− 800
1861	− 2,500	− 2,400	− 4,000	+ 200	− 8,700
1862	− 1,000	− 900	− 1,200	+ 200	− 2,900
1863	− 100	− 100	− 200	+ 200	− 200
1864	− 800	− 700	− 700	+ 200	− 2,000
1865	− 707	− 609	− 701	+ 63	− 1,954

tion from Akershus between 1769 and 1801 of 10,250; of 9,200 from Kristiansand, of 9,200 from Bergen and a gain from immigration of 10,250 by Trondheim. My main reason for doing this was so as not to have to allow for a rate of immigration into the Trondheim diocese which, on the basis of the nineteenth-century material seemed implausibly high.

Of the other censuses I have assumed the total of 1815 to be deficient by 20,000, again for the reasons given above. Although those of 1825, 1835, 1845, 1855 and 1865 were undoubtedly deficient to a greater or lesser degree I have let them stand. Finally, I have not amended further the totals of births and deaths appearing in tables 2 and 3.

These assumptions involved one further calculation, namely the production of estimates of inter-diocesan migration. These represent the difference between the natural increase and the actual increase recorded in the censuses. Obviously there is a possibility of a wide margin of error here. For this reason no attempt has been made to give a false impression of accuracy by modifying either the sharp breaks that result around census years, or the somewhat bizarre totals that emerge as one set of data is made to fit another. From the mid-1840s the annual returns of emigrants from Norway have been taken into account. One aspect of the table which follows calls for comment, namely the very sharp break in the migration pattern of the Trondheim diocese around 1800.

In the 1790s we have relatively heavy immigration. During the 1800s it is negligible. Although the changeover would undoubtedly have been less severe there is reason to believe it took place. For the high death rates and low birth rates in this diocese in the 1800s would suggest that the area was then less attractive to immigrants than in the 1790s.

TABLE 2   *Births in the dioceses of Norway 1735–1865*

Year	Akershus	Kristiansand	Bergen	Trondheim	Norway
1735	8,879	2,748	3,318	2,905	17,850
1736	9,368	2,179	3,393	3,905	18,845
1737	8,980	2,714	3,313	3,853	18,860
1738	8,576	2,420	3,407	3,002	17,405
1739	9,152	3,346	3,732	3,070	19,300
1740	8,904	3,175	3,269	3,053	18,401
1741	8,381	2,780	2,784	3,036	16,981
1742	6,786	2,520	3,379	3,304	15,989
1743	7,784	3,141	3,661	2,429	17,015

169

TABLE 2 (*cont.*)

Year	Akershus	Kristiansand	Bergen	Trondheim	Norway
1744	8,883	3,088	3,534	2,671	18,176
1745	8,723	3,437	3,910	3,791	19,861
1746	8,578	2,707	3,542	3,524	18,351
1747	9,232	3,217	3,860	4,000	20,309
1748	9,688	3,507	3,425	3,658	20,278
1749	9,334	2,983	3,811	4,344	20,472
1750	7,835	3,048	3,814	4,386	19,083
1751	9,977	3,385	3,944	4,600	21,906
1752	9,241	3,490	3,623	4,759	21,113
1753	9,971	3,557	3,839	4,780	22,147
1754	10,150	3,561	4,014	5,008	22,733
1755	9,695	3,350	3,817	5,020	21,882
1756	10,938	3,644	4,038	5,035	23,655
1757	10,031	3,613	3,915	5,305	22,864
1758	9,966	3,441	3,928	5,146	22,481
1759	9,494	3,354	3,894	5,137	21,879
1760	10,739	3,967	3,780	5,454	23,940
1761	11,024	3,589	3,933	4,834	23,380
1762	10,691	3,711	3,730	5,401	23,533
1763	10,128	3,643	3,538	5,205	22,514
1764	10,712	3,700	3,797	5,405	23,614
1765	10,268	3,603	3,669	4,996	22,536
1766	10,271	3,852	3,650	4,597	22,370
1767	10,994	3,879	3,845	4,726	23,444
1768	10,433	3,604	3,540	4,563	22,140
1769	10,468	3,680	3,754	4,944	22,846
1770	10,772	4,033	3,982	4,728	23,515
1771	10,989	3,846	3,707	4,783	23,325
1772	9,318	3,472	3,612	4,534	20,936
1773	7,129	3,299	3,266	3,713	17,407
1774	8,928	3,565	3,681	4,433	20,607
1775	10,881	4,095	4,083	5,365	24,424
1776	10,128	3,539	3,499	4,756	21,922
1777	10,580	3,583	3,973	5,195	23,331
1778	10,998	3,870	3,889	4,855	23,612
1779	11,124	3,837	3,867	5,034	23,862
1780	11,149	4,142	4,187	5,233	24,711

TABLE 2 (*cont.*)

Year	Akershus	Kristiansand	Bergen	Trondheim	Norway
1781	11,250	3,975	4,045	4,783	24,053
1782	10,839	3,876	3,919	5,310	23,944
1783	8,816	3,642	3,844	5,252	21,554
1784	10,591	4,003	3,924	5,356	23,874
1785	10,404	3,994	3,625	4,634	22,657
1786	10,578	4,135	3,976	5,290	23,979
1787	10,368	3,514	4,002	5,186	23,070
1788	10,699	3,914	4,306	5,486	24,405
1789	11,421	3,918	4,114	4,912	24,365
1790	11,858	3,783	4,233	5,722	25,596
1791	11,718	3,993	4,551	6,107	26,369
1792	12,903	4,268	4,674	6,401	28,246
1793	12,750	4,297	4,805	6,187	28,039
1794	12,788	4,251	4,642	6,388	28,069
1795	12,432	4,121	4,509	6,187	27,249
1796	12,016	4,102	4,498	6,402	27,018
1797	13,282	4,239	4,392	6,260	28,173
1798	12,960	4,432	4,370	6,248	28,010
1799	12,544	4,625	4,348	7,023	28,540
1800	11,544	4,045	4,326	6,500	26,415
1801	10,044	3,956	4,604	6,349	24,953
1802	9,723	4,172	4,334	5,792	24,021
1803	11,456	4,320	4,415	5,614	25,805
1804	10,963	4,103	4,096	5,139	24,301
1805	12,232	4,426	4,698	5,512	26,868
1806	12,519	4,404	4,484	6,040	27,447
1807	12,159	4,456	4,339	5,986	26,940
1808	11,323	4,165	4,423	5,424	25,335
1809	7,430	3,919	3,880	4,943	20,172
1810	10,974	4,040	3,991	5,078	24,083
1811	11,906	4,239	3,943	4,717	24,805
1812	12,798	4,603	4,120	5,091	26,612
1813	10,443	4,113	4,259	4,710	23,525
1814	10,169	4,350	3,772	3,794	22,085
1815	12,958	4,629	4,690	5,373	27,650
1816	15,055	4,985	5,200	7,019	32,259
1817	13,670	5,096	5,091	6,443	30,300

Population and Society in Norway 1735–1865

TABLE 2 (cont.)

Year	Akershus	Kristiansand	Bergen	Trondheim	Norway
1818	12,975	4,773	4,945	6,409	29,102
1819	13,322	4,889	5,532	6,794	30,537
1820	14,311	5,366	5,466	7,166	32,309
1821	16,369	5,302	5,287	7,208	34,166
1822	15,071	5,219	5,494	7,085	32,869
1823	16,028	5,591	5,580	7,176	34,375
1824	15,250	5,283	5,617	7,238	33,388
1825	16,813	5,786	5,535	7,722	35,856
1826	17,039	6,266	6,066	7,635	37,006
1827	15,383	5,800	5,726	7,629	34,538
1828	15,665	5,671	5,720	7,711	34,767
1829	16,751	6,158	6,268	8,103	37,280
1830	16,090	5,757	6,091	8,369	36,307
1831	14,961	5,741	5,917	8,606	35,225
1832	14,174	5,995	6,039	8,192	34,400
1833	15,210	6,346	6,131	8,031	35,718
1834	16,279	6,166	6,365	8,430	37,240
1835	16,814	6,915	6,643	8,408	38,780
1836	15,530	6,268	5,777	7,792	35,367
1837	15,189	6,255	5,542	7,856	34,842
1838	15,202	7,009	6,646	8,241	37,098
1839	13,671	5,964	5,731	7,515	32,881
1840	14,829	6,305	5,693	7,721	34,548
1841	15,330	6,822	6,523	8,697	37,372
1842	16,799	6,774	6,302	9,181	39,056
1843	16,313	7,025	6,758	8,704	38,800
1844	16,547	6,916	6,618	8,892	38,973
1845	17,700	7,299	6,800	9,251	41,200
1846	18,428	6,785	6,874	9,441	41,528
1847	18,019	7,024	7,023	9,544	41,610
1848	18,139	6,956	6,314	9,145	40,554
1849	19,946	7,753	6,698	9,716	44,113
1850	19,526	7,615	6,766	9,175	43,082
1851	20,061	7,543	7,248	10,047	44,899
1852	19,356	7,687	7,074	10,102	44,219
1853	20,993	7,670	7,363	10,013	46,039
1854	23,106	8,078	7,610	11,102	49,896
1855	22,880	8,023	7,399	11,136	49,438

TABLE 2 (*cont.*)

Year	Akershus	Kristiansand	Bergen	Trondheim	Norway
1856	22,792	7,722	7,187	10,610	48,311
1857	23,192	8,272	7,727	11,007	50,198
1858	24,222	8,130	7,972	11,347	51,671
1859	25,501	8,416	8,111	12,528	54,556
1860	24,459	8,314	8,067	12,234	53,074
1861	22,497	7,635	7,684	11,730	49,546
1862	23,410	8,014	7,731	13,035	52,190
1863	24,874	8,457	7,985	12,589	53,905
1864	23,703	8,463	7,921	13,071	53,158
1865	24,295	8,740	8,219	12,685	53,939

TABLE 3 *Deaths in the dioceses of Norway 1735–1865*

Year	Akershus	Kristiansand	Bergen	Trondheim	Norway
1735	5,765	1,776	2,158	2,027	11,726
1736	5,969	1,601	2,597	2,624	12,791
1737	8,398	1,686	2,750	2,503	15,337
1738	7,681	1,674	2,680	2,358	14,393
1739	7,071	2,099	2,974	2,345	14,489
1740	8,089	2,508	3,029	2,383	16,009
1741	11,446	6,458	5,030	2,973	25,907
1742	17,690	4,225	3,911	6,631	32,457
1743	8,783	2,355	2,971	3,295	17,404
1744	5,974	2,069	2,762	2,392	13,197
1745	4,790	1,996	2,339	2,227	11,352
1746	5,599	1,940	2,109	3,295	12,943
1747	6,736	2,238	2,264	3,500	14,738
1748	10,812	3,184	2,560	3,918	20,474
1749	6,582	3,166	4,277	3,272	17,297
1750	5,799	1,963	4,080	4,542	16,384
1751	7,719	1,994	2,907	4,268	16,888
1752	6,447	2,557	2,821	4,173	15,998
1753	6,193	2,642	2,465	3,592	14,892
1754	7,488	2,580	2,735	2,723	15,526
1755	7,953	2,497	2,698	3,492	16,640

TABLE 3 (*cont.*)

Year	Akershus	Kristiansand	Bergen	Trondheim	Norway
1756	8,095	2,443	2,621	4,662	17,821
1757	6,592	2,077	2,362	3,641	14,672
1758	5,819	3,036	3,731	3,899	16,485
1759	7,803	3,438	2,813	4,150	18,204
1760	6,435	2,514	2,739	4,142	15,830
1761	6,927	2,675	2,590	3,835	16,027
1762	7,190	2,978	2,756	3,703	16,627
1763	10,354	5,275	4,193	5,733	25,555
1764	8,989	3,369	2,900	4,128	19,386
1765	8,310	2,878	3,797	5,256	20,241
1766	9,135	2,915	3,118	4,842	20,010
1767	6,716	2,448	2,541	4,431	16,136
1768	7,477	2,743	2,560	3,560	16,340
1769	7,261	2,582	2,522	3,735	16,100
1770	9,362	2,564	2,510	3,170	17,606
1771	6,845	3,185	3,788	3,358	17,176
1772	8,567	3,167	3,952	4,545	20,231
1773	20,604	4,162	2,884	7,712	35,362
1774	9,053	3,288	2,683	3,760	18,784
1775	8,039	2,816	2,423	3,655	16,933
1776	6,373	2,372	2,748	3,777	15,270
1777	7,104	2,176	2,612	3,763	15,655
1778	6,045	2,682	2,493	4,012	15,232
1779	8,493	3,059	3,506	5,710	20,768
1780	9,009	2,932	3,315	4,267	19,523
1781	7,776	2,427	2,297	3,551	16,051
1782	8,096	2,676	3,177	3,614	17,563
1783	8,600	3,195	3,451	4,111	19,357
1784	8,654	2,974	2,915	4,282	18,825
1785	11,913	4,257	3,663	6,311	26,144
1786	8,740	3,012	3,042	4,370	19,164
1787	8,278	2,625	2,992	4,139	18,034
1788	9,935	3,201	3,351	4,347	20,834
1789	12,552	3,738	3,066	4,959	24,315
1790	8,035	3,067	3,018	4,251	18,371
1791	8,212	3,087	3,074	4,201	18,574
1792	8,446	3,335	3,955	3,828	19,564

TABLE 3 *(cont.)*

Year	Akershus	Kristiansand	Bergen	Trondheim	Norway
1793	8,457	3,001	2,985	3,784	18,227
1794	7,302	2,797	3,175	4,125	17,399
1795	8,418	2,837	3,030	4,725	19,010
1796	8,539	2,582	2,780	4,575	18,476
1797	8,491	2,635	3,567	4,643	19,336
1798	8,484	3,069	3,506	4,521	19,580
1799	7,531	3,503	3,444	3,876	18,354
1800	10,463	3,514	3,383	5,200	22,560
1801	12,832	3,030	3,242	5,063	24,167
1802	9,624	2,645	4,061	5,947	22,277
1803	8,084	2,861	4,522	6,607	22,074
1804	7,753	3,333	3,674	6,119	20,879
1805	8,031	3,078	3,137	4,279	18,525
1806	8,558	3,027	3,278	4,143	19,006
1807	8,966	3,091	3,215	5,188	20,460
1808	12,679	2,946	2,721	5,437	23,783
1809	21,391	3,247	3,235	4,613	32,486
1810	11,323	3,854	3,527	5,325	24,029
1811	9,137	3,418	3,653	6,636	22,844
1812	7,701	2,835	3,266	5,401	19,203
1813	12,413	3,169	3,658	7,358	26,598
1814	8,577	2,839	3,216	5,702	20,334
1815	7,565	2,769	3,677	3,942	17,953
1816	7,275	3,023	3,563	3,906	17,767
1817	7,075	2,833	2,949	3,630	16,487
1818	8,216	2,965	2,844	3,991	18,016
1819	9,427	2,757	2,713	3,962	18,859
1820	8,439	2,654	3,117	4,130	18,340
1821	8,329	3,544	3,452	4,802	20,127
1822	7,903	3,465	3,570	4,483	19,421
1823	7,847	2,982	3,052	4,077	17,958
1824	8,670	3,104	3,237	3,970	18,981
1825	8,255	2,836	2,971	4,139	18,201
1826	8,462	3,100	3,530	4,517	19,609
1827	8,170	3,000	3,591	4,630	19,391
1828	9,383	3,343	3,591	4,900	21,217
1829	9,477	3,389	3,442	5,149	21,457
1830	9,704	3,890	3,793	4,774	22,161

TABLE 3 (*cont.*)

Year	Akershus	Kristiansand	Bergen	Trondheim	Norway
1831	9,538	3,604	4,567	4,793	22,502
1832	9,136	3,205	3,649	5,264	21,254
1833	11,371	3,200	3,760	5,325	23,656
1834	11,193	4,269	4,666	6,228	26,356
1835	9,293	4,176	3,753	5,929	23,151
1836	9,584	3,978	4,199	5,373	23,134
1837	10,396	4,097	4,615	6,110	25,218
1838	10,966	4,133	4,674	6,808	26,581
1839	12,388	3,820	3,835	6,609	26,652
1840	10,050	4,076	3,921	6,546	24,593
1841	9,019	3,862	3,712	5,056	21,649
1842	9,826	3,969	4,110	4,942	22,847
1843	9,099	3,607	4,602	5,761	23,069
1844	9,096	3,954	4,255	4,992	22,297
1845	8,802	3,686	4,596	5,219	22,303
1846	9,535	4,404	4,543	5,405	23,887
1847	12,123	4,174	4,781	6,411	27,489
1848	11,293	4,076	5,458	7,089	27,916
1849	10,077	4,114	5,260	5,775	25,226
1850	9,803	3,665	4,291	6,212	23,971
1851	10,238	4,106	3,837	5,911	24,092
1852	10,993	4,192	4,329	6,051	25,565
1853	12,667	4,139	3,878	5,707	26,391
1854	10,085	3,785	3,930	5,562	23,362
1855	10,934	4,117	4,436	5,875	25,362
1856	10,931	4,463	4,298	5,665	25,357
1857	11,231	4,379	4,094	6,313	26,017
1858	10,566	4,026	3,908	6,296	24,796
1859	12,118	4,600	4,163	5,857	26,738
1860	11,902	4,261	4,325	6,910	27,398
1861	13,269	5,171	4,906	8,147	31,493
1862	14,371	4,510	4,443	9,178	32,502
1863	13,793	4,940	4,936	7,407	31,076
1864	13,215	5,153	4,686	6,638	29,692
1865	11,943	4,683	4,126	7,314	28,066

TABLES 2 AND 3

What follows is an indication of the discrepancies between the various sources listed above together with the reasons for choosing the totals appearing in tables 2 and 3. Where possible the bishops' returns have been relied upon for the years 1735–1800. When no comment is made on the figures for a particular year it can be assumed that the various sources are in agreement, although minor discrepancies have been ignored. From 1801 onwards I have used the material in the official publications listed above. It would be possible to check these official figures against the bishops' returns for many years, as after 1815 they are to be found in the riksarkiv, Oslo and from 1801 to 1814 in the statsarkiv of Oslo, Kristiansand and Bergen, but not in Trondheim.

Diocese of Akershus

1744, 1757, 1760, 1781—no bishops' return. Births and deaths from *Materialien zur Statistik der Dänischen Staaten*, II, tables X and XI (subsequently abbreviated to *Materialien*).

1786, 1787, 1789, 1790, 1793, 1795, 1796 no bishops' return. Totals reconstructed by Fru Sogner from either deans' or parsons' lists or, in the case of 1786, 1787 and 1793 by estimating the proportions of the national totals given by Catteau-Calleville, that might be expected to come from Akershus.

Diocese of Kristiansand

Here there are no surviving bishops' returns before 1762. Till this date totals are taken from *Materialien* with the following exceptions.

1740. In the manuscripts found in the Dansk rigsarkiv (subsequently to be abbreviated to DRA) and the Norsk statistisk sentralbyrå (subsequently abbreviated to NSSB) births are given as 2,380 and deaths as 1,888. In both cases these totals are described as defective. They derive, so it would appear, from a table contained in a letter from bishop Jakob Kærup of Kristiansand to Geheime-Conferentz-Raad J. L. von Holstein dated 12 May 1741. A copy of this letter is in the Christiania bispearkiv. Ministerielle forretninger. Innberetninger. Rekke I. Biskopene 1733–1814. Box 6, now in the statsarkiv, Oslo. Here the nature of the defect is explained, namely that returns had not come in from certain deans and parsons in the diocese. In *Materialien*, 1,000 has been added to each of the totals. By calculating a little more closely (using the returns in 1742 to estimate the gaps in 1740), I have added 795 to the total of births and 620 to that of deaths.

1742. DRA and NSSB give 1,411 births and 2,578 deaths. The bishops' kopibok (Kristiansand bispearkiv. Kopibok nr. 10. 1742–44, pp. 101–2 in statsarkivet Kristiansand) gives 1,411 births and 2,578 deaths as totals for seven of the ten deaneries into which the diocese was divided. *Materialien* gives 2,580 births and 14,011 deaths! According to the kopibok, the totals of births in all deaneries but that of Øvre Telemark, for which there was no return, amounted to 2,167 and 3,525 respectively. Assuming that the Øvre Telemark total of births was 353, the same as in 1740, and that of deaths, 700, double the 1740 figure (likely totals in view of the position in neighbouring deaneries), then the total of births for the diocese as a whole would be 2,520, and that of deaths 4,225.

1743. Births and deaths from *Materialien*. When sending me a photo-copy of the part of the bishops' kopibok referred to above, the statsarkivar of Kristiansand pointed out that in 1743 also there was no return of either births or deaths from Øvre Telemark. Through an oversight I failed to allow for this before tables 2 and 3 had been prepared and the calculations made in tables 1, 5 and 7.

1750. Both DRA and *Materialien* give 3,000 births and 2,500 deaths. Both figures would seem to be estimates based on the totals for 1749 and 1751. The manuscript 'General-tabelle over fødde og døde udi Danmark og Norge fra anno 1743 til anno 1756' in the statsarkiv, Oslo, gives 3,048 births and 1,963 deaths.

1766, 1767, 1769, 1774 and 1777 from *Materialien* due to lacunæ in bishops' lists.

1798. Provided by Fru Sogner.

Diocese of Bergen

1735. Figures from *Materialien*. Bishops' list begins in 1736.

1741. According to bishop's list, 2,784 births and 5,030 deaths. *Materialien* and DRA give same number of births, but 2,246 deaths. This latter figure is, of course, the *excess* of deaths over births.

1746. *Materialien* and DRA give 2,429 births and 3,295 deaths; the same figure as they give for the Trondheim diocese in 1743.

1760, 1762, 1766, 1768, 1769, 1771, 1773, 1774 from *Materialien*. No bishops' returns.

1772. No bishops' list. *Materialien* gives 3,612 births and 3,788 deaths. DRA gives 3,687 births and 3,952 deaths. Latter figure adopted here as 3,788 also appears in *Materialien* for 1771.

1775. Bishop's list and DRA give 4,083 births and 2,423 deaths. *Materialien* has 5,365 births and 3,655 deaths, the figures given by the DRA for Trondheim. It would appear that the compiler of the table in the *Materialien* has inadvertently switched the figures for the two dioceses.

1776. The above mistake repeated. The figures given in the bishop's list for Bergen are ascribed in the *Materialien* to Trondheim.

1795, 1798, 1799, 1800 reconstructed by Fru Sogner from partial returns.

Diocese of Trondheim

No bishops' returns have survived. With the exceptions noted below all figures for the years 1735-84 have been taken directly from *Materialien.*

1738. Births and deaths in *Materialien* and DRA are the same. But letter from Bishop E. Hagerup of Trondheim enclosing the return for 1738 notes that they do not include any totals for the deaneries of Storfosen, Numedal or Vesterålen. A copy of this letter is in the Christiania bispearkiv. Ministerielle forretninger. Innberetninger. Rekke I. Biskopene 1733-1814. Box 6 in the statsarkiv, Oslo.

1740. The letter from Bishop Hagerup (see note above for 1738) also enclosed a return for 1740. This was even more deficient than that of 1738. The total of 1,653 births and 1,383 deaths given in the DRA was marked 'defect'. It did not, we learn from the letter, include totals from Romsdal, Storfosen, Innherad, Numedal or Vesterålen, i.e. 5 of the 13 deaneries. As Romsdal had 206 births and 196 deaths in 1738, whilst Indherred had 664 births and 505 deaths, the estimate given in *Materialien* for the diocese as a whole of 3,053 births and 2,383 deaths seems reasonable.

1772. DRA total of births adopted. *Materialien* gives 3,952, the figure given by the DRA for Bergen.

1773. *Materialien* gives 4,713 births, whilst DRA gives 3,713. I have used the latter on the grounds that this was a year of high mortality here as well as in the three other dioceses. In the other three dioceses a fall in the number of births was recorded between 1772 and 1773. There is no reason to believe that Trondheim went against the trend. I assume the compiler of *Materialien* added 1,000 to the total as he did on earlier occasions when he felt a total to be defective.

1775 and 1776. See notes on these years for the Bergen diocese.

1785, 1789, 1790, 1791, 1792, 1798. Fru Sogner reached these totals by subtracting the sum of the other dioceses from the national figures in Catteau-Calleville.

1786, 1787. The above-mentioned procedure was not possible in these years as there was no return from Akershus. Fru Sogner, therefore, estimated the proportion of the national total that might be expected to come from Trondheim.

1799. Here there was no return from Kristiansand. Fru Sogner, therefore, followed the practice adopted for 1786 and 1787.

Population and Society in Norway 1735–1865

1793, 1794, 1795, 1796, 1797. Fru Sogner reconstructed the diocesan totals from the parsons' and deans' returns in the statsarkiv, Trondheim.
1788. Totals taken from a stray manuscript giving them for this one year only. See Folkemengdens bevegelse, pakke 2 in the library of the statistisk sentralbyrå, Oslo.
1800. My calculation based on totals for 1799 and 1801.
1801. N.O.S. Fjerde række, *Tabel over ægteviede, fødte og døde i Norge for aarene 1801 til 1835 inclusive* (Christiania, 1839), p. 2. I suspect the totals of births, marriages and deaths given here are too high; the reason being a double count of the returns from the northern part of the diocese. This area—Nordland and Finnmark—was taken out of the Trondheim diocese in 1803 to form the new diocese of Tromsø. Returns from it, however, appear separately in the N.O.S. Fjerde række, *op. cit.* from 1801 onwards. The total of births for the old Trondheim diocese (the area used throughout for reasons of comparability) for 1801 appears at 8,499, a higher figure than in any year from 1735 to 1831. The total of marriages, at 2,123 is higher than that of any year from 1735 to 1841. This latter figure is, however, very close to what we would get in 1802 and 1803 were we to double the totals from Nordland–Finnmark and add them to those from the remainder of the old Trondheim diocese. In 1802 the calculation would be $1,068 + 559 + 559 = 2,186$ and in 1803, $942 + 598 + 598 = 2,138$. What then, in the official publication purport to be totals of births, marriages and deaths for the new diocese of Trondheim are, in 1801 at least, those for the older and much larger diocese of the same name.

TABLE 4 *Marriages in the dioceses of Norway 1735–1865*

Year	Akershus	Kristiansand	Bergen	Trondheim	Norway
1735	2,150	—	—	—	—
1736	2,071	—	987	—	—
1737	2,050	—	981	—	—
1738	2,197	—	1,024	—	—
1739	2,227	—	967	—	—
1740	2,026	—	881	—	—
1741	1,825	—	886	—	—
1742	1,904	—	1,179	—	—
1743	2,246	—	1,147	—	—
1744	—	—	1,101	—	—
1745	2,360	—	1,088	—	—

TABLE 4 (*cont.*)

Year	Akershus	Kristiansand	Bergen	Trondheim	Norway
1746	2,154	—	1,042	—	—
1747	2,295	—	1,047	—	—
1748	2,308	—	871	—	—
1749	1,865	—	986	—	—
1750	2,145	—	1,162	—	—
1751	2,386	—	1,063	—	—
1752	2,561	—	1,093	—	—
1753	2,584	—	1,095	—	—
1754	2,568	—	1,085	—	—
1755	2,309	—	1,141	—	—
1756	2,491	—	1,054	—	—
1757	2,092	—	1,049	—	—
1758	2,143	—	939	—	—
1759	2,090	—	1,004	—	—
1760	—	—	—	—	—
1761	2,403	—	978	—	—
1762	2,210	946	—	—	—
1763	2,250	830	965	—	—
1764	2,888	1,226	1,255	—	—
1765	2,560	1,040	1,095	—	—
1766	2,728	—	—	—	—
1767	2,506	—	946	—	—
1768	2,463	811	—	—	—
1769	2,356	—	—	—	—
1770	2,303	827	978	1,288	5,396
1771	2,172	795	—	—	5,007
1772	1,898	771	—	—	4,433
1773	1,839	772	—	—	4,410
1774	2,892	—	—	—	6,200
1775	3,072	1,028	1,059	1,639	6,798
1776	2,954	982	952	1,343	6,231
1777	2,746	—	1,102	—	6,249
1778	2,760	867	1,071	1,315	6,013
1779	2,756	963	1,048	1,360	6,127
1780	2,562	956	1,026	1,319	5,863
1781	—	955	1,045	—	6,177
1782	2,208	900	1,006	1,355	5,469

TABLE 4 (*cont.*)

Year	Akershus	Kristiansand	Bergen	Trondheim	Norway
1783	2,620	1,095	1,202	1,396	6,313
1784	2,561	1,058	1,171	—	—
1785	2,510	1,009	1,093	—	—
1786	—	949	1,191	—	—
1787	—	917	1,195	—	—
1788	2,650	—	1,199	—	—
1789	—	825	1,097	—	—
1790	—	1,077	1,244	—	—
1791	3,275	1,163	1,286	—	—
1792	3,404	1,102	1,315	—	—
1793	—	—	1,285	—	—
1794	3,117	1,069	1,274	—	—
1795	—	943	—	—	6,531
1796	—	1,024	1,172	—	6,695
1797	3,006	985	1,199	1,760	6,950
1798	3,127	—	—	—	7,227
1799	2,788	1,016	—	—	6,910
1800	2,638	1,053	1,084	—	—
1801	2,369	965	1,186	1,569	6,089
1802	2,785	1,109	1,221	1,627	6,742
1803	3,059	1,041	1,150	1,540	6,790
1804	2,955	1,043	1,327	1,744	7,069
1805	3,023	1,065	1,339	1,800	7,227
1806	3,031	1,084	1,322	1,846	7,283
1807	2,609	1,001	1,222	1,499	6,331
1808	1,794	801	1,045	1,665	5,305
1809	2,332	846	926	1,266	5,370
1810	3,503	1,010	1,097	1,490	7,100
1811	3,799	1,155	1,284	1,616	7,854
1812	3,619	1,269	1,424	1,538	7,850
1813	2,971	1,027	1,206	1,249	6,453
1814	2,371	1,006	1,103	1,321	5,801
1815	4,251	1,406	1,444	2,070	9,171
1816	4,360	1,406	1,550	2,111	9,427
1817	3,610	1,183	1,372	1,845	8,010
1818	3,352	1,218	1,428	1,715	7,713
1819	3,116	1,179	1,479	1,947	7,721
1820	3,862	1,273	1,471	2,106	8,712

TABLE 4 (*cont.*)

Year	Akershus	Kristiansand	Bergen	Trondheim	Norway
1821	3,988	1,318	1,426	2,163	8,895
1822	4,254	1,339	1,416	1,940	8,949
1823	3,740	1,373	1,537	2,191	8,841
1824	3,658	1,266	1,444	2,008	8,376
1825	3,887	1,446	1,492	2,195	9,020
1826	3,766	1,446	1,600	1,993	8,805
1827	3,271	1,256	1,504	2,056	8,087
1828	3,370	1,275	1,512	2,201	8,358
1829	3,626	1,306	1,460	2,247	8,639
1830	3,473	1,351	1,545	2,300	8,669
1831	3,162	1,272	1,471	2,285	8,190
1832	3,052	1,327	1,415	2,045	7,839
1833	3,425	1,389	1,611	2,123	8,548
1834	3,755	1,481	1,626	2,010	8,872
1835	3,816	1,428	1,565	1,975	8,784
1836	3,590	1,516	1,431	1,887	8,424
1837	3,373	1,429	1,450	1,871	8,123
1838	3,386	1,464	1,473	2,092	8,415
1839	3,151	1,330	1,415	2,053	7,949
1840	3,554	1,477	1,499	2,071	8,601
1841	3,975	1,580	1,578	2,462	9,595
1842	4,240	1,645	1,615	2,462	9,962
1843	4,323	1,636	1,778	2,436	10,173
1844	4,394	1,654	1,838	2,404	10,290
1845	4,616	1,696	1,856	2,402	10,570
1846	4,970	1,642	1,880	2,660	11,152
1847	4,225	1,502	1,797	2,366	9,890
1848	4,456	1,611	1,659	2,461	10,187
1849	4,629	1,747	1,829	2,424	10,629
1850	4,706	1,723	1,846	2,373	10,648
1851	4,549	1,668	1,912	2,446	10,575
1852	4,479	1,642	1,647	2,411	10,179
1853	4,973	1,682	1,907	2,695	11,257
1854	5,803	1,843	1,940	2,893	12,479
1855	5,596	1,813	1,738	2,862	12,009
1856	5,338	1,733	1,798	2,730	11,599
1857	5,137	1,785	1,874	2,651	11,447

Population and Society in Norway 1735-1865

TABLE 4 (cont.)

Year	Akershus	Kristiansand	Bergen	Trondheim	Norway
1858	5,179	1,817	1,914	2,812	11,722
1859	5,328	1,751	1,972	3,032	12,083
1860	4,752	1,720	1,834	3,107	11,413
1861	4,395	1,618	1,860	3,066	10,939
1862	4,568	1,779	1,834	3,040	11,221
1863	4,926	1,840	1,959	3,083	11,808
1864	4,731	1,845	1,952	2,843	11,371
1865	4,793	1,947	1,969	2,884	11,593

TABLE 4

For most years in the eighteenth century our only source of marriage totals are the bishops' lists. For the years 1770-83 and 1795-9 the N.O.S. Ældre række C., no. 1. *Tabeller vedkommende folkemængdens bevægelse i aarene 1856-65* (Christiania, 1868-9), table 10, p. 194, give national totals. By subtracting from these the sum total of marriages in the dioceses of Akershus, Kristiansand and Bergen, we are able, for certain of these years, to arrive at a figure for the diocese of Trondheim.

From 1801 to 1865 the totals of marriages are taken from N.O.S. Fjerde række, *Tabel over ægteviede, fødte og døde i Norge for aarene 1801 til 1835 inclusive* (Christiania, 1839); N.O.S. Ottende række, *Tabeller over folkemængden i Norge den 31te December 1845 samt over de i tidsrummet 1836-45 ægteviede, fødte og døde* (Christiania, 1847); N.O.S. Sextende række, *Tabeller over folkemængden i Norge den 31te December 1855 samt over de i tidsrummet 1846-55 ægteviede, fødte og døde* (Christiania, 1857); N.O.S. Ældre række, C., no. 1. *Tabeller vedkommende folkemængdens bevægelse i aarene 1856-65* (Christiania, 1868-9).

TABLE 5   *Births per 1,000 mean population in the dioceses of Norway 1735-1865*

Year	Akershus	Kristiansand	Bergen	Trondheim	Norway
1735	33·9	29·0	30·4	19·3	29·0
1736	35·3	22·8	30·8	25·8	30·3
1737	33·6	28·1	29·9	25·3	30·1
1738	32·0	24·9	30·5	19·5	27·6
1739	34·0	34·0	33·2	19·9	30·4
1740	32·9	32·0	29·0	19·7	28·8

TABLE 5 (*cont.*)

Year	Akershus	Kristiansand	Bergen	Trondheim	Norway
1741	31·1	28·4	24·9	19·5	26·8
1742	25·8	26·5	30·6	21·5	25·7
1743	30·3	33·2	33·1	16·0	27·7
1744	34·5	32·3	31·8	17·7	29·5
1745	33·4	35·5	34·8	24·9	31·9
1746	32·4	27·6	31·1	23·0	29·1
1747	34·5	32·6	33·4	26·1	32·0
1748	36·1	35·3	29·4	23·8	31·8
1749	34·7	30·0	32·6	28·2	32·0
1750	28·9	30·5	32·7	28·4	29·7
1751	36·5	33·5	33·8	29·7	33·9
1752	33·5	34·1	30·8	30·7	32·4
1753	35·7	34·4	32·3	30·6	33·7
1754	36·0	34·2	33·4	31·7	34·2
1755	34·1	31·9	31·4	31·4	32·6
1756	38·2	34·3	32·9	31·3	35·0
1757	34·7	33·6	31·5	32·7	33·5
1758	34·0	31·7	31·4	31·4	32·6
1759	32·1	30·9	31·0	31·1	31·5
1760	35·9	36·3	29·8	32·8	34·2
1761	36·4	32·5	30·8	28·8	33·0
1762	34·9	33·4	29·0	31·9	32·9
1763	32·9	33·0	27·5	30·7	31·4
1764	34·7	33·7	29·5	31·7	32·9
1765	33·1	32·7	28·4	29·2	31·3
1766	33·0	34·7	28·2	26·9	31·0
1767	35·0	34·6	29·6	27·6	32·2
1768	32·9	31·9	27·0	26·5	30·2
1769	32·7	32·3	28·4	28·6	30·9
1770	33·4	35·0	29·9	27·1	31·5
1771	33·8	33·2	27·7	27·1	31·1
1772	28·5	29·9	27·1	25·6	27·8
1773	22·3	28·5	24·5	21·1	23·4
1774	28·5	30·9	27·5	25·4	28·0
1775	34·6	35·3	30·3	30·5	33·0
1776	31·9	30·3	25·7	26·8	29·3
1777	33·0	30·4	29·1	29·1	30·9

TABLE 5 (*cont.*)

Year	Akershus	Kristiansand	Bergen	Trondheim	Norway
1778	33·9	32·5	28·2	27·0	31·0
1779	33·9	32·0	27·9	27·9	31·1
1780	33·7	34·3	30·1	28·9	32·1
1781	33·8	32·6	28·9	26·2	31·0
1782	32·3	31·5	27·8	28·8	30·6
1783	26·2	29·5	27·2	28·3	27·4
1784	31·4	32·3	27·7	28·6	30·2
1785	30·8	32·2	25·5	24·7	28·7
1786	31·4	33·3	28·0	28·2	30·3
1787	30·6	28·2	28·0	27·5	29·0
1788	31·5	31·3	30·0	28·9	30·6
1789	33·7	31·2	28·5	25·7	30·5
1790	34·8	30·1	29·2	29·8	31·9
1791	34·1	31·7	31·2	31·5	32·6
1792	37·2	33·7	31·9	32·5	34·6
1793	36·3	33·8	32·6	31·0	34·0
1794	36·0	33·2	31·2	31·6	33·6
1795	34·5	31·9	30·1	30·2	32·3
1796	33·1	31·5	29·8	31·0	31·7
1797	36·2	32·3	28·9	30·0	32·8
1798	34·9	33·5	28·7	29·6	32·3
1799	33·4	34·7	28·5	32·9	32·6
1800	30·5	30·3	28·2	30·0	30·0
1801	26·6	29·5	29·9	29·1	28·3
1802	25·9	30·9	28·0	26·5	27·2
1803	30·4	31·7	28·6	25·8	29·1
1804	28·9	29·9	26·5	23·7	27·4
1805	31·9	32·1	30·3	25·4	30·1
1806	32·4	31·7	28·7	27·6	30·5
1807	31·2	31·8	27·6	27·2	29·7
1808	29·0	29·5	28·0	24·6	27·8
1809	19·4	27·6	24·4	22·4	22·3
1810	29·3	28·4	25·0	23·0	26·9
1811	31·7	29·8	24·7	21·5	27·7
1812	33·8	32·1	25·8	23·3	29·5
1813	27·5	28·5	26·6	21·7	26·1
1814	26·8	29·9	23·5	17·7	24·5
1815	33·9	31·5	29·1	25·0	30·6

TABLE 5 (*cont.*)

Year	Akershus	Kristiansand	Bergen	Trondheim	Norway
1816	38·7	33·6	32·1	32·4	35·2
1817	34·5	33·8	31·0	29·3	32·5
1818	32·3	31·3	29·8	28·8	30·8
1819	32·8	31·6	32·8	30·1	32·0
1820	34·8	34·2	31·9	31·3	33·4
1821	39·2	33·3	30·5	31·1	34·8
1822	35·4	32·4	31·4	30·2	33·0
1823	37·0	34·2	31·5	30·2	34·0
1824	34·7	31·9	31·2	30·0	32·5
1825	37·6	34·4	30·3	31·6	34·4
1826	37·4	36·6	32·8	30·8	34·9
1827	33·2	33·2	30·6	30·3	32·1
1828	33·3	32·1	30·2	30·2	31·8
1829	35·1	34·3	32·7	31·4	33·7
1830	33·3	31·7	31·3	31·9	32·4
1831	30·6	31·2	30·1	32·3	31·0
1832	28·7	32·2	30·5	30·3	29·9
1833	30·5	33·6	30·6	29·4	30·7
1834	32·4	32·2	31·4	30·5	31·7
1835	33·0	35·7	32·4	30·1	32·7
1836	30·1	31·9	27·9	27·6	29·4
1837	29·2	31·5	26·6	27·6	28·7
1838	29·0	34·9	31·7	28·7	30·3
1839	25·9	29·3	27·1	26·0	26·7
1840	28·0	30·7	26·7	26·5	27·8
1841	28·6	32·8	30·3	29·5	29·8
1842	31·0	32·2	29·0	30·6	30·8
1843	29·7	33·0	30·8	28·6	30·2
1844	29·8	32·0	29·9	28·7	29·9
1845	31·4	33·4	30·5	29·4	31·2
1846	32·3	30·7	30·5	29·6	31·1
1847	31·2	31·5	30·9	29·5	30·8
1848	31·2	30·8	27·7	28·0	29·8
1849	33·9	34·0	29·3	29·5	32·1
1850	32·7	32·9	29·4	27·5	30·9
1851	33·1	32·2	31·2	29·7	31·9
1852	31·6	32·6	30·1	29·5	31·0

TABLE 5 (*cont.*)

Year	Akershus	Kristiansand	Bergen	Trondheim	Norway
1853	33·9	32·2	31·1	28·9	32·0
1854	36·8	33·6	31·8	31·6	34·2
1855	35·8	33·0	30·6	31·2	33·4
1856	35·1	31·6	29·4	29·3	32·2
1857	35·2	33·5	31·3	30·0	33·0
1858	36·1	32·5	32·0	30·5	33·5
1859	37·3	33·1	32·1	33·1	34·8
1860	35·1	32·3	31·5	31·9	33·3
1861	31·8	29·4	29·9	30·2	30·7
1862	32·8	30·7	30·0	33·2	32·1
1863	34·4	32·0	30·7	31·7	32·8
1864	32·3	31·7	30·2	32·4	31·9
1865	32·6	32·4	30·9	31·0	31·9

TABLE 6 *Marriages per 1,000 mean population in the dioceses of Norway 1735–1865*

Year	Akershus	Kristiansand	Bergen	Trondheim	Norway
1735	8·2	—	—	—	—
1736	7·8	—	8·9	—	—
1737	7·7	—	8·8	—	—
1738	8·2	—	9·2	—	—
1739	8·3	—	8·6	—	—
1740	7·5	—	7·8	—	—
1741	6·8	—	7·9	—	—
1742	7·2	—	10·7	—	—
1743	8·7	—	10·4	—	—
1744	—	—	9·9	—	—
1745	9·0	—	9·7	—	—
1746	8·1	—	9·1	—	—
1747	8·6	—	9·1	—	—
1748	8·6	—	7·5	—	—
1749	6·9	—	8·4	—	—
1750	7·9	—	10·0	—	—
1751	8·7	—	9·1	—	—
1752	9·3	—	9·3	—	—

TABLE 6 (*cont.*)

Year	Akershus	Kristiansand	Bergen	Trondheim	Norway
1753	9·3	—	9·2	—	—
1754	9·1	—	9·0	—	—
1755	8·1	—	9·4	—	—
1756	8·7	—	8·6	—	—
1757	7·2	—	8·4	—	—
1758	7·3	—	7·5	—	—
1759	7·1	—	8·0	—	—
1760	—	—	—	—	—
1761	7·9	—	7·7	—	—
1762	7·2	8·5	—	—	—
1763	7·3	7·5	7·5	—	—
1764	9·4	11·2	9·7	—	—
1765	8·3	9·4	8·5	—	—
1766	8·8	—	—	—	—
1767	8·0	—	7·3	—	—
1768	7·8	7·2	—	—	—
1769	7·4	—	—	—	—
1770	7·1	7·2	7·3	7·4	7·2
1771	6·7	6·9	—	—	6·7
1772	5·8	6·6	—	—	5·9
1773	5·7	6·7	—	—	5·9
1774	9·2	—	—	—	8·4
1775	9·8	8·9	7·8	9·3	9·2
1776	9·3	8·4	7·0	7·6	8·3
1777	8·6	—	8·1	—	8·3
1778	8·5	7·3	7·8	7·3	7·9
1779	8·4	8·0	7·6	7·5	8·0
1780	7·7	7·9	7·4	7·3	7·6
1781	—	7·8	7·5	—	8·0
1782	6·6	7·3	7·1	7·4	7·0
1783	7·8	8·9	8·5	7·5	8·0
1784	7·6	8·5	8·3	—	—
1785	7·4	8·1	7·7	—	—
1786	—	7·6	8·4	—	—
1787	—	7·3	8·4	—	—
1788	7·8	—	8·4	—	—
1789	—	6·6	7·6	—	—
1790	—	8·6	8·6	—	—

TABLE 6 (*cont.*)

Year	Akershus	Kristiansand	Bergen	Trondheim	Norway
1791	9·5	9·2	8·8	—	—
1792	9·8	8·7	9·0	—	—
1793	—	—	8·7	—	—
1794	8·8	8·3	8·6	—	—
1795	—	7·3	—	—	7·7
1796	—	7·9	7·8	—	7·8
1797	8·2	7·5	7·9	8·4	8·1
1798	8·4	—	—	—	8·3
1799	7·4	7·6	—	—	7·9
1800	7·0	7·9	7·1	—	—
1801	6·3	7·2	7·7	7·2	6·9
1802	7·4	8·2	7·9	7·4	7·6
1803	8·1	7·6	7·4	7·1	7·7
1804	7·8	7·6	8·6	8·0	8·0
1805	7·9	7·7	8·6	8·3	8·1
1806	7·8	7·8	8·5	8·4	8·1
1807	6·7	7·1	7·8	6·8	7·0
1808	4·6	5·7	6·6	7·5	5·8
1809	6·1	6·0	5·8	5·7	5·9
1810	9·3	7·1	6·9	6·7	7·9
1811	10·1	8·1	8·0	7·4	8·8
1812	9·5	8·8	8·9	7·0	8·7
1813	7·8	7·1	7·5	5·7	7·1
1814	6·2	6·9	6·9	6·1	6·4
1815	11·1	9·6	9·0	9·6	10·1
1816	11·2	9·5	9·6	9·7	10·3
1817	9·1	7·8	8·4	8·4	8·6
1818	8·3	8·0	8·6	7·7	8·2
1819	7·7	7·6	8·8	8·6	8·1
1820	9·4	8·1	8·6	9·2	9·0
1821	9·5	8·3	8·2	9·3	9·0
1822	10·0	8·3	8·1	8·3	9·0
1823	8·6	8·4	8·7	9·6	8·7
1824	8·3	7·6	8·0	8·3	8·2
1825	8·7	8·6	8·2	9·0	8·6
1826	8·3	8·4	8·7	8·0	8·3
1827	7·0	7·2	8·0	8·2	7·5

TABLE 6 (*cont.*)

Year	Akershus	Kristiansand	Bergen	Trondheim	Norway
1828	7·2	7·2	8·0	8·6	7·6
1829	7·6	7·3	7·6	8·7	7·8
1830	7·2	7·4	7·9	8·8	7·7
1831	6·5	6·9	7·5	8·6	7·2
1832	6·2	7·1	7·1	7·6	6·8
1833	6·9	7·3	8·0	7·8	7·3
1834	7·5	7·7	8·0	7·3	7·6
1835	7·5	7·4	7·6	7·1	7·4
1836	7·0	7·7	6·9	6·7	7·0
1837	6·5	7·2	7·0	6·6	6·7
1838	6·4	7·3	7·0	7·3	6·9
1839	6·0	6·5	6·7	7·1	6·4
1840	6·7	7·2	7·0	7·1	6·9
1841	7·4	7·6	7·3	8·3	7·6
1842	7·8	7·8	7·4	8·2	7·8
1843	7·9	7·7	8·1	8·0	7·9
1844	7·9	7·7	8·3	7·8	7·9
1845	8·2	7·7	8·3	7·6	8·0
1846	8·7	7·4	8·3	8·3	8·3
1847	7·3	6·7	7·9	7·3	7·3
1848	7·7	7·1	7·3	7·5	7·5
1849	7·9	7·6	8·0	7·3	7·7
1850	7·9	7·4	8·0	7·1	7·6
1851	7·5	7·1	8·2	7·2	7·5
1852	7·3	6·9	7·0	7·0	7·1
1853	8·0	7·1	8·0	7·8	7·8
1854	9·2	7·7	8·1	8·2	8·5
1855	8·8	7·4	7·2	8·0	8·1
1856	8·2	7·1	7·3	7·5	7·7
1857	7·8	7·2	7·6	7·2	7·5
1858	7·7	7·3	7·7	7·6	7·6
1859	7·8	6·9	7·8	8·0	7·7
1860	6·8	6·7	7·2	8·1	7·2
1861	6·2	6·2	7·2	7·9	6·8
1862	6·4	6·8	7·1	7·7	6·9
1863	6·8	7·0	7·5	7·8	7·2
1864	6·5	6·9	7·4	7·1	6·8
1865	6·4	7·2	7·4	7·0	6·9

Population and Society in Norway 1735–1865

TABLE 7 Deaths per 1,000 mean population in the dioceses of Norway 1735–1865

Year	Akershus	Kristiansand	Bergen	Trondheim	Norway
1735	22·0	18·7	19·8	13·5	19·0
1736	22·5	16·7	23·6	17·3	20·5
1737	31·4	17·5	24·8	16·4	24·5
1738	28·7	17·2	24·0	15·4	22·8
1739	26·2	21·3	26·5	15·2	22·8
1740	29·9	25·2	26·8	15·4	25·1
1741	42·4	66·0	45·0	19·1	40·8
1742	67·3	44·4	35·4	43·2	52·2
1743	34·2	24·9	26·9	21·7	28·4
1744	23·2	21·6	24·8	15·8	21·4
1745	18·3	20·6	20·8	14·6	18·2
1746	21·2	19·8	18·5	21·5	20·6
1747	25·2	22·7	19·6	22·8	23·2
1748	40·3	32·0	21·9	25·5	32·1
1749	24·5	31·8	36·6	21·2	27·1
1750	21·4	19·6	35·0	29·4	25·5
1751	28·2	19·7	24·9	27·6	26·1
1752	23·4	25·0	24·0	26·9	24·6
1753	22·2	25·6	20·7	23·0	22·7
1754	26·4	24·8	22·8	17·2	23·4
1755	28·0	23·7	22·2	21·8	24·8
1756	28·3	23·0	21·4	28·9	26·3
1757	22·8	19·3	19·0	22·4	21·5
1758	19·8	28·0	29·8	23·8	23·9
1759	26·4	31·6	22·4	25·2	26·2
1760	21·5	23·0	21·6	24·9	22·6
1761	22·9	24·2	20·3	22·9	22·6
1762	23·5	26·8	21·4	21·9	23·2
1763	33·6	47·7	32·5	33·8	35·6
1764	29·2	30·7	22·5	24·2	27·0
1765	26·8	26·1	29·4	30·7	28·1
1766	29·3	26·3	24·1	28·3	27·7
1767	21·4	21·8	19·5	25·9	22·2
1768	23·6	24·3	19·5	20·7	22·3
1769	22·7	22·7	19·1	21·6	21·8
1770	29·1	22·3	18·8	18·1	23·6

192

TABLE 7 (*cont.*)

Year	Akershus	Kristiansand	Bergen	Trondheim	Norway
1771	21·1	27·5	28·3	19·0	22·9
1772	26·2	27·2	29·6	25·6	26·8
1773	64·3	36·0	21·6	43·9	47·5
1774	28·9	28·5	20·1	21·6	25·5
1775	25·6	24·3	18·0	20·8	22·9
1776	20·1	20·3	20·2	21·3	20·4
1777	22·1	18·4	19·1	21·1	20·8
1778	18·6	22·5	18·1	22·3	20·0
1779	25·9	25·5	25·3	31·6	27·1
1780	27·3	24·3	23·8	23·6	25·3
1781	23·4	19·9	16·4	19·5	20·7
1782	24·1	21·8	22·5	19·6	22·4
1783	25·5	25·9	24·4	22·1	24·6
1784	25·6	24·0	20·6	22·9	23·8
1785	35·3	34·4	25·8	33·7	33·1
1786	25·9	24·3	21·4	23·3	24·2
1787	24·4	21·0	21·0	21·9	22·7
1788	29·2	25·6	23·4	22·9	26·1
1789	37·0	29·8	21·3	26·0	30·4
1790	23·6	24·4	20·8	22·1	22·9
1791	23·9	24·5	21·1	21·6	22·9
1792	24·3	26·4	27·0	19·5	23·9
1793	24·1	23·6	20·2	19·0	22·1
1794	20·5	21·8	21·3	20·4	20·8
1795	23·4	22·0	20·2	23·1	22·5
1796	23·5	19·8	18·4	22·1	21·7
1797	23·1	20·1	23·5	22·2	22·5
1798	22·8	23·2	23·0	21·4	22·6
1799	20·0	26·3	22·5	18·1	21·0
1800	27·7	26·3	22·1	24·0	25·6
1801	34·0	22·6	21·0	23·2	27·4
1802	25·6	19·6	26·3	27·2	25·2
1803	21·5	21·0	29·3	30·3	24·9
1804	20·4	24·3	23·8	28·2	23·5
1805	21·0	22·3	20·2	19·7	20·7
1806	22·1	21·8	21·0	18·9	21·1
1807	23·0	22·1	20·5	23·6	22·6

TABLE 7 (*cont.*)

Year	Akershus	Kristiansand	Bergen	Trondheim	Norway
1808	32·5	20·9	17·2	24·7	26·1
1809	56·0	22·9	20·3	20·9	35·9
1810	30·2	27·1	22·1	24·1	26·8
1811	24·3	24·0	22·9	30·2	25·5
1812	20·3	19·8	20·4	24·7	21·3
1813	32·6	21·9	22·8	33·9	29·5
1814	22·6	19·5	20·0	26·5	22·6
1815	19·8	18·9	22·8	18·4	19·8
1816	18·7	20·3	22·0	18·0	19·4
1817	17·9	18·8	18·0	16·5	17·7
1818	20·4	19·4	17·1	17·9	19·1
1819	23·2	17·8	16·1	17·5	19·7
1820	20·5	16·9	18·2	18·0	18·9
1821	19·9	22·2	19·9	20·7	20·5
1822	18·6	21·5	20·4	19·1	19·5
1823	18·1	18·3	17·2	17·2	17·8
1824	19·7	18·7	18·0	16·5	18·5
1825	18·4	16·9	16·3	16·9	17·5
1826	18·6	18·1	19·1	18·2	18·5
1827	17·6	17·2	19·2	18·4	18·0
1828	19·9	18·9	19·0	19·2	19·4
1829	19·9	18·9	17·9	19·9	19·4
1830	20·1	21·4	19·5	18·2	19·7
1831	19·5	19·6	23·3	18·0	19·8
1832	18·5	17·2	18·4	19·5	18·5
1833	22·8	16·9	18·7	19·5	20·4
1834	22·3	22·3	23·0	22·5	22·5
1835	18·3	21·5	18·3	21·2	19·5
1836	18·6	20·3	20·3	19·0	19·3
1837	20·0	20·6	22·2	21·4	20·8
1838	20·9	20·6	22·3	23·7	21·7
1839	23·5	18·8	18·1	22·8	21·6
1840	18·9	19·8	18·4	22·5	19·8
1841	16·8	18·6	17·2	17·1	17·3
1842	18·1	18·9	18·9	16·5	18·0
1843	16·6	16·9	21·0	18·9	17·9
1844	16·4	18·3	19·2	16·1	17·1
1845	15·6	16·8	20·6	16·6	16·9

TABLE 7 (*cont.*)

Year	Akershus	Kristiansand	Bergen	Trondheim	Norway
1846	16·7	19·9	20·2	16·9	17·9
1847	21·0	18·7	21·1	19·8	20·4
1848	19·4	18·1	23·9	21·7	20·5
1849	17·1	18·0	23·0	17·5	18·3
1850	16·4	15·8	18·6	18·6	17·2
1851	16·9	17·5	16·5	17·5	17·1
1852	17·9	17·7	18·4	17·7	17·9
1853	20·5	17·4	16·4	16·5	18·3
1854	16·1	15·7	16·4	15·8	16·0
1855	17·1	16·9	18·3	16·5	17·1
1856	16·8	18·2	17·6	15·6	16·9
1857	17·0	17·7	16·6	17·2	17·1
1858	15·7	16·1	15·7	16·9	16·1
1859	17·7	18·1	16·5	15·5	17·0
1860	17·1	16·5	16·9	18·0	17·2
1861	18·8	19·9	19·1	21·0	19·5
1862	20·1	17·3	17·3	23·4	20·0
1863	19·1	18·7	19·0	18·6	18·9
1864	18·0	19·3	17·8	16·5	17·8
1865	16·0	17·3	15·5	17·9	16·6

Kiær and Gille on birth and death rates

Before calculating the Norwegian birth and death rates for the years 1735–1865, Anders Kiær made certain assumptions. The first of these was that the figures published in *Materialien* and by Catteau-Calleville were acceptable. The second, that this was also true of the totals of births and deaths in the various nineteenth-century official publications, with the exception of those for 1801–15. These he modified slightly without giving his reasons for doing so. Kiær also took the census of 1769 and 1801 to be substantially correct. The only reason for doing this seems to have been the fact that the excess of births over deaths for the period 1769–1801 was almost the same as the amount by which the population in the census of 1801 exceeded that in the census of 1769. In fact Kiær believed that the natural increase of population in Norway all but equalled the actual increase until as late as 1845. Working backwards from the 1801 census Kiær calculated a population figure for each of the years 1735–1800 by subtracting the excess of births over deaths in the one year from the population of the succeeding year and by making a small allowance for losses through emigration (*c.* 150 per annum). He adopted the same technique for the years after 1801 assuming, where necessary, that the census totals were deficient rather than those of births and deaths. Kiær also considered the question of still births. Initially, as noted in the text, he believed them to have been included amongst both the births and deaths. Later he believed they had been omitted from both. It seems impossible to resolve this problem now. There is, however, one piece of evidence suggesting that Kiær's earlier position may have been the correct one. In the bishop of Akershus's return of 1801 the totals of births and deaths are given as 10,403 and 13,191 respectively. They are subsequently amended, however, to 10,044 and 12,832 by subtracting the number of still-births (359) from both.

In 1949 Dr Halvor Gille reworked the eighteenth-century statistics. Like Kiær he too accepted the totals of births and deaths in *Materialien* and in the work of Catteau-Colleville. He took issue with Kiær however on the reliability of the 1769 census; reckoning that the population was nearer 750,000 than the 723,000 officially recorded. To get agreement between this revised figure, that of the census of 1801 and the totals of births and deaths in the intervening years, Dr Gille made two further assumptions. The first was that still births had been recorded as deaths. He, therefore, reduced the number of deaths by 2 per cent of the births registered in the same year, except during the last two decades of the century, when he used a reduction factor of 1 per cent. Second, he assumed that the population was reduced through emigration by about 1·6 per 1,000 (approximately 1,300 persons) each year. Similar reduction factors were applied to the period before 1769.

If we go behind the national aggregate we find neither the Kiær nor the Gille position wholly satisfactory. For as the following table shows, if we accept the totals of births and deaths and the census totals, then we must also accept quite considerable interregional migration. Akershus diocese would appear to have lost 4,000 people, Kristiansand 8,000 and Bergen 7,000. The most surprising feature of the table is, however, the immigration into the Trondheim diocese of 19,000 people. Such a high rate of migration into the Trondheim diocese is what we would expect in the 1840s when population pressure in the southern part of the country was eased to some extent by the colonisation of waste land in the northern counties. Even if we accept the Gille assumption on the misregistration of still births, the position is not radically altered with regard to the Trondheim diocese, although it more than doubles the rate of emigration from Akershus.

The 'natural' and the 'actual' increase of population in the dioceses of Norway 1769–1801*

	Akershus	Kristiansand	Bergen	Trondheim	Norway
Population in 1801	378,646	133,711	153,556	217,115	883,028
Population in 1769	315,043	113,024	130,352	164,703	723,122
Increase 1769–1801	63,603	20,687	23,204	52,412	159,906
Excess of births 1769–1801	67,341	28,473	30,064	33,121	158,999
Emigration (−) or immigration (+)	− 3,738	− 7,786	− 6,860	+ 19,291	+ 907

* Population census of 1769 (manuscript copy in the library, statistisk sentralbyrå, Oslo); Census of 1801 in *Den Norske Rigstidende*. Appendix to no. 29 (Christiania, 1815). This gives totals by dioceses and counties. The total for the diocese of Trondheim is given as 217,115. After the calculations were made in tables 1–7 I discovered this was a printing error. The proper total was 217,125 and the national total, therefore, 883,038. The *Budstikken*, nos. 12–15 (Christiania, 1826), pp. 107–8 gives the following totals of population for the dioceses in 1801: Akershus (378,646); Kristiansand (133,515); Bergen (153,752); Trondheim (138,690); Nordland (78,435). Excess of births for 1769–1801 calculated from the figures in statistical appendix, tables 2 and 3.

It is tempting to assume that the Trondheim figures are at fault. To allow for a 10 per cent under registration of births here would leave us with a more plausible immigration of about 2,500. On the other hand as the same clergy registered the births as took the censuses it would seem logical to assume that the censuses were also inaccurate. To alter the totals of births arbitrarily in the one diocese also raises the question of what to do in the others.

For most years the national rates shown in tables 5–7 are very close to those calculated by Kiær and Gille, as the illustration below shows.

The very close agreement between the rates in 1735 and 1795, both of which are representative of the intervening years, suggests that the different allowances made by Kiær, Gille and myself for migration or the misregistration of still births, have had little significant effect. The rates for 1765 show that the inclusion by Kiær and Gille of the Icelandic returns in the Norwegian totals had the effect of raising their rates by 2–3 per 1,000 between 1761 and 1769. Finally, the sharp differences between Kiær–Gille rates and mine in 1742 and 1759 add a note of caution. For there is a possibility that a re-examination of the primary material would bring to light similarly gross mistakes.

*Births and deaths per 1,000 mean population according
to Kiær,* Gille† and Drake‡*

Year	Births			Deaths		
	Kiær	Gille	Drake	Kiær	Gille	Drake
1735	29·4	31·5	29·0	19·3	20·1	19·0
1765	34·5	35·7	31·3	30·2	30·5	28·1
1795	32·4	32·7	32·3	22·6	22·5	22·5
1825	34·3	—	34·4	17·4	—	17·5
1855	33·4	—	33·4	17·1	—	17·1
1741	—	—	—	36·9	38·7	40·8
1742	—	—	—	69·3	73·2	52·2
1759	—	—	—	19·5	19·7	26·2

* *Norges offisielle statistikk,* **10,** 178 *Statistiske oversikter 1948* (Oslo, 1949), table 14.

† H. Gille, 'The demographic history of the Northern European countries in the eighteenth century', *Population Studies,* **3** (1949–50).

‡ Tables 5 and 7 above.

TABLE 8 Some nuptiality and fertility measures of the population of six inland and six coastal deaneries in Norway 1769*

Deaneries	Marital status	Men 16–24 years	24–32 years	32–40 years	40–48 years	16–48 years	Women 16–24 years	24–32 years	32–40 years	40–48 years	16–48 years	Annual births 1770 (Mean 1768–70)	70	Mean Children 0–8 years in 1769	Births in 1770 per 1,000 women aged 16–48 years in 1769 — All women	Married and widowed women	Children 0–8 years per 1,000 women aged 16–48 years in 1769 — All women	Married and widowed women
Inland																		
Nedre Romerike	Total	975	604	685	586	2,850	1,176	816	750	624	3,366	502 (14)	501 (14)	3,367	149	306	1,000	2,050
	Ever married	157	332	523	495	1,507	169	462	551	460	1,642							
	Percentage ever married	16·1	55·0	76·3	84·5	52·9	14·4	56·6	73·5	73·7	48·8							
Øvre Romerike	Total	2,058	1,354	1,562	1,233	6,207	2,367	1,808	1,756	1,322	7,253	1,023 (58)	1,010 (51)	7,013	141	283	967	1,944
	Ever married	175	728	1,289	1,131	3,323	295	1,003	1,296	1,014	3,608							
	Percentage ever married	8·5	53·8	82·5	91·7	53·5	12·5	55·5	73·8	76·7	49·7							
Hedemarken	Total	1,346	935	848	769	3,898	1,551	1,086	1,036	868	4,541	564 (17)	509 (18)	3,635	124	234 (247)	800	1,508 (1,591)
	Ever married	369 (153)	549	673	693	2,284 (2,068)	356 (229)	589	766	700	2,411 (2,284)							
	Percentage ever married	27·4 (11·4)	58·7	79·4	90·1	58·6 (53·0)	23·0 (14·8)	54·2	73·9	80·6	53·1 (50·3)							
Gudbrands-dalen	Total	1,872	1,231	1,108	906	5,117	1,976	1,401	1,244	943	5,564	751 (53)	735 (44)	5,121	135	286	920	1,949
	Ever married	268	563	822	756	2,409	338	674	888	727	2,627							
	Percentage ever married	14·3	45·7	74·2	83·4	47·1	17·1	48·1	71·4	77·1	47·2							
Østerdalen	Total	951	661	635	497	2,744	1,028	783	629	515	2,955	371 (23)	375 (19)	2,719	126	248	920	1,821
	Ever married	110	302	472	428	1,312	173	430	475	415	1,493							
	Percentage ever married	11·6	45·7	74·3	86·1	47·8	16·8	54·9	75·5	80·6	50·5							

199

TABLE 8 (cont.)

Deaneries	Marital status	Men 16–24 years	24–32 years	32–40 years	40–48 years	16–48 years	Women 16–24 years	24–32 years	32–40 years	40–48 years	16–48 years	Annual births 1770	Mean 1768–70	Mean Children 0–8 years in 1769	Births in 1770 per 1,000 women aged 16–48 years in 1769 — All women	Married and widowed women	Children 0–8 years per 1,000 women aged 16–48 years in 1769 — All women	Married and widowed women
Inland (cont.)																		
Toten and Valdres	Total	1,624	1,155	1,181	881	4,841	1,811	1,351	1,273	1,071	5,506	707 (26)	691 (23)	5,077	128	263	922	1,891
	Ever married	185	560	953	737	2,435	285	675	806	828	2,684							
	Percentage ever married	11·4	48·5	80·7	83·7	50·3	15·7	50·0	70·4	77·3	48·7							
Coastal																		
Sunnhordland	Total	1,166	878	923	723	3,690	1,349	1,244	978	745	4,316	603 (8)		3,662	140	271	848	1,646
	Ever married	105	406	737	653	1,901	199	663	732	630	2,224							
	Percentage ever married	9·0	46·2	79·8	90·3	51·5	14·8	53·3	74·8	84·6	51·5							
Nordhordland	Total	2,033	1,421	1,341	1,267	6,062	2,233	1,826	1,475	1,260	6,794	933 (7)		5,639	137	289	830	1,744
	Ever married	146	715	1,080	1,136	3,077	217	882	1,127	1,007	3,233							
	Percentage ever married	7·2	50·3	80·5	89·7	50·7	9·7	48·3	76·3	79·9	47·6							
Sogn	Total	1,014	729	716	595	3,054	1,114	983	813	597	3,507	498 (42)		2,869	142	300	818	1,731
	Ever married	52	281	600	552	1,485	108	461	600	488	1,657							
	Percentage ever married	5·1	38·5	83·8	92·8	48·6	9·7	46·9	73·8	81·7	47·2							
Sunnfjord	Total	941	741	588	515	2,785	1,036	871	628	475	3,010	314 (4)		2,753	104	239	915	2,098
	Ever married	39	307	494	469	1,309	62	381	470	399	1,312							
	Percentage ever married	4·1	41·4	84·0	91·1	47·0	6·0	43·7	74·8	84·0	43·6							
Nordfjord	Total	890	642	620	459	2,611	975	778	655	500	2,908	381 (6)		2,354	131	276	809	1,707
	Ever married	137	313	535	396	1,381	147	371	451	410	1,379							
	Percentage ever married	15·4	48·7	86·3	86·3	52·9	15·1	47·7	68·8	82·0	47·4							

Sunnmøre Total	1,424	1,124	1,006	835	4,389	1,598	1,288	1,152	835	4,873	616	3,858	126	255	792	1,597
Ever married	200	695	886	771	2,552	189	626	882	719	2,416	(12)					
Percentage ever married	14·0	61·8	88·1	92·3	58·1	11·8	48·6	76·6	86·1	49·6						
Inland deaneries Total	8,826	5,940	6,019	4,872	25,657	9,909	7,245	6,688	5,343	29,185	3,821	26,932	134	273	923	1,878
Ever married	1,264 (1,048)	3,034	4,732	4,240	13,270 (13,054)	1,616 (1,489)	3,833	4,872	4,144	14,465 (14,338)	3,918 (191) (169)					
Percentage ever married	14·3 (11·9)	51·1	78·6	87·0	51·7 (50·9)	16·3 (15·0)	52·9	72·8	77·6	49·6 (49·1)						
Coastal deaneries Total	7,468	5,535	5,194	4,394	22,591	8,305	6,990	5,701	4,412	25,408	3,345	21,135	132	274	832	1,729
Ever married	679	2,717	4,332	3,977	11,705	922	3,384	4,262	3,653	12,221 (79)						
Percentage ever married	9·1	49·1	83·4	90·5	51·8	11·1	48·4	74·8	82·8	48·1						

* Population totals from census of Norway 1769; manuscript copy in the library of the Central Statistical Office, Oslo. Birth totals for the inland deaneries from Bishop of Åkershus' returns; microfilm in *Riksarkivet*, Oslo. Birth totals for the coastal deaneries from Bishop of Bergen's returns; microfilm in *Riksarkivet*, Oslo. I have made only a few changes in the original returns. First I have assumed that the 16-24 year age group in Hedemarken was a mistake and have inserted, in parenthesis, more likely figures; these being the means of those for the neighbouring deaneries of Øvre Romerike and Gudbrandsdalen.

Second, it appears that in Sogn either the 0-8 group is too large, possibly because it is in fact the 0-9 group, or the total of births is too low. Unfortunately, there are a number of gaps in the deanery returns of the Bergen diocese during the 1760s, so that it is not possible to resolve this problem. Third, the census of Sunnmøre gives no data on marital status for the parish of Hareid. The figures in the table represent, therefore, Sunnmøre without Hareid. I have made a corresponding adjustment in the total of births for this deanery. Births in parenthesis are illegitimate.

TABLE 9   *Median age at first marriage (bachelor–spinster) in
the deaneries of Norway 1841–55* *

Deanery		Number of marriages			Median age in years		
		1841–1845	1846–1850	1851–1855	1841–1845	1846–1850	1851–1855
Nedre Borgesyssel	Male	502	848	1,000	27·4	27·4	27·7
	Female				25·4	25·4	25·7
Mellem Borgesyssel	Male	506	717	752	26·7	26·5	27·6
	Female				24·2	24·8	25·5
Vestre Borgesyssel	Male	492	720	795	26·5	26·5	27·5
	Female				24·2	24·9	25·6
Øvre Borgesyssel	Male	425	633	689	27·4	27·9	28·1
	Female				25·2	25·6	26·2
Nedre Romerike	Male	N.D.	792	887	N.D.	27·2	27·9
	Female				N.D.	25·5	26·0
Oslo diocesan	Male	1,589	1,823	2,077	27·3	27·6	27·9
deanery	Female				26·0	26·4	26·9
Øvre Romerike,	Male	N.D.	2,101	2,492	N.D.	26·9	27·5
Solør and Odalen	Female				N.D.	25·5	25·5
Østerdalen	Male	500	633	724	28·4	28·7	28·8
	Female				25·9	25·7	26·1
Hedemarken	Male	826	1,199	1,253	26·6	26·8	27·3
	Female				25·5	25·9	26·5
Gudbrandsdalen	Male	1,097	985	1,145	27·4	27·4	27·9
	Female				24·8	25·0	26·1
Toten and Valdres	Male	1,584	2,008	2,158	26·6	27·0	27·3
	Female				24·4	25·1	25·3
Hadeland, Ringerike	Male	1,007	1,279	1,361	27·1	27·3	27·5
and Hallingdal	Female				24·9	24·7	25·4
Kongsberg	Male	973	1,274	1,316	26·4	27·2	27·6
	Female				24·8	24·8	25·5
Drammen	Male	658	1,001	1,061	27·0	27·3	27·8
	Female				25·3	25·9	25·7
Jarlsberg	Male	945	1,337	1,594	27·1	27·8	27·9
	Female				25·9	25·9	26·2
Larvik	Male	628	764	841	27·0	27·4	27·7
	Female				25·3	25·8	26·3
Nedre Telemark	Male	1,098	1,535	1,720	26·7	26·8	27·1
and Bamble	Female				24·9	25·7	25·2
Øvre Telemark	Male	769	770	726	27·3	27·7	28·0
	Female				24·6	24·6	25·4

TABLE 9 (*cont.*)

Deanery		Number of marriages			Median age in years		
		1841–1845	1846–1850	1851–1855	1841–1845	1846–1850	1851–1855
Østre Nedenæs	Male	509	572	646	27·4	27·5	27·7
	Female				24·3	25·0	25·1
Vestre Nedenæs	Male	832	893	969	27·9	28·0	28·1
	Female				25·3	25·6	25·8
Råbygdelaget	Male	339	416	430	26·6	27·4	27·3
	Female				23·3	23·7	24·2
Kristiansand	Male	245	280	341	26·0	26·6	26·9
diocesan deanery	Female				24·8	24·7	25·8
Mandal	Male	527	592	639	27·9	28·2	28·0
	Female				25·1	24·9	25·1
Lister	Male	680	632	671	28·0	27·8	28·4
	Female				25·4	25·2	25·1
Dalane	Male	505	506	499	27·4	28·1	28·1
	Female				24·2	24·8	24·5
Jæren	Male	391	431	437	27·9	28·1	27·9
	Female				24·5	24·4	25·0
Stavanger	Male	700	713	812	26·6	26·9	27·1
	Female				24·0	24·6	25·0
Karmsund	Male	450	485	513	26·6	27·4	27·6
	Female				23·8	24·3	25·3
Ryfylke	Male	694	603	564	27·7	27·3	27·7
	Female				24·2	24·9	24·8
Hardanger and Voss	Male	767	748	709	28·7	28·4	28·8
	Female				24·8	25·2	25·5
Sunnhordland	Male	937	1,121	1,041	28·1	27·8	28·1
	Female				25·1	25·6	25·7
Bergen diocesan	Male	750	784	925	27·2	27·3	27·6
deanery	Female				26·1	26·3	26·5
Nordhordland	Male	1,058	1,241	1,219	26·8	27·2	27·1
	Female				25·4	25·7	25·6
Ytre Sogn	Male	476	432	494	28·1	27·9	28·0
	Female				26·2	26·4	27·3
Indre Sogn	Male	595	545	581	28·0	28·1	28·4
	Female				25·3	26·1	26·3
Sunnfjord	Male	670	703	709	27·2	27·5	28·0
	Female				24·9	25·4	26·0
Nordfjord	Male	548	561	583	27·8	27·7	28·0
	Female				26·0	26·6	26·4

TABLE 9 (*cont.*)

Deanery		Number of marriages			Median age in years		
		1841–1845	1846–1850	1851–1855	1841–1845	1846–1850	1851–1855
Søndre Sunnmøre	Male	368	399	398	27·5	27·7	28·0
	Female				26·5	26·1	26·7
Nordre Sunnmøre	Male	551	500	527	27·6	28·0	28·6
	Female				25·1	25·8	26·2
Romsdal	Male	551	520	571	28·1	28·2	29·1
	Female				25·5	25·7	27·0
Nordmøre	Male	900	946	964	27·9	28·2	28·7
	Female				25·5	25·7	26·6
Fosen	Male	717	707	862	27·9	27·9	28·4
	Female				24·4	24·8	25·6
Trondheim	Male	399	453	463	27·6	27·9	28·0
diocesan deanery	Female				26·4	27·1	27·4
Dalerne	Male	1,457	1,421	1,490	28·1	28·1	29·0
	Female				26·0	26·0	26·7
Innherad	Male	1,415	1,580	1,704	27·5	27·6	28·2
	Female				25·7	26·2	26·5
Namdalen	Male	490	417	557	28·7	27·7	28·6
	Female				26·4	25·4	26·3
Helgeland	Male	978	988	1,100	28·1	28·0	28·5
	Female				26·1	26·0	26·6
Salten	Male	585	636	698	27·6	27·8	28·4
	Female				25·0	26·2	26·6
Lofoten and	Male	376	556	648	27·9	27·8	28·1
Vesterålen	Female				25·7	25·1	25·3
Senja	Male	486	606	748	27·5	27·8	27·7
	Female				24·3	24·7	24·8
Tromsø	Male	451	602	635	26·5	27·1	27·3
	Female				23·8	24·4	24·5
Øst-Finnmark	Male	115	161	213	25·1	26·5	26·8
	Female				23·2	24·0	24·7
Vest-Finnmark	Male	326	384	361	24·5	25·5	25·1
	Female				22·8	23·0	23·4

* SOURCE: The returns of age at marriage by deanery and by five year age groups have been published for the years 1846–50 and 1851–5 in Norges Officielle Statistik, Sextende række, *Tabeller over folkemængden i Norge den 31te December 1855 samt over de i tidsrummet 1846–55 ægtviede fødte og døde* (Christiania, 1857). Ages at marriage in the years after 1855 are not classified according to first and subsequent marriages. We are able to make good the gaps in the official statistics by drawing on the original

TABLE 10   *Births and deaths, under age 5 years,*
in Herøy, Hallingdal and Hedemarken 1816–65*

	Births			Deaths under 5 years		
	Herøy	Hallingdal	Hede-marken	Herøy	Hallingdal	Hede-marken
1816–25	775	3,636	3,430	198	528	623
1826–35	829	3,554	3,231	201	658	581
1836–45	834	4,340	3,228	176	778	517
1846–55	969	4,225	3,884	193	569	523
1856–65	1,050	2,328	3,518	207	324	549
1816–65	4,457	18,083	17,291	975	2,857	2,793

* See below, bibliography, unprinted sources, riksarkivet, Oslo, item 3. Data not available for every year.

TABLE 11   *Births and deaths, under age 1 year,*
in Herøy, Hallingdal and Hedemarken 1832–65*

	Births			Deaths under 1 year		
	Herøy	Hallingdal	Hede-marken	Herøy	Hallingdal	Hede-marken
1832–45	1,110	5,517	4,209	195	687	420
1846–55	969	4,225	3,884	111	392	288
1856–65	1,050	2,328	3,518	114	191	295
1832–65	3,129	12,070	11,611	420	1,270	1,003

* As above, table 10.

returns made by the vicars and deans in the years 1841–5. These returns are in the riksarkiv, Oslo in *Folkemengdens bevegelse*, pakker 37–63. The gaps cannot, however, be filled completely. Damp has destroyed those from the Akershus diocese for 1844, and those for the deaneries of Nedre Romerike and Øvre Romerike have been lost. There are no deanery returns for the Bergen diocese, so the parish returns have been used here. As for the years after 1855, so many of the returns have been rendered illegible by damp that it was not felt worth while to make use of the ones that are available.

Population and Society in Norway 1735–1865

TABLE 12   Births in 1835, 1836, 1844, 1845, 1846, 1854,
1856 and women 21–50 years in 1835, 1845, and 1855 in
Herøy, Hallingdal and Hedemarken*

	Births		
Years	Herøy	Hallingdal	Hedemarken
1835, 1836	162	845	724
1844, 1845, 1846	296	1,394	1,138
1854, 1856	240	1,010	1,041
Women 21–50 years			
1835	636	2,326	2,325
1845	708	2,495	2,578
1855	867	2,441	2,861

* Births, as above, table 10. Women aged 21–50 from censuses of population in 1835,
1845 and 1855. For detailed reference see bibliography, official publications, items
1, 4 and 5.

TABLE 13   Age of spinster-brides (marrying bachelor-
bridegrooms) in Herøy, Hallingdal and Hedemarken in
various years from 1839 to 1865*

	Herøy		Hallingdal		Hedemarken	
Spinster-brides (marrying bachelor-bridegrooms) in the years 1839–45						
	Total	%	Total	%	Total	%
Under 20	4	3·2	73	12·9	15	3·0
20–25	42	33·3	217	38·2	200	40·1
25–30	50	39·7	167	29·4	199	39·9
30–35	21	16·7	64	11·3	60	12·0
35–40	4	3·2	27	4·7	18	3·6
40–45	2	1·6	12	2·1	4	0·8
45–50	3	2·3	5	0·9	3	0·6
Over 50	0	0	3	0·5	0	0
Total	126	100·0	568	100·0	499	100·0

TABLE 13 (*cont.*)

	Herøy		Hallingdal		Hedemarken	
	Total	%	Total	%	Total	%
Spinster-brides (marrying bachelor-bridegrooms) in the years 1846–54						
Under 20	8	4·3	73	9·6	30	3·6
20–25	72	38·9	333	43·6	331	39·6
25–30	63	34·2	231	30·3	319	38·2
30–35	26	14·0	85	11·1	110	13·2
35–40	11	5·9	25	3·3	28	3·3
40–45	5	2·7	6	0·8	11	1·3
45–50	0	0	9	1·2	6	0·7
Over 50	0	0	1	0·1	1	0·1
Total	185	100·0	763	100·0	836	100·0
Spinster-brides (marrying bachelor-bridegrooms) in the years 1856–65						
Under 20	8	4·1	40	9·4	27	4·4
20–25	53	27·2	178	42·0	248	40·6
25–30	65	33·4	125	29·6	194	31·8
30–35	45	23·1	54	12·8	99	16·2
35–40	19	9·7	18	4·3	32	5·2
40–45	2	1·0	7	1·7	8	1·3
45–50	3	1·5	1	0·2	3	0·5
Over 50	0	0	0	0	0	0
Total	195	100·0	423	100·0	611	100·0
Spinster-brides (marrying bachelor-bridegrooms) in the years 1839–65						
Under 20	20	3·9	186	10·6	72	3·7
20–25	167	33·0	728	41·5	779	40·0
25–30	178	35·2	523	29·8	712	36·6
30–35	92	18·2	203	11·6	269	13·8
35–40	34	6·7	70	4·0	78	4·1
40–45	9	1·8	25	1·4	23	1·2
45–50	6	1·2	15	0·9	12	0·6
Over 50	0	0	4	0·2	1	0
Total	506	100·0	1,754	100·0	1,946	100·0

* Calculated from marriage totals in the same source as used for table 10 above.

Population and Society in Norway 1735–1865

TABLE 14 *Age of bachelor-bridegrooms (marrying spinster-brides) in Herøy, Hallingdal and Hedemarken in various years from 1839 to 1865**

	Herøy		Hallingdal		Hedemarken	
	Total	%	Total	%	Total	%
Bachelor-bridegrooms (marrying spinster-brides) in the years 1839–45						
	Total	%	Total	%	Total	%
Under 20	1	0·8	15	2·6	4	0·8
20–25	34	27·0	148	26·1	168	33·7
25–30	59	46·8	214	37·7	210	42·1
30–35	26	20·6	116	20·4	81	16·2
35–40	4	3·2	44	7·7	22	4·4
40–45	1	0·8	17	3·0	10	2·0
45–50	1	0·8	8	1·4	3	0·6
Over 50	0	0	6	1·1	1	0·2
Total	126	100·0	568	100·0	499	100·0
Bachelor-bridegrooms (marrying spinster-brides) in the years 1846–54						
Under 20	1	0·5	10	1·3	6	0·6
20–25	39	21·1	165	21·6	294	35·2
25–30	95	51·4	354	46·4	327	39·2
30–35	35	18·9	148	19·4	139	16·7
35–40	12	6·5	50	6·6	48	5·7
40–45	2	1·1	22	2·9	12	1·4
45–50	1	0·5	6	0·8	9	1·1
Over 50	0	0	8	1·0	1	0·1
Total	185	100·0	763	100·0	836	100·0
Bachelor-bridegrooms (marrying spinster-brides) in the years 1856–65						
Under 20	2	1·0	4	0·9	18	2·9
20–25	36	18·5	84	19·9	197	32·2
25–30	83	42·5	177	41·9	236	38·6
30–35	51	26·2	107	25·3	112	18·3
35–40	16	8·2	36	8·5	32	5·3
40–45	5	2·6	11	2·6	14	2·3
45–50	1	0·5	3	0·7	1	0·2
Over 50	1	0·5	1	0·2	1	0·2
Total	195	100·0	423	100·0	611	100·0

TABLE 14 (*cont.*)

	Herøy		Hallingdal		Hedemarken	
	Total	%	Total	%	Total	%
Under 20	4	0·8	29	1·7	28	1·4
20–25	109	21·6	397	22·6	659	33·9
25–30	237	46·8	745	42·5	773	39·7
30–35	112	22·1	371	21·2	332	17·1
35–40	32	6·3	130	7·4	102	5·2
40–45	8	1·6	50	2·8	36	1·8
45–50	3	0·6	17	1·0	13	0·7
Over 50	1	0·2	15	0·8	3	0·2
Total	506	100·0	1,754	100·0	1,946	100·0

Bachelor-bridegrooms (marrying spinster-brides) in the years 1839–65

* Calculated from marriage totals in the same source as used for table 10 above.

TABLE 15 *Occupations of men aged 21–50 in the rural districts of Norwegian counties in 1801**

	Number in each occupation						
	Farmers	Husmenn with land	Craftsmen	Seamen, fisherman	Servants	Husmenn without land	Day labourers	(a)
Østfold	3,011	2,271	309	168	1,079	233	316	7,748
Akershus	3,229	3,019	536	189	1,795	420	541	10,412
Hedmark	3,863	3,477	686	3	1,484	309	371	10,830
Oppland	3,985	4,321	656	—	1,606	289	524	12,199
Buskerud	3,270	2,463	429	52	991	508	715	9,297
Vestfold	2,929	812	374	705	632	230	327	6,527
Telemark	2,798	1,946	292	515	858	208	572	7,748
Aust-Agder	2,422	584	318	842	487	391	444	5,799
Vest-Agder	3,664	308	234	845	291	112	369	6,065
Rogaland	3,901	1,031	93	520	1,076	127	148	7,242
Hordaland	6,833	1,016	36	89	1,851	546	311	11,117
Sogn and Fjordane	5,147	945	59	99	2,363	544	171	9,815
Møre and Romsdal	5,757	1,202	135	183	2,744	377	218	11,102
Sør-Trøndelag	3,888	2,202	293	338	1,451	279	553	9,799
Nord-Trøndelag	3,315	1,987	303	142	1,386	192	404	8,256
Nordland	5,024	750	75	703	2,234	291	93	9,578
Troms and Finnmark	2,114	629	44	819	763	179	31	4,988
Norway	65,150	28,963	4,872	6,222	23,091	5,235	6,107	148,508

	Percentage in each occupation							(b)
Østfold	38·9	29·3	4·0	2·2	13·9	3·0	4·1	95·4
Akershus	31·0	29·0	5·1	1·9	17·2	4·0	5·2	93·4
Hedmark	35·7	32·1	6·3	—	13·7	2·8	3·4	94·0
Oppland	32·7	35·4	5·4	0·6	13·2	2·4	4·3	93·4
Buskerud	35·2	26·5	4·6	10·8	10·6	5·5	7·7	90·7
Vestfold	44·9	12·4	5·7	6·6	9·7	3·5	5·0	92·0
Telemark	36·1	25·1	3·8	14·5	11·1	2·7	7·4	92·8
Aust-Agder	41·8	10·1	5·5	13·9	8·4	6·7	7·6	94·6
Vest-Agder	60·4	5·1	3·8	7·2	4·8	1·8	6·1	95·9
Rogaland	53·9	14·2	1·3	0·8	14·8	1·7	2·0	95·1
Hordaland	61·5	9·1	0·3	1·1	16·6	4·9	2·8	96·0
Sogn and Fjordane	52·4	9·6	0·6	1·6	24·1	5·5	1·7	95·0
Møre and Romsdal	51·8	10·8	1·2	1·6	24·7	3·4	2·0	95·5
Sør-Trøndelag	39·7	22·5	3·0	3·4	14·8	2·8	5·6	91·8
Nord-Trøndelag	40·1	24·1	3·7	1·7	16·8	2·3	4·9	93·6
Nordland	52·4	7·8	0·8	7·3	23·3	3·0	1·0	95·6
Troms and Finnmark	42·4	12·6	0·9	16·4	15·3	3·6	0·6	91·8
Norway	43·9	19·5	3·3	4·2	15·5	3·5	4·1	94·0

(a) Total men in county.
(b) Men in the occupations listed as a percentage of all men in county.
* Calculated from 1801 census of Norway. See bibliography, official publications no. 14. Figures include sons living in home of their fathers.

Population and Society in Norway 1735–1865

TABLE 16   *Distribution of households of farmers and crofters by number of inhabitants in Herøy, Hallingdal and Hedemarken in 1801**

No. of inhabitants	Farmers' households			Crofters' households		
	Herøy	Hallingdal	Hede-marken	Herøy	Hallingdal	Hede-marken
1	—	—	2	2	1	—
2	13	16	16	39	80	133
3	36	19	35	29	146	208
4	70	63	52	15	156	239
5	87	81	63	5	180	190
6	64	100	85	2	118	121
7	55	117	83	2	87	56
8	20	111	90	—	30	30
9	13	76	55	1	19	14
10	5	63	37	—	10	4
11	2	31	43	—	2	2
12	—	21	36	—	1	2
13	—	9	18	—	—	—
14	—	6	15	—	—	—
15	—	5	7	—	—	1
16	—	4	8	—	—	—
17	—	—	4	—	—	—
18	—	—	1	—	—	—
19	—	—	1	—	—	—
Total	365	722	651	95	830	1,000

* Calculated from ennumerators' returns of census of 1801 in parishes of Herøy, (Sunnmøre), Nes and Ål (Hallingdal); Nes and Ringsaker (Hedemarken).

TABLE 17 *Marital status of farmers and crofters in Herøy, Hallingdal and Hedemarken in 1801**

	Farmers			Crofters		
	Herøy	Hallingdal	Hede-marken	Herøy	Hallingdal	Hede-marken
Single men	7	28	16	1	14	4
Single women	—	—	—	—	—	2
Married†						
I i	210	514	478	50	655	809
I ii	51	56	58	7	30	36
I iii	7	5	5	—	2	2
I iv	1	—	—	1	—	—
II i	53	57	46	15	51	77
II ii	5	5	8	5	9	15
II iii	2	1	—	1	—	1
III i	7	4	2	1	4	9
III ii	2	—	2	2	—	3
IV i	1	—	1	—	—	3
IV ii	—	—	1	—	—	—
Total married	339	642	601	82	751	955
Widowers	12	26‡	8	5	27	11
Widows	7	18	18	7	29	24
Not classified	0	8	2	—	9	4
Total	365	722	645	95	830	1,000

* Source as in table 16.

† The numerals specify the current marital status of the marriage partners. Hence a woman in her third marriage is entered here as iii, whilst a man in his second is entered II.

‡ Includes one married man who at the time of the census was separated from his wife.

TABLE 18 *The age and social composition of farm households in Herøy in 1801*

Age	Farmers Male U	Farmers Male M	Farmers Male W	Farmers Female U	Farmers Female M	Farmers Female W	Farmers' wives M	Children Male U	Children Male M	Children Male W	Children Female U	Children Female M	Children Female W	Other rel. Male U	Other rel. Male M	Other rel. Male W	Other rel. Female U	Other rel. Female M	Other rel. Female W	Lodgers Male U	Lodgers Male M	Lodgers Male W	Lodgers Female U	Lodgers Female M	Lodgers Female W	Servants Male U	Servants Male M	Servants Male W	Servants Female U	Servants Female M	Servants Female W	Total
0–4	·	·	·	·	·	·	·	107	·	·	102	·	·	1	·	·	1	·	·	1	·	·	3	·	·	·	·	·	·	·	·	215
5–9	·	·	·	·	·	·	·	84	·	·	101	·	·	3	·	·	6	·	·	4	·	·	4	·	·	·	·	·	1	·	·	204
10–14	·	·	·	·	·	·	·	67	·	·	74	·	·	9	·	·	10	·	·	1	·	·	5	·	·	21	·	·	19	·	·	206
15–19	1	·	·	·	·	·	2	44	·	·	47	·	·	7	·	·	10	·	·	1	·	·	2	·	·	36	·	·	31	·	·	181
20–24	1	9	·	·	·	·	12	13	·	·	17	·	·	11	2	·	10	·	·	2	·	·	1	·	·	36	·	·	48	·	·	164
25–29	2	40	1	·	·	·	27	11	·	·	9	·	·	5	·	·	11	·	·	3	1	·	1	·	·	16	1	·	23	·	·	153
30–34	3	49	·	·	·	·	50	1	·	·	5	·	·	4	2	·	9	·	·	2	·	·	2	·	·	8	·	·	25	1	·	161
35–39	·	74	1	·	·	·	58	1	1	·	2	·	·	1	·	·	4	·	2	·	2	·	4	2	·	4	1	1	13	·	·	168
40–44	·	41	2	·	·	2	54	·	·	·	·	·	·	·	·	·	1	2	2	·	1	·	3	·	2	·	2	·	4	1	·	119
45–49	·	45	1	·	·	2	46	1	·	·	·	·	·	·	·	·	2	3	1	1	·	·	1	5	3	·	·	·	2	4	1	121
50–54	·	25	1	·	·	2	36	·	·	·	·	·	·	·	·	·	1	·	2	·	·	·	1	3	3	·	2	1	2	2	2	84
55–59	·	21	1	·	·	·	17	·	·	·	·	·	·	·	1	·	3	1	4	1	1	1	3	2	4	·	·	·	·	1	·	61
60–64	·	14	1	·	·	·	21	·	·	·	·	·	·	·	1	·	·	1	4	·	·	·	·	1	6	·	·	·	·	·	·	47
65–69	·	12	3	·	·	·	12	·	·	·	·	·	·	1	·	·	1	1	·	·	1	1	2	1	2	·	·	·	·	·	·	37
70–74	·	6	·	·	·	·	2	·	·	·	·	·	·	·	2	·	·	1	2	·	·	·	·	1	3	·	2	·	·	·	·	24
75–79	·	2	·	·	·	·	·	·	·	·	·	·	·	·	·	·	·	·	2	·	·	·	·	·	3	·	·	·	·	·	·	7
80–84	·	1	1	·	·	·	1	·	·	·	·	·	·	·	·	2	·	·	·	·	·	·	·	·	·	·	·	·	·	·	·	8
85–89	·	·	·	·	·	·	1	·	·	·	·	·	·	·	·	·	·	·	·	·	·	·	·	·	3	·	·	·	·	·	·	4
90–94	·	·	·	·	·	·	·	·	·	·	·	·	·	·	·	·	·	·	·	·	·	·	·	·	·	·	·	·	·	·	·	·
95–99	·	·	·	·	·	·	·	·	·	·	·	·	·	·	·	·	·	·	·	·	·	·	·	·	·	·	·	·	·	·	·	·
Total	7	339	12	·	·	7	339	329	1	·	357	·	·	41	8	2	69	11	22	14	6	3	32	12	36	124	11	1	170	6	5	1,964

TABLE 18 (cont.) *The age and social composition of crofter households in Herøy in 1801*

Age	Crofters Male U	Crofters Male M	Crofters Male W	Crofters Female U	Crofters Female M	Crofters Female W	Crofters' wives M	Crofters' wives W	Children Male U	Children Male M	Children Male W	Children Female U	Children Female M	Children Female W	Other rel. Male U	Other rel. Male M	Other rel. Male W	Other rel. Female U	Other rel. Female M	Other rel. Female W	Lodgers Male U	Lodgers Male M	Lodgers Male W	Lodgers Female U	Lodgers Female M	Lodgers Female W	Servants Male U	Servants Male M	Servants Male W	Servants Female U	Servants Female M	Servants Female W	Total
0–4	·	·	·	·	·	·	·	·	10	·	·	5	·	·	1	·	·	·	·	·	1	·	·	·	·	·	·	·	·	·	·	·	17
5–9	·	·	·	·	·	·	·	·	18	·	·	13	·	·	·	·	·	·	·	·	1	·	·	1	·	·	·	·	·	·	·	·	33
10–14	·	·	·	·	·	·	·	·	11	·	·	8	·	·	1	·	·	·	·	·	1	·	·	·	·	·	1	·	·	·	·	·	22
15–19	·	·	·	·	·	·	·	·	2	·	·	·	·	·	·	·	·	1	·	·	·	·	·	·	·	·	1	·	·	·	·	·	3
20–24	·	2	·	·	·	·	·	·	1	·	·	2	·	·	·	·	·	1	·	·	·	·	·	·	·	·	2	·	·	2	·	·	7
25–29	·	5	·	·	·	·	3	·	·	·	·	·	·	·	1	·	·	·	·	·	1	·	·	2	·	·	·	·	·	·	·	·	5
30–34	·	7	·	·	·	·	11	·	·	·	·	·	·	·	·	·	·	·	·	·	·	·	·	·	·	·	·	·	·	2	·	·	9
35–39	·	7	·	·	·	·	9	·	·	·	·	·	·	·	1	·	·	·	·	·	·	·	·	1	·	·	·	·	·	2	·	·	19
40–44	·	10	·	·	·	2	16	·	·	·	·	·	·	·	·	·	·	·	·	·	·	·	·	1	·	1	·	·	·	·	·	·	23
45–49	·	14	·	·	·	1	15	·	·	·	·	·	·	·	1	·	·	·	·	·	1	·	·	1	1	·	1	·	·	·	·	·	32
50–54	·	13	3	·	·	1	11	·	·	·	·	·	·	1	·	1	·	·	·	1	·	·	·	1	1	·	·	·	·	·	·	·	33
55–59	1	9	2	·	·	1	4	·	·	·	·	·	·	·	1	·	·	·	·	·	1	·	·	1	·	3	·	·	·	·	·	·	34
60–64	·	6	·	·	·	·	5	·	·	·	·	·	·	·	·	·	·	1	·	·	·	·	·	·	·	3	·	·	·	·	·	·	19
65–69	·	5	·	·	·	·	4	·	·	·	·	·	·	·	·	·	1	·	·	·	·	·	·	·	·	·	·	·	·	·	·	·	11
70–74	·	3	·	·	·	2	2	·	·	·	·	·	·	·	·	·	·	·	·	·	·	·	·	·	·	·	·	·	·	·	·	·	12
75–79	·	·	·	·	·	·	1	·	·	·	·	·	·	·	·	·	·	·	·	·	·	·	·	·	·	·	·	·	·	·	·	·	5
80–84	·	·	·	·	·	·	·	·	·	·	·	·	·	·	·	·	·	·	·	·	·	·	·	·	·	·	·	·	·	·	·	·	1
85–89	·	·	·	·	·	·	1	·	·	·	·	·	·	·	·	·	·	·	·	·	·	·	·	·	·	·	·	·	·	·	·	·	·
90–94	·	1	·	·	·	·	·	·	·	·	·	·	·	·	·	·	·	·	·	·	·	·	·	·	·	·	·	·	·	·	·	·	1
95–99	1	·	·	·	·	·	·	·	·	·	·	·	·	·	·	·	·	·	·	·	·	·	·	·	·	·	·	·	·	·	·	·	1
Total	1	82	5	·	·	7	82	·	42	·	·	28	·	1	6	1	1	3	·	1	6	·	·	8	2	7	5	·	·	4	·	·	287

215

Age	Farmers					Farmers' children				Other relatives					Livorefolk						Lodgers						Servants					Total
	Male			Female	Farmers' wives	Male		Female		Male		Female			Male			Female			Male			Female			Male		Female			
	U	M	W	W	M	U	M	U	M	U	M	U	M	W	U	M	W	U	M	W	U	M	W	U	M	W	U	M	U	M	W	
0–4	.	.	.	.	.	349	.	329	.	18	.	10	.	.	.	.	.	.	.	.	12	.	.	13	.	.	.	.	.	.	.	731
5–9	.	.	.	.	.	281	.	286	.	15	.	8	.	.	.	.	.	.	.	.	15	.	.	11	.	.	.	.	.	.	.	620
10–14	2	.	.	.	.	249	.	216	.	9	.	13	.	.	1	.	.	.	.	.	12	.	.	7	.	.	4	.	48	.	.	575
15–19	3	1	.	1	4	160	2	151	1	14	.	10	4	1	1	.	.	.	.	.	22	.	.	21	.	.	21	.	106	.	.	576
20–24	9	15	.	1	55	99	3	72	.	18	2	13	3	.	.	1	.	1	.	.	42	.	.	26	.	.	83	1	75	1	.	486
25–29	7	36	1	1	90	53	.	31	.	14	1	11	.	.	1	1	.	1	.	.	48	2	.	12	.	.	51	.	50	.	.	407
30–34	4	92	4	1	104	18	.	9	.	8	1	4	.	.	1	1	.	1	.	.	30	4	.	20	.	.	37	1	22	.	.	344
35–39	2	97	4	.	95	3	.	2	.	5	.	4	1	1	.	2	1	1	1	.	21	3	.	6	.	.	9	.	21	.	.	282
40–44	.	102	3	1	81	.	.	1	.	6	.	4	.	.	1	2	3	.	1	.	9	.	.	8	.	.	6	.	5	.	1	232
45–49	1	101	5	4	75	.	.	.	.	4	1	2	.	.	.	4	3	.	3	2	10	1	.	17	2	2	6	.	6	.	.	250
50–54	1	73	4	5	63	.	.	.	.	2	.	1	.	3	.	4	3	.	4	6	12	1	2	5	6	6	5	.	5	.	1	200
55–59	.	66	5	.	51	.	.	.	.	1	.	1	.	.	1	13	7	2	9	7	8	2	1	4	7	9	3	.	3	.	.	190
60–64	.	33	1	.	18	.	.	.	.	1	.	1	.	2	1	14	4	.	8	12	6	2	1	6	1	7	3	.	.	.	1	129
65–69	1	16	1	1	9	.	.	.	.	1	.	2	.	1	1	7	4	1	16	12	4	1	3	10	.	5	1	.	1	.	.	101
70–74	1	11	.	1	3	.	.	.	.	.	.	.	.	2	.	7	8	.	13	18	3	1	1	4	.	5	1	.	.	.	.	101
75–79	.	5	1	.	2	.	.	.	.	.	.	.	.	.	.	5	5	1	5	13	.	2	1	2	.	3	.	.	1	.	.	83
80–84	.	1	.	.	.	.	.	.	.	.	.	.	.	.	.	2	5	.	3	9	.	.	1	2	.	3	.	.	.	.	.	58
85–89	.	.	.	.	.	.	.	.	.	.	.	.	.	.	.	.	2	.	1	3	.	.	3	.	.	2	.	.	.	.	.	31
90–94	.	.	.	.	.	.	.	.	.	.	.	.	.	.	.	.	1	.	1	1	.	.	1	.	.	.	.	.	.	.	.	8
95–99	.	.	.	.	.	.	.	.	.	.	.	.	.	.	.	.	.	.	.	1	.	.	.	.	.	.	.	.	.	.	.	1
Total	29	650	27	17	650	1,212	5	1,097	1	124	5	84	8	12	8	62	46	8	64	84	268	19	14	174	16	42	230	2	343	1	3	5,305

TABLE 18 (cont.) *The age and social composition of crofter households in Hallingdal in 1801*

Age	Crofters Male U	Crofters Male M	Crofters Male W	Crofters Female U	Crofters Female M	Crofters Female W	Crofters' wives M	Crofters' children Male U	Crofters' children Male M	Crofters' children Female U	Livørefolk Male U	Livørefolk Male M	Livørefolk Male W	Livørefolk Female U	Livørefolk Female M	Livørefolk Female W	Other relatives Male U	Other relatives Male M	Other relatives Male W	Other relatives Female U	Other relatives Female M	Other relatives Female W	Lodgers Male U	Lodgers Male M	Lodgers Male W	Lodgers Female U	Lodgers Female M	Lodgers Female W	Servants Male U	Servants Female U	Total
0–4	·	·	·	·	·	·	·	276	·	269	·	·	·	·	·	·	7	·	·	5	·	·	21	·	·	24	·	·	·	·	602
5–9	·	·	·	·	·	·	·	245	·	248	·	·	·	·	·	·	2	·	·	3	·	·	15	·	·	20	·	·	·	1	534
10–14	·	·	·	·	·	·	·	172	·	148	·	·	·	·	·	·	7	·	·	2	·	·	18	·	·	14	·	·	6	9	376
15–19	1	1	·	·	·	·	3	89	1	71	·	·	·	·	·	·	5	·	·	4	·	·	21	·	·	12	·	·	7	8	222
20–24	1	10	·	·	·	·	30	51	·	34	·	·	·	·	·	·	2	·	·	4	·	·	28	·	·	15	·	·	3	4	188
25–29	·	56	1	·	·	·	79	22	·	18	·	·	·	·	·	·	1	·	·	2	1	·	14	2	·	30	2	1	2	2	229
30–34	4	96	1	·	·	·	91	5	·	6	·	·	·	·	·	·	·	·	·	2	1	·	12	2	·	15	3	1	2	1	245
35–39	3	100	2	·	·	·	107	1	·	·	·	·	·	·	·	·	·	·	·	1	1	·	11	4	·	19	2	2	1	1	258
40–44	1	99	2	·	·	2	90	1	·	4	·	·	·	·	·	·	1	·	1	1	1	·	4	2	·	9	2	2	·	·	216
45–49	2	113	1	·	·	4	137	·	·	1	·	·	·	·	·	·	·	·	·	1	·	·	10	1	·	17	3	3	·	·	297
50–54	·	87	4	·	·	6	67	·	·	·	1	2	·	1	·	·	·	·	1	1	·	1	3	1	·	10	3	5	·	·	189
55–59	·	76	6	·	·	5	66	·	·	·	·	·	2	·	1	1	·	1	1	1	·	·	8	1	2	14	2	7	·	·	206
60–64	·	41	2	·	·	6	38	·	·	·	·	2	·	1	1	3	·	2	·	1	·	1	3	4	·	10	4	8	·	·	127
65–69	1	44	2	·	·	2	26	·	·	·	·	3	·	·	5	3	·	1	·	1	·	·	6	5	3	9	1	11	·	·	122
70–74	·	15	3	·	·	2	10	·	·	·	·	1	·	·	2	2	·	·	·	1	·	1	4	3	·	11	1	6	·	·	65
75–79	·	15	2	·	·	2	6	·	·	·	·	1	1	·	1	2	·	·	1	1	·	·	1	1	1	10	1	6	·	·	65
80–84	·	3	1	·	·	1	4	·	·	·	·	1	2	·	1	1	·	·	·	·	·	1	·	1	·	2	·	6	·	·	30
85–89	·	3	1	·	·	·	2	·	·	·	·	·	·	·	·	1	·	·	·	·	·	·	·	·	·	1	·	3	·	·	11
90–94	·	·	·	·	·	·	·	·	·	·	·	·	·	·	·	·	·	·	·	·	·	·	·	·	·	1	·	·	·	·	2
95–99	·	·	·	·	·	·	·	·	·	·	·	·	·	·	·	·	·	·	·	·	·	·	·	·	·	·	·	·	·	·	·
Total	13	759	28	·	·	30	756	862	1	799	1	10	5	2	11	13	25	4	4	31	4	4	182	27	6	242	29	62	21	26	3,984

217

TABLE 18 (cont.) The age and social composition of farm households in Hedemarken in 1801

Age	Farmers Male U	Farmers Male M	Farmers Male W	Farmers Female M	Farmers Female W	Farmers' wives M	Farmers' children Male U	Farmers' children Male M	Farmers' children Female U	Farmers' children Female M	Livorefolk Male U	Livorefolk Male M	Livorefolk Male W	Livorefolk Female U	Livorefolk Female M	Livorefolk Female W	Other relatives Male U	Other relatives Male M	Other relatives Female U	Other relatives Female M	Other relatives Female W	Lodgers Male U	Lodgers Male M	Lodgers Male W	Lodgers Female U	Lodgers Female M	Lodgers Female W	Servants Male U	Servants Male M	Servants Male W	Servants Female U	Servants Female M	Servants Female W	Total
0–4	·	·	·	·	·	·	210	·	233	·	·	·	·	·	·	·	8	·	16	·	·	10	·	·	9	·	·	·	·	·	·	·	·	486
5–9	·	·	·	·	·	·	238	·	210	·	·	·	·	·	·	·	11	·	14	·	·	17	·	·	17	·	·	·	·	·	2	·	·	509
10–14	·	·	·	·	·	·	201	·	168	·	·	·	·	·	·	·	17	·	18	1	·	42	·	·	27	·	·	23	·	·	47	·	·	543
15–19	·	·	·	·	·	2	119	1	101	·	·	·	·	·	·	·	17	·	19	3	·	14	·	·	16	·	·	99	3	·	154	·	·	543
20–24	4	11	·	·	·	40	84	2	75	2	·	·	·	·	·	·	11	2	17	3	·	17	2	·	5	2	·	95	3	·	187	1	·	564
25–29	3	31	·	·	·	43	41	1	29	2	·	·	·	·	·	·	10	1	13	3	·	14	3	·	7	2	·	32	2	·	83	1	·	316
30–34	4	55	·	·	1	83	15	·	10	1	·	·	·	·	·	·	10	1	3	·	·	16	7	·	4	6	·	18	1	·	42	1	3	285
35–39	3	86	·	·	1	111	3	1	2	·	·	·	·	·	·	·	3	1	4	1	·	3	1	·	9	2	·	8	1	·	22	1	2	269
40–44	1	107	1	·	5	87	1	·	·	·	1	4	·	·	1	·	4	2	5	·	·	1	3	1	13	2	2	8	1	·	12	1	3	262
45–49	1	100	3	·	3	84	·	·	·	·	1	8	·	·	3	3	2	1	2	1	3	5	1	1	9	1	5	3	1	·	9	1	2	251
50–54	·	99	2	·	5	63	·	·	·	·	1	8	2	·	11	5	3	2	5	·	·	1	2	·	3	3	7	1	·	·	6	1	1	227
55–59	·	52	1	·	1	40	·	·	·	·	1	18	6	·	8	9	3	1	3	1	·	4	1	1	4	3	5	1	·	2	2	·	2	171
60–64	·	35	1	·	·	26	·	·	·	·	1	24	7	·	17	18	1	1	2	·	·	6	3	4	6	3	5	·	·	·	2	·	·	161
65–69	·	15	·	·	1	17	·	·	·	·	·	14	7	·	18	21	·	·	·	·	4	5	5	8	5	3	12	1	·	·	·	·	·	127
70–74	·	8	·	·	·	5	·	·	·	·	·	18	7	·	24	19	·	1	1	·	2	4	4	2	2	2	14	·	·	·	2	·	·	111
75–79	·	3	·	·	·	·	·	·	·	·	·	8	7	1	18	17	1	·	·	·	·	3	2	3	3	1	8	·	·	·	·	·	·	82
80–84	·	·	·	·	·	·	·	·	·	·	1	6	6	1	14	7	·	·	·	·	1	3	2	1	3	1	4	·	·	·	·	·	·	44
85–89	·	·	·	·	·	·	·	·	·	·	1	3	1	·	4	5	·	·	·	·	1	·	·	·	1	·	·	·	·	·	·	·	·	17
90–94	·	·	·	·	·	·	·	·	·	·	·	·	·	·	·	·	·	·	·	·	·	·	·	·	1	·	·	·	·	·	·	·	·	1
95–99	·	·	·	·	·	·	·	·	·	·	·	·	·	·	·	·	·	·	·	·	·	·	·	·	·	·	·	·	·	·	·	·	·	·
Total	**16**	**602**	**8**	**1**	**18**	**601**	**912**	**5**	**828**	**5**	**5**	**111**	**43**	**2**	**118**	**104**	**98**	**13**	**122**	**13**	**12**	**146**	**36**	**21**	**142**	**31**	**63**	**289**	**12**	**2**	**570**	**6**	**14**	**4,969**

TABLE 18 (cont.)   The age and social composition of crofter households in Hedemarken 1801

Age	Crofters						Crofters' wives	Crofters' children				Liverefolk				Other relatives						Lodgers						Servants			Total
	Male			Female				Male		Female		Male		Female		Male			Female			Male			Female			Male	Female		
	U	M	W	U	M	W	M	U	M	U	M	M	W	M	W	U	M	W	U	M	W	U	M	W	U	M	W	U	U	W	
0–4	.	.	.	.	.	.	.	318	.	281	.	.	.	.	.	15	.	.	20	.	.	17	.	.	26	.	.	.	.	.	677
5–9	.	.	.	.	.	.	.	295	.	288	.	.	.	.	.	12	.	.	13	.	.	20	.	.	14	.	.	.	.	.	642
10–14	.	.	.	.	.	.	.	187	.	147	.	.	.	.	.	2	.	.	5	.	.	13	.	.	11	.	.	3	6	.	374
15–19	1	.	.	.	.	.	1	84	1	49	.	.	.	.	.	2	.	.	6	.	.	11	2	.	8	1	.	3	7	.	166
20–24	1	33	.	.	.	.	35	45	1	15	.	.	.	.	.	2	1	.	5	2	.	6	2	.	11	2	.	3	6	.	182
25–29	1	76	1	.	.	.	81	17	2	9	3	.	.	.	.	2	2	.	2	1	.	2	2	1	6	2	.	2	6	.	217
30–34	1	123	1	.	1	3	122	4	.	2	1	.	.	.	.	1	.	.	2	1	.	2	1	.	14	7	3	2	3	1	295
35–39	.	144	2	.	1	3	150	1	1	2	1	.	.	.	.	1	.	.	2	1	.	2	1	.	16	5	2	.	.	.	334
40–44	.	123	1	1	.	2	130	.	.	5	.	.	.	.	.	1	1	.	2	.	1	2	1	2	10	.	5	.	.	.	284
45–49	.	144	1	1	1	2	152	.	.	.	.	.	.	.	.	1	.	.	2	1	1	2	1	3	12	2	12	1	1	.	328
50–54	.	108	1	.	1	7	95	.	.	.	.	1	.	2	1	3	1	.	3	2	8	3	1	1	7	3	5	.	.	.	248
55–59	.	85	1	.	.	3	85	.	.	.	.	.	.	2	2	1	2	1	.	3	.	3	1	3	13	7	12	.	1	.	219
60–64	.	52	2	.	.	2	42	.	.	.	.	2	.	3	1	1	2	2	2	4	5	2	2	3	7	4	17	.	.	.	145
65–69	.	37	1	.	.	3	33	.	.	.	.	1	.	1	1	2	3	.	2	4	8	1	5	.	2	4	19	.	.	.	123
70–74	.	20	.	.	.	1	16	.	.	.	.	1	3	2	4	1	1	3	1	2	4	2	.	.	3	2	9	.	.	.	73
75–79	.	6	.	.	.	.	11	.	.	.	.	.	.	.	1	1	.	.	1	.	5	4	.	.	.	.	.	.	.	.	42
80–84	.	4	1	.	.	1	2	.	.	.	.	2	.	1	1	1	1	.	.	1	6	5	2	1	.	2	5	.	.	.	24
85–89	.	1	.	.	.	.	.	.	.	.	.	.	.	.	.	.	.	1	.	.	1	6	1	1	.	1	1	.	.	.	4
90–94	.	.	.	.	.	.	.	.	.	.	.	.	.	.	.	.	.	.	.	.	.	.	.	.	.	.	.	.	.	.	.
95–99	.	.	.	.	.	.	.	.	.	.	.	.	.	.	.	.	.	.	.	.	.	.	.	.	.	.	.	.	.	.	.
Total	4	956	11	2	3	24	955	951	5	798	5	6	6	12	7	39	14	7	65	18	39	95	23	16	157	31	99	11	24	1	4,377

Population and Society in Norway 1735–1865

NOTE TO TABLE 18

This table is drawn from the enumerators' returns for the 1801 censuses of the parishes of Herøy (Sunnmøre), Nes and Ål (Hallingdal) and Nes and Ringsaker (Hedemarken) now in the riksarkiv, Oslo.

Columns marked U contain unmarried people, while M and W contain the married and widowed respectively. The livørefolk were people who had some claim on the income of the farm—or more rarely the croft. They were usually the retired parents of the farmer or crofter. People in the column headed 'Other relatives' were related to the head of the household or to his wife, but were not either his children or in receipt of livøre. Some members of this group were described as servants in the census schedules. The 'lodgers' were not related to the head of the household or to his wife.

Because of the size of parts of table 18, certain of the columns headed U, M and W have been omitted when they contained no entries.

There are a few discrepancies between the numbers in table 18 and those of tables presented either in the text or the statistical appendix. These arise partly because it was possible to include some people in one table, but not in another, as, for instance, when age or marital status was given but not occupation. Mainly, however, the errors are mine in drawing up the tables. It will be noted that the Hedemarken farm households in table 18 do not contain six 'gentlemen farmers' included in the other tables in the statistical appendix.

TABLE 19 *Marriages between bachelors and widows together with total marriages in Herøy, Hallingdal and Hedemarken, 1827–65**

	Herøy marriages		Hallingdal marriages		Hedemarken marriages	
	Total	Bachelor/ widow	Total	Bachelor/ widow	Total	Bachelor/ widow
1827–35	192	27	706	42	651	42
1836–45	226	23	1,019	84	810	38
1846–55	256	25	890	49	935	26
1856–65	280	33	484	19	708	21
1827–65	954	108	3,099	194	3,104	127

* As in table 10 above.

TABLE 20   *Distribution of farmers' and crofters' children living at home in Herøy, Hallingdal and Hedemarken in 1801**

No. of children	Farmers			Crofters		
	Herøy	Hallingdal	Hedemarken	Herøy	Hallingdal	Hedemarken
0	90	99	93	51	178	226
1	77	82	106	26	191	275
2	83	109	121	11	157	206
3	52	127	109	5	156	158
4	38	99	107	2	79	94
5	15	94	66	—	48	27
6	8	61	28	—	13	12
7	2	32	15	—	6	1
8	—	11	2	—	2	1
9	—	6	4	—	—	—
10	—	2	—	—	—	—
Total	365	722	651	95	830	1,000

* Source as above, table 16.

TABLE 21   *Children of farmers and crofters aged 11–20 and 20 years and over living with their parents in Herøy, Hallingdal and Hedemarken in 1801**

	Farmers' children				Crofters' children			
	Sons		Daughters		Sons		Daughters	
	11–20	Over 20	11–20	Over 20	11–20	Over 20	11–20	Over 20
Herøy	111	28	121	33	—	—	—	—
Hallingdal	409	178	368	115	261	81	219	63
Hedemarken	321	148	269	121	271	72	196	38

* As above, table 16.

TABLE 22 *Distribution of servants ('tjenestefolk') amongst the households of farmers and crofters in Herøy, Hallingdal and Hedemarken in 1801**

No. of servants	Farmers			Crofters		
	Herøy	Hallingdal	Hedemarken	Herøy	Hallingdal	Hedemarken
0	160	437	319	87	792	975
1	124	127	97	7	31	20
2	59	82	87	1	5	2
3	16	44	51	—	2	1
4	3	19	45	—	—	1
5	3	9	23	—	—	—
6	—	1	14	—	—	1
7	—	1	7	—	—	—
8	—	—	3	—	—	—
9	—	2	2	—	—	—
10	—	—	2	—	—	—
11	—	—	1	—	—	—
Total	365	722	651	95	830	1,000

* As above, table 16.

TABLE 23 *Distribution of relatives, other than children, of the heads of households or of their wives, amongst the households of farmers and crofters in Herøy, Hallingdal and Hedemarken in 1801**

No. of relatives	Farmers			Crofters		
	Herøy	Hallingdal	Hedemarken	Herøy	Hallingdal	Hedemarken
0	270	476	330	89	729	860
1	59	108	138	5	67	89
2	21	75	112	1	25	42
3	7	36	38	—	6	6
4	7	15	14	—	3	3
5	1	6	10	—	—	—
6	—	2	4	—	—	—
7	—	3	3	—	—	—
8	—	—	1	—	—	—
9	—	1	1	—	—	—
Total	365	722	651	95	830	1,000

* As above, table 16.

TABLE 24   *Distribution of lodgers, who were not related to the heads of households or their wives, amongst the households of farmers and crofters in Herøy, Hallingdal and Hedemarken in 1801* *

No. of lodgers	Farmers			Crofters		
	Herøy	Hallingdal	Hedemarken	Herøy	Hallingdal	Hedemarken
0	293	406	368	80	546	745
1	50	184	182	10	146	152
2	15	76	68	4	71	70
3	6	32	22	—	37	18
4	1	16	6	—	19	7
5	—	4	2	1	5	2
6	—	3	—	—	3	4
7	—	1	1	—	3	1
8	—	—	—	—	—	—
9	—	—	2	—	—	1
Total	365	722	651	95	830	1,000

* As above, table 16.

TABLE 25   *The age gap separating farmers and crofters from their respective wives in Sunnmøre, Ryfylke, Hallingdal, Hedemarken and Østerdalen in 1801* *

	Same age	1–4 years	5–9 years	10–14 years	15 and over	All ages
Sunnmøre	47	287	201	138	112	785
Ryfylke	103	607	463	301	244	1,718
Hallingdal	63	479	429	266	156	1,393
Hedemarken	91	586	497	229	153	1,556
Østerdalen	116	656	491	247	107	1,617
All areas	420	2,615	2,081	1,181	772	7,069

* Bibliography, unprinted sources, riksarkiv, Oslo, item 1.

TABLE 26   *The age gap separating farmers and crofters from their respective wives in parts of Norway in 1801 classified according to whether wife or husband the elder partner**

		Age gap (years)								
		1–4		5–9		10–14		15+		
	Same age	Husband older	Wife older	Husband older	Wife older	Husband older	Wife older	Husband older	Wife older	Total
Sunnmøre	47	140	147	94	107	74	64	56	56	785
Ryfylke	103	353	254	294	169	190	111	141	103	1,718
Hallingdal	63	297	182	319	110	208	58	119	37	1,393
Hedemarken	91	305	281	307	190	145	84	106	47	1,556
Østerdalen	116	411	245	356	135	177	70	81	26	1,617
All areas	420	1,506	1,109	1,370	711	794	387	503	269	7,069

* For the parishes covered by this analysis see bibliography, unprinted sources, riksarkivet, no. 1.

TABLE 27   *Marital status of farmers and crofters in Sunnmøre, Ryfylke, Hallingdal, Hedemarken and Østerdalen in 1801**

Marital status†	Ryfylke	Sunnmøre	Hallingdal	Hedemarken	Østerdalen
		Farmers			
I i	760	429	514	478	797
I ii	139	84	56	58	80
I iii	10	12	5	5	1
I iv	1	1	—	—	—
II i	136	89	57	46	77
II ii	21	10	5	8	8
II iii	2	2	1	—	—
III i	12	15	4	2	4
III ii	3	2	—	2	1
III iii	1	1	—	—	—
III iv	—	1	—	—	—
IV i	2	1	—	1	1
IV ii	—	1	—	1	—
Total marriages	1,087	648	642	601	969

TABLE 27 (*cont.*)

Marital status†	Ryfylke	Sunnmøre	Hallingdal	Hedemarken	Østerdalen
		Crofters			
I i	474	82	655	809	573
I ii	37	12	30	36	25
I iii	2	—	2	2	—
I iv	1	1	—	—	—
II i	63	28	51	77	41
II ii	22	7	9	15	3
II iii	2	3	—	1	1
III i	21	2	4	9	4
III ii	5	2	—	3	—
IV i	1	—	—	3	—
IV ii	2	—	—	—	—
V iii	1	—	—	—	—
Total marriages	631	137	751	955	647
Population of all areas in 1801	11,056	4,368	9,585	9,603	12,596

* For the parishes covered by this analysis see bibliography, unprinted sources, riks-arkivet, Oslo, no. 1.

† The numerals specify the current marital status of the marriage partners. Hence a woman in her third marriage is entered here as iii, whilst a man in his second is entered II.

TABLE 28 *Age gap separating farmers from their wives in marriages where neither partner previously married in parts of Norway in 1801 classified according to whether the wife or the husband the elder partner**

		Age gap (years)								
		1–4		5–9		10–14		15+		
	Same age	Hus-band	Wife	Hus-band	Wife	Hus-band	Wife	Hus-band	Wife	Total
		older		older		older		older		
Sunnmøre	35	92	103	56	66	36	28	7	6	429
Ryfylke	46	208	125	159	67	86	26	33	10	760
Hallingdal	29	114	55	156	24	92	6	36	2	514
Hedemarken	34	110	63	127	34	68	9	31	2	478
Østerdalen	67	219	119	202	54	92	14	27	3	797
All areas	211	743	465	700	245	374	83	134	23	2,978

* As in table 26.

225

TABLE 29 *Age gap separating crofters from their wives in marriages where neither partner previously married in parts of Norway in 1801 classified according to whether the wife or the husband the elder partner**

		Age gap (years)								
		1–4		5–9		10–14		15+		
	Same age	Husband older	Wife	Husband older	Wife	Husband older	Wife	Husband older	Wife	Total
Sunnmøre	5	17	12	9	12	8	11	5	3	82
Ryfylke	40	99	87	73	63	42	38	14	18	474
Hallingdal	28	163	103	138	65	83	32	29	14	655
Hedemarken	49	158	193	143	119	48	49	27	23	809
Østerdalen	40	156	93	117	60	51	32	21	3	573
All areas	162	593	488	480	319	232	162	96	61	2,593

* As in table 26.

TABLE 30 *Children 1–10 per 100 women 21–50 in the rural districts of Norwegian counties 1801–65**

	Children 1–10					
	1801	1825	1835	1845	1855	1865
Østfold	11,700	13,537	15,051	14,559	17,562	21,441
Akershus	14,906	17,757	18,445	17,736	22,880	29,199
Hedmark	15,489	19,279	20,176	20,079	26,245	32,082
Oppland	17,270	22,335	24,648	23,713	29,555	31,852
Buskerud	13,606	15,931	16,880	16,940	19,508	21,215
Vestfold	9,033	11,235	12,493	12,306	15,134	16,022
Telemark	11,604	13,932	16,137	15,099	16,548	17,161
Aust-Agder	7,979	9,477	10,556	11,552	12,446	14,676
Vest-Agder	8,485	9,476	10,988	12,086	13,155	13,678
Rogaland	9,264	13,765	15,648	16,919	20,157	19,740
Hordaland	14,706	18,539	20,957	21,351	25,626	27,151
Sogn and Fjordane	12,317	15,418	17,122	18,231	19,105	21,362
Møre and Romsdal	12,273	14,011	16,350	16,848	19,264	22,418
Sør-Trøndelag	12,733	14,120	15,899	16,989	17,684	20,816
Nord-Trøndelag	10,426	12,365	14,138	14,237	16,191	18,700
Nordland	13,048	13,157	14,508	14,785	18,666	22,774
Troms and Finnmark	7,146	7,838	9,574	9,907	13,307	15,879
Norway	201,967	242,172	269,570	273,337	323,033	366,166

Appendix 1

TABLE 30 (cont.)

	1801	1825	1835	1845	1855	1865
			Women 21–50			
Østfold	8,637	9,584	9,954	11,603	13,342	14,994
Akershus	11,854	12,395	12,761	14,831	17,256	20,143
Hedmark	12,234	14,587	15,080	17,341	19,634	22,186
Oppland	13,332	16,683	17,810	20,192	22,266	23,111
Buskerud	10,274	11,951	12,289	13,596	14,134	14,473
Vestfold	7,564	8,952	9,464	10,598	12,213	12,220
Telemark	9,031	10,268	11,322	12,168	12,624	12,976
Aust-Agder	6,864	7,771	8,091	9,098	10,888	11,656
Vest-Agder	7,365	7,673	8,457	9,432	10,305	10,834
Rogaland	8,407	10,224	11,192	12,786	14,793	15,295
Hordaland	12,680	15,019	16,438	18,703	21,217	22,706
Sogn and Fjordane	11,078	13,108	13,864	15,639	16,616	17,155
Møre and Romsdal	12,499	12,916	13,541	15,399	17,033	18,938
Sør-Trøndelag	10,649	12,448	13,129	14,783	16,230	18,134
Nord-Trøndelag	9,057	11,090	11,767	13,190	14,539	15,710
Nordland	11,046	11,891	11,781	13,556	16,131	17,957
Troms and Finnmark	5,474	6,497	6,856	8,087	9,766	11,218
Norway	168,049	193,057	203,796	231,002	257,987	279,706
		Children 1–10 per 100 women 21–50				
Østfold	135	141	151	125	131	143
Akershus	126	143	145	119	133	149
Hedmark	127	132	134	116	134	145
Oppland	129	134	139	118	130	138
Buskerud	132	133	138	125	138	147
Vestfold	119	126	132	116	124	131
Telemark	128	136	143	124	131	132
Aust-Agder	116	122	131	127	114	126
Vest-Agder	115	123	130	128	128	126
Rogaland	110	134	140	132	136	129
Hordaland	116	123	127	114	121	120
Sogn and Fjordane	111	117	124	117	115	124
Møre and Romsdal	98	108	121	110	113	118
Sør-Trøndelag	120	113	121	115	109	115
Nord-Trøndelag	115	112	120	108	111	119
Nordland	118	111	123	109	116	127
Troms and Finnmark	130	121	140	123	136	141
Norway	120	126	132	118	125	131

* For the source material of these calculations see bibliography, official publications, nos. 1, 4, 5, 14 and 15.

227

15-2

TABLE 31   *Number of marriages between bachelors and spinsters, bachelors and widows, widowers and spinsters, widowers and widows in Norwegian 'counties' in the years 1841–55**

	Number of marriages between					
	Bachelors and spinsters			Bachelors and widows		
	1841–5	1846–50	1851–5	1841–5	1846–50	1851–5
Østfold	1,498	2,285	2,547	107	128	153
Akershus	2,014	3,248	3,653	157	197	208
Hedmark	1,327	3,933	4,466	55	167	155
Oppland	2,682	2,993	4,705	139	115	140
Buskerud	2,638	3,554	3,738	171	148	167
Vestfold	1,562	2,101	2,435	114	125	117
Telemark	1,867	2,305	2,446	118	82	86
Aust-Agder	1,680	1,881	2,045	87	72	88
Vest-Agder	1,452	1,504	1,651	94	79	90
Rogaland	2,740	2,738	2,825	145	142	163
Hordaland	3,513	3,894	3,894	328	357	323
Sogn and Fjordane	2,289	2,241	2,367	201	237	190
Møre and Romsdal	2,373	2,365	2,460	309	268	270
Sør-Trøndelag	2,572	2,581	2,815	235	178	151
Nord-Trøndelag	1,907	1,997	2,261	193	144	131
Nordland	1,939	2,180	2,446	223	201	217
Troms and Finnmark	1,378	1,753	1,957	171	184	179
	Widowers and spinsters			Widowers and widows		
Østfold	164	267	273	64	73	61
Akershus	205	280	403	48	86	98
Hedmark	138	297	390	36	120	99
Oppland	263	243	363	92	63	78
Buskerud	280	333	358	100	122	96
Vestfold	167	241	265	47	56	46
Telemark	275	272	268	89	78	57
Aust-Agder	193	213	233	39	41	38
Vest-Agder	223	173	172	48	37	41
Rogaland	363	309	338	107	110	89
Hordaland	542	550	537	148	164	166
Sogn and Fjordane	310	302	321	71	64	80
Møre and Romsdal	372	321	344	132	109	117
Sør-Trøndelag	313	240	259	99	60	65
Nord-Trøndelag	235	207	210	106	68	69
Nordland	330	284	276	132	105	92
Troms and Finnmark	180	182	200	64	59	54

TABLE 31 (*cont.*)

	Total marriages			Percentage of marriages between bachelors and spinsters		
	1841–5	1846–50	1851–5	1841–5	1846–50	1851–5
Østfold	1,833	2,753	3,034	81·6	83·0	83·9
Akershus	2,424	3,811	4,362	83·0	85·3	83·7
Hedmark	1,556	4,517	5,110	85·3	86·9	87·4
Oppland	3,176	3,414	5,286	84·5	87·7	89·0
Buskerud	3,189	4,157	4,359	82·6	85·4	85·7
Vestfold	1,890	2,523	2,863	82·6	83·3	84·9
Telemark	2,349	2,737	2,857	79·4	84·3	85·6
Aust-Agder	1,999	2,207	2,404	84·0	85·1	85·0
Vest-Agder	1,817	1,793	1,954	80·0	83·8	84·5
Rogaland	3,355	3,299	3,415	81·7	83·0	82·7
Hordaland	4,531	4,965	4,920	77·5	78·3	79·1
Sogn and Fjordane	2,871	2,844	2,958	79·7	78·8	80·0
Møre and Romsdal	3,186	3,063	3,191	74·4	77·2	77·1
Sør-Trøndelag	3,219	3,059	3,290	79·8	84·4	85·5
Nord-Trøndelag	2,441	2,416	2,671	78·2	82·7	84·7
Nordland	2,624	2,770	3,031	73·8	78·7	80·8
Troms and Finnmark	1,793	2,178	2,390	76·8	80·5	81·8

	Percentage of marriages between					
	Bachelors and widows			Widowers and spinsters		
Østfold	5·8	4·6	5·0	8·9	9·7	9·0
Akershus	6·5	5·2	4·8	8·5	7·3	9·2
Hedmark	3·5	3·7	3·0	8·9	6·6	7·6
Oppland	4·4	3·4	2·6	8·3	7·1	6·9
Buskerud	5·4	3·6	3·8	8·8	8·0	8·2
Vestfold	6·0	4·9	4·1	8·8	9·5	9·3
Telemark	5·0	3·0	3·1	11·7	9·9	9·4
Aust-Agder	4·4	3·3	3·7	9·6	9·6	9·7
Vest-Agder	5·2	4·4	4·6	12·3	9·6	8·8
Rogaland	4·3	4·3	4·7	10·8	9·4	9·9
Hordaland	7·2	7·2	6·6	12·0	11·1	10·9
Sogn and Fjordane	7·0	8·3	6·4	10·8	10·6	10·9
Møre and Romsdal	9·7	8·7	8·5	11·7	10·5	10·8
Sør-Trøndelag	7·3	5·8	4·6	9·7	7·8	7·9
Nord-Trøndelag	7·9	6·0	4·9	9·6	8·6	7·9
Nordland	8·5	7·2	7·2	12·6	10·2	9·1
Troms and Finnmark	9·6	8·5	7·5	10·0	8·4	8·4

TABLE 31 (*cont.*)

	Percentage of marriages between widowers and widows		
	1841–5	1846–50	1851–5
Østfold	3·5	2·7	2·0
Akershus	2·0	2·3	2·2
Hedmark	2·3	2·7	1·9
Oppland	2·9	1·8	1·5
Buskerud	3·1	2·9	2·2
Vestfold	2·5	2·2	1·6
Telemark	3·8	2·9	2·0
Aust-Agder	2·0	1·9	1·6
Vest-Agder	2·6	2·1	2·1
Rogaland	3·2	3·3	2·6
Hordaland	3·3	3·3	3·4
Sogn and Fjordane	2·5	2·3	2·7
Møre and Romsdal	4·1	3·5	3·7
Sør-Trøndelag	3·1	2·0	2·0
Nord-Trøndelag	4·3	2·8	2·6
Nordland	5·0	3·8	3·0
Troms and Finnmark	3·6	2·7	2·3

* As for table 9. The 'counties' here are not the official ones but are composed of the deaneries lying as nearly as possible within the proper county boundaries. The divisions have been made as follows:

'County'	Deaneries
Østfold	Mellem, Vestre and Nedre Borgesyssel.
Akershus	Nedre Romerike, Øvre Borgesyssel, Oslo diocesan deanery.
Hedmark	Hedemarken, Østerdalen, Øvre Romerike.
Oppland	Gudbrandsdalen, Toten and Valdres.
Buskerud	Hadeland, Hallingdal, Ringerike, Drammen, Kongsberg.
Vestfold	Jarlsberg, Larvik.
Telemark	Øvre and Nedre Telemark.
Aust-Agder	Østre and Vestre Nedenæs, Råbygdelaget.
Vest-Agder	Lister, Mandal, Kristiansand diocesan deanery.
Rogaland	Ryfylke, Stavanger, Karmsund, Jæren, Dalane.
Hordaland	Sunn- and Nordhordland, Hardanger and Voss, Bergen diocesan deanery.
Sogn and Fjordane	Ytre and Indre Sogn, Sunnfjord, Nordfjord.
Møre and Romsdal	Nordre and Søndre Sunnmøre, Nordmøre, Romsdal.
Sør-Trøndelag	Dalerne, Fosen, Trondheim diocesan deanery.
Nord-Trøndelag	Innherad, Numedal.
Nordland	Helgeland, Salten, Lofoten and Vesterålen.
Troms and Finnmark	Senja, Tromsø, Øst- and Vest-Finnmark.

2 *Questionnaires completed by Norwegian clergy*

Examples of forms annually completed by Norwegian parish priests. The first of these—to be found in Bragernes Prosti: Innkomne Saker 1817–18, 1–34, statsarkiv, Oslo—contained columns for the number of marriages, for the male and female legitimate and illegitimate births, and for male and female still-births. The dead were divided into the age groups under 5, 5–9, 10–19, 20–29 and so on up to 90–99. The still-births were entered only once, i.e. not amongst the totals of births and deaths. Nine questions had to be answered. They were:

1 How many twins, etc., born?
2 In which month was mortality greatest?
3 What sicknesses or epidemics prevailed?
4 Is vaccination widely known and practised?
5 How many people died as a result of an accident, and what kind?
6 Were there any suicides?
7 Were there any murders?
8 How many marriages took place between bachelors and widows?
9 What source of employment was the most important?

The following form was introduced in the 1830s, probably in 1832 when the *Tabelkontoret* was set up as a separate office in the Ministry of Finance to collect statistics. It will be seen that the questions were both greater in number and more complicated than in the form above.

1 How many marriages in each month?
2 How many marriages took place between:
   A Men not previously married and widows?
   B Widowers and women previously unmarried?
   C Widowers and widows?
3 How many legitimate and how many illegitimate children born each month?
4 How many twins, triplets or quads amongst the births?
5 How many of the still-births were of illegitimate children?
6 How many abnormal children born, and of what kind?

231

7   How many people died in each month?
8   How many of those who died were illegitimate children:
    A   under 1 year old?
    B   between 1 and 3 years?
    C   between 3 and 5 years?
    D   between 5 and 10 years?
9   What sicknesses were the most prevalent?
10 How many children are reported to have been baptised during the year?
11 Has anyone died during pregnancy, and if so how many and how old?
12 How many people, and of which sex, died as a result of an accident? What were these accidents?
13 Have any children been overlaid by their mothers, and if so how many and of what class were their parents?
14 Were any of the children overlaid illegitimate, and if so, how many?
15 Has anyone committed suicide, and if so how many, of what sex, by what means, and at what time of the year?
16 Are the reasons for the suicides known, and if so what were they?
17 Was anyone killed or murdered and if so how?

Bibliography

I. UNPRINTED SOURCES

Riksarkivet, Oslo

1. Census of Norway, 1 February 1801. Original returns from the parishes (*prestegjeldene*) of Nes and Ål (Hallingdal); Nes and Ringsaker (Hedemarken); Herøy, Ulstein (less Hareid), Vanylven (Sunnmøre); Torvastad, Avaldsnes, Skudenes, Skjold, Nedstrand, Vikedal, (Ryfylke); Elverum, Åmot, Tynset, Tolga, Trysil (Østerdalen).
2. Census of Norway, 30 April 1815. Returns from all parishes.
3. Returns of births, marriages, deaths and other information of a demographic character made annually by all Norwegian parish priests for the years 1815–65 (pakker FB 6–63). Due to the ravages of damp certain of these are not available. For the country as a whole this is the case with the returns covering 1834 and 1855. The returns from Herøy (Sunnmøre); Nes, Ål and Gol (Hallingdal); Nes and Ringsaker (Hedemarken) have been used extensively in this study. Returns from Herøy are not available for 1834, 1855, 1859 and 1865. For Nes, Ål and Gol (Hallingdal) this is the case with the years 1834, 1855, 1857, 1860, 1863, 1864 and 1865. The Nes and Ringsaker (Hedemarken) returns are not available for 1834, 1855, 1857, 1860 and 1863.

Statsarkivet, Oslo

1. Bragernes Prosti, Indkomne Sager 1817–18, 1–34.
2. Parish registers of births, marriages and deaths from the following: Nes and Ål (Hallingdal) for the years 1815–60 and Gol (Hallingdal) for the years 1837–60.
3. Letters of Bishop Jakob Kærup of Kristiansand (12 May 1741): Bishop O. C. Bornemann of Bergen (10 March 1742) and Bishop E. Hagerup of Trondheim to Geheime-conferentz-raad J. L. von Holstein. Copies in Christiania bispearkiv. Ministerielle forretninger. Innberetninger. Rekke 1. Biskopene 1733–1814. Box 6.
4. Bishops' returns of births, marriages and deaths in the deaneries of Akershus (1733–1814); Kristiansand (1762–1814 on microfilm); Bergen (1736–1814 on microfilm).

Statistisk Sentralbyrå, Oslo

1. Census of Norway, 15 August 1769. Manuscript copy.
2. Returns of births, marriages and deaths from various parts of Norway in the years 1735–1800 (*pakker FB 1–5*).

Norsk Historisk Kjeldeskrift-institutt, Oslo

1. Kjeldeskriftfondets manuskripter 175–86.

II. OFFICIAL PUBLICATIONS [Norges Offisielle Statistikk]

1. *Første række, tabeller over folkemængden i Norge den 29de november 1835.* Christiania, 1838.
2. *Anden række, tabeller over udsæd og avl samt kreaturhold i Norge den 29de november 1835.* Christiania, 1839.
3. *Fjerde række, tabeller over ægteviede, fødte og døde i Norge for aarene 1801 til 1835 inclusive.* Christiania, 1839.
4. *Ottende række, tabeller over folkemængden i Norge den 31te december 1845 samt over de i tidsrummet 1836–1845 ægteviede, fødte og døde.* Christiania, 1847.
5. *Sextende række, tabeller over folkemængden i Norge den 31te december 1855 samt over de i tidsrummet 1846–1855 ægteviede, fødte og døde.* Christiania, 1857.
6. *Oversigt over de af amtmændene afgivne rapporter angaaende Norges œconomiske tilstand m.m. ved udgangen af aaret 1829.* Christiania, 1831.
7. *Beretninger om den œconomiske tilstand m.m. i Norge ved udgangen af aaret 1835, underdanigst afgivne af rigets amtmænd.* Christiania, 1836.
8. *Beretning om kongeriget Norges œkonomiske tilstand i aarene 1836–1840.* Christiania, 1843.
9. *Beretning om kongeriget Norges œkonomiske tilstand i aarene 1840–1845.* Christiania, 1847.
10. *Beretning om kongeriget Norges œkonomiske tilstand i aarene 1846–1850.* Christiania, 1853.
11. *Beretning om kongeriget Norges œkonomiske tilstand i aarene 1851–1855.* Christiania, 1858.
12. *Ældre række, C, no. 2, Beretning om kongeriget Norges œkonomiske tilstand i aarene 1856–60.* Christiania, 1863.
13. *Ældre række, C, no. 2, Beretning om kongeriget Norges œkonomiske tilstand i aarene 1861–65.* Christiania, 1867–9.
14. *Ældre række, C, no. 1, Tabeller vedkommende folketællingerne i Norge i aarene 1801 og 1825.* Christiania, 1874.

15. *Ældre række, C, no. 1, Resultaterne af folketællingen i Norge 1 Januar 1866.* Christiania, 1868–9.
16. *Ældre række, C, no. 1, Tabeller vedkommende folkemængdens bevægelse i aarene 1856–1865.* Christiania, 1868–9.
17. *Tredie række, no. 106, Oversigt over de vigtigste resultater af de statistiske tabeller vedkommende folkemængdens bevægelse 1866–1885.* Kristiania, 1890.
18. *Norway. Official publication for the Paris exhibition 1900.* Kristiania, 1900.
19. *Statistiske oversikter for Norge 1926.* Oslo, 1926.
20. *Statistik Årbok for Norge 1940.* Oslo, 1940.
21. *Statistiske oversikter for Norge 1948.* Oslo, 1949.
22. *Census of Ireland, 1841, reports of commissioners,* Parl. Papers, London, 1843, xxiv.
23. *Reports of the commissioners for inquiring into the conditions of the poorer classes in Ireland, reports from commissioners,* Parl. Papers, London, 1836, xxx–xxxiv.

III. BOOKS AND ARTICLES

Allwood, Martin S. *Eilert Sundt, a pioneer in sociology and social anthropology.* Oslo, 1957.
Armengaud, André and Reinhard, Marcel. *Histoire générale de la population mondiale.* Paris, 1961.
Aschehoug, T. H. 'Om Norges Folkemængde i aarene 1664–66', *Norsk Tidsskrift for Videnskab og Litteratur,* **2** (Christiania, 1848), 305–407.
Backer, Julie E. 'Population statistics and population registration in Norway. Part I. The vital statistics of Norway, an historical review', *Population Studies,* **1** (London, 1947–8), 212–26: part II (no title), *Population Studies,* **2** (1948–9), 318–38.
Baalsrud, A. 'Veivesenets og veibygningens utvikling i Norge', *Norsk Geografisk Tidsskrift,* **11** (Oslo, 1928–9).
Barclay, G. W. Techniques of population analysis. London, 1958.
Berg, Wessel. *Kongelige reskripter, resolutioner, og collegial-breve for Norge i tidsrummet 1660–1813,* vol. IV, 1797–1813. Christiania, 1845.
Biographie Universelle, ancienne et moderne, vol. 36. Paris, 1823.
Bjørklund, Oddvar. *Marcus Thrane: en stridsmann for menneskerett og fri tanke.* Oslo, 1951.
Petitionen fra 1850: Thraneforeningenes bønnskrift til Kongen. Oslo, 1957.
Bloch, Hofman Gevel, *Reise-Iagttagelser eller udtog af en dagbog holden paa en reise fra Throndhjem til Christiania i aaret 1806.* Kjøbenhavn, 1808.

Blom, G. P. *Underdanigst indberetning om en reise i udlandet til under-søgelse av fattigvæsenet og dets lovgivning.* Drammen, 1844.

Bødtker, Provst. 'Om letsindige ægteskaber blandt landalmuen', *Morgenbladet.* Christiania, 20 December 1850.

Boulding, Kenneth E. (ed.). *Thomas Robert Malthus. The first essay.* Ann Arbor, 1959.

Bremner, Robert. *Excursions in Denmark, Norway, Sweden including notices of the state of public opinion in those countries and anecdotes of their courts,* 2 vols. London, 1840.

Broch, O. J. *Kongeriget Norge og det norske folk, dets sociale forhold, sundhetstilstand, næringsveie, samfærdselsmidler og ekonomi.* Kristiania, 1876.

Brooke, A. de Capell. *Travels through Sweden, Norway and Finmark to the North Cape in the summer of 1820.* London, 1823.

Buch, Leopold von. *Travels through Norway and Lapland during the years 1806, 1807 and 1808,* translated from the German by John Black. London, 1813.

Bull, Edvard. *Arbeidermiljø under det industrielle gjennombrudd,* Oslo, 1958.
'Industrial workers and their employers in Norway circa 1900', *Scandinavian Economic History Review,* **3**, no. 1 (Copenhagen, 1955), 64–84.
'Norway: industrialisation as a factor in economic growth', *Contributions to the first international conference of economic history Stockholm 1960,* pp. 261–71. Paris–The Hague, 1960.

Carr-Saunders, A. M. *World population: past growth and present trends.* Oxford, 1936.

Catteau-Colleville, J. P. G. *Tableau statistique des états danois envisagés sous les rapports du mécanisme social,* 3 vols. Paris, 1802.

Chambers, J. D. *The vale of Trent 1670–1800.* Economic History Review Supplement, **3**. London, 1957.

Chrichton, Andrew and Wheaton, Henry. *Scandinavia ancient and modern: being a history of Denmark, Sweden and Norway.* Edinburgh, 1838.

Christie, Nils. *Eilert Sundt som fanteforsker og sosial statistiker.* Institute of Sociology, University of Oslo, Stencil series. Oslo, 1958.

Christopherson, H. O. *Eilert Sundt, Humanist og samfunnsforsker.* Oslo, 1959.
Eilert Sundt. En dikter i kjensgjerninger. Oslo, 1962.

Cipolla, Carlo. *The economic history of world population.* Harmondsworth, 1962.

Clark, George. *War and society in the seventeenth century.* Cambridge, 1958.

Clarke, Edward Daniel. *Travels in various countries of Europe, Asia and Africa*, part III, *Scandinavia*. London, 1819.

Coale, Ansley J. and Hoover, Edgar M. *Population growth and economic development in low income countries. A case study of India's prospects.* Oxford, 1959.

Collin Nils. 'Nogle reisebemerkninger nedskrevne 1757', *Norsk Historisk Tidsskrift*, 4 (Kristiania, 1877), 503–11.

Connell, K. H. *The population of Ireland, 1750–1845.* Oxford, 1950.
'Some unsettled problems in English and Irish population history', 1750–1845', *Irish Historical Studies*, 7 (Dublin, 1951).
'Peasant marriage in Ireland: its structure and development since the famine', *Economic History Review*, 2nd ser. 14 (London, 1962).

Daae, Ludvig, L. 'Uaar og hungersnød i Norge 1740–43', *Videnskabs-Selskabets Forhandlinger*. Christiania, 1868.

Dahl, N. *Anviisning til at føre et lykkeligt liv. En haandbog for de mere oplyste blandt almuens ungdom.* Bergen, 1837.

Demographic yearbook, 1961. United Nations—New York, 1961.

Derry, Thomas Kingston. *A short history of Norway*, London. 1957.

Drachmann, Poul. *The industrial development and commercial policies of the three Scandinavian countries.* Oxford, 1915.

Djupedal, Reidar. 'Den store innsamlinga av topografisk historisk og språkleg tilfang ved embetsmennene 1743 og "Det Kongerige Norge"', *Heimen*. Oslo, 1955–7.

Drake, M. 'An elementary exercise in parish register demography', *Economic History Review*, 2nd ser. 14 (London, 1961), 427–45.
'Marriage and population growth in Ireland, 1750–1845', *Economic History Review*, 2nd ser. 16 (London, December 1963), 301–13.

Dybvik, Daniel. 'Husmannsvesenet i Numedal', *Norsk Geografisk Tidsskrift*, 14, 7–8 (Oslo, 1954), 369–463.

Edwards, R. Dudley and Williams, T. Desmond (eds.). *The great famine.* Dublin, 1956.

'Efterretning om potatos—avling og bruk', *Nordske Intelligens Sedler*. Kristiania, 20 March 1765.

Eversley, D. E. C. 'A survey of population in an area of Worcestershire from 1660–1850', *Population Studies*, 10 (London, 1956–7), 253–79.
Social theories of fertility and the Malthusian debate. Oxford, 1959.

Falk, Hjalmar, Reichborn-Kjennerud, I. and Lid, Nils. 'Innsamling av norsk folkemedisin. Rettledning og ordliste', *Maal og Minne*. Kristiania, 1921.

'Om fattiges giftermaal', *Morgenbladet*. Christiania, 13 March 1853.

Fine, B. C. de. 'Beskrivelse over Stavanger amt 1743', *Norsk Magasin, Skrifter og Optegnelser angaaende Norge og Forfattede efter Reforma-*

tionen, samlede og udgivne af N. Nicolaysen, pp. 103–244. Christiania, 1870.

Fogel, Robert William. *Railroads and American economic growth: essays in econometric history*. Baltimore, 1964.

Folkevennen. *Et Tidsskrift udgivet af Selskabet for Folkeoplysningens Fræmme*. Kristiania, 1852–1900.

Forester, Thomas. *Norway in 1848 and 1849*. London, 1850.

Frimannslund, R. 'Gårds- og grannesamfunnsundersøkelsen' stencilled by Institutt for sammenlignende kulturforskning, Oslo.

Gille, H. 'The demographic history of the northern European countries in the eighteenth century', *Population Studies*, 3 (London, 1949–50), 3–65.

Glass, D. V. and Eversley, D. E. C. (eds.), *Population in history*. London, 1965.

Glass, D. V. and Grebenik, E. 'World population 1800–1950' in H. J. Habakkuk and M. Postan (eds.), *The Cambridge economic history of Europe*, VI. Cambridge, 1965.

Griffith, G. T. *Population problems of the age of Malthus*. Cambridge, 1926.

'Rickman's second series of eighteenth century population figures', *Journal of the Royal Statistical Society*, 92 (London, 1929).

Grøn, Fredrik. 'Folkemedisin i Setersdalen', *Maal og Minne*, pp. 65–80. Kristiania, 1909.

'Om kostholdet i Norge fra omkring 1500-tallet og op til vår tid', *Norsk videnskaps Akademiets Skrifter*, II, *Historisk-filosofisk klasse*. Oslo, 1941.

Habakkuk, H. J. 'English population in the eighteenth century', *Economic History Review*, 2nd ser. 6 (London, 1953), 117–33.

Harsin, Paul and Hélin Etienne. *Actes du colloque international de démographie historique, Liège 18–20, April 1963*. Paris, 1963.

Heckscher, Eli F. 'Swedish population trends before the industrial revolution', *Economic History Review*, 2nd ser. 2 (London, 1949), 266–77.

An economic history of Sweden, translated from the Swedish by Gøran Ohlin. Harvard, 1954.

Helland, Amund. *Norges land og folk. Topografisk-statistisk beskrevet*. Kristiania, 1885–1918.

Hertzberg, J. N. *Høifjeldsliv og Fjeldfolk 1863–1875*. Kristiania, 1900.

Hertzberg, Peder Harboe. *Underretning for bønder i Norge om den meget nyttige jord-frugt potatos at plante og bruge*. Bergen, 1774.

Hillman, Arthur. 'Eilert Sundt. Social surveyor extraordinary', *Sociological Review*, 43 (Keele, 1951).

Holm, Peter. 'Forsøg til en beskrivelse over Lister og Mandals amter',

Bibliography

Topographisk Journal for Norge, **2**, 8, pp. 35–114 and **3**, 9, pp. 57–128 (Christiania, 1793–4).
Holmsen, Andreas. 'The old Norwegian peasant community. General survey and introduction', *Scandinavian Economic History Review*, **4**, 1 (Copenhagen, 1956).
'Landowners and tenants in Norway', *Scandinavian Economic History Review*, **6**, 2 (Copenhagen, 1958).
Holst, Fredrik D. 'Om folketællingen i Norge i aaret 1825', *Budstikken*, pp. 633–64. Christiania, 1827.
Holst, Peter M. 'Helseforholdene i Norge omkring 1880', *Tidsskrift for Den Norske Lægeforening*. Oslo, 1955.
Hovde, B. J. *The Scandinavian countries 1720–1865*, II. Boston, 1943.
Hoven, E. Holmer. *Slik var vår barndoms hvite by Mandal i gamle dager*. Oslo, 1946.
'Hvilke forføininger kan og bør statsstyrelsen træffe for at indskrænke udgifterne til fattigvæsenet', *Morgenbladet*. Christiania, 25 August 1858.
Inglis, H. D. *A personal narrative of a journey through Norway, part of Sweden and the islands and states of Denmark*, 4th edn. London, 1837.
Jahn, Gunnar. 'Folketellingene 1801 og 1815 og befolkningsforholdene dengang', *Statsøkonomisk Tidsskrift*, **43** (Oslo, 1929), 201–18.
'Ennu engang folketellingen av 1801. Tilsvar til dr. Keilhau', *Statsøkonomisk Tidsskrift*, **44** (Oslo, 1930), 121–5.
James, Patricia (ed.). *The travel diaries of T. R. Malthus*. Cambridge, 1966.
Jensen, Magnus. *Norges historie II, Fra 1660 til våre dager*. Oslo, 1938.
Johnsen, Oscar Albert. *Norges Bønder. Utsyn over den norske bondestands historie*, 2nd ed. Oslo, 1936.
Keilhau, Wilhelm. *Det Norske folks liv og historie gjennem tidene*, **8** (1814–40), Oslo, 1929 and **9** (1840–70), Oslo, 1931.
'Folketellinger, Norges historie og logikk: svar til Gunnar Jahn', *Statsøkonomisk Tidsskrift*, **44** (Oslo, 1930), 33–45.
'Siste svar til Gunnar Jahn', *Statsøkonomisk Tidsskrift*, **44** (Oslo, 1930), 208–11.
Kiær, Anders Nicolai. 'Nogle oplysninger om forholdet mellem ægteskaber og fødsler med særligt hensyn til ægteskabernes stiftelsestid', *Det norske videnskabs-selskabets Forhandlinger*. Christiania, 1873.
'Nye bidrag til belysning av frugtbarhedsforholdene inden ægteskabet i Norge, *Det norske videnskaps-selskapets avhandlinger og skrifter*. Kristiania, 1902.
Kiær, A. Th. 'Det norske folks hovederhverv 1801 samt 1865–1900', *Statsøkonomisk Tidsskrift*, pp. 264–78. Kristiania, 1904.

Kraft, Jens. *Topographisk-statistisk beskrivelse over kongeriget Norge*, I–VI. Christiania, 1820–35.

Det søndenfjeldske Norge. Topographisk-statistisk beskrevet. Christiania, 1840.

Krause, John T. 'The medieval household: large or small?' *Economic History Review*, 2nd ser. 9 (London, 1956–7), 420–32.

'Changes in English fertility and mortality, 1781–1850', *Economic History Review*, 2nd ser. 11 (London, 1958), 52–70.

'Some implications of recent work in historical demography', *Comparative studies in Society and History*, 1 (The Hague, 1958–9), 164–88.

'Some neglected factors in the English industrial revolution', *Journal of Economic History*, 19 (New York, 1959), 528–40.

Kuczynski, R. R. *The measurement of population growth.* London, 1935.

Lady, A. *My Norske note book.* London, 1859.

Laing, Samuel. *Journal of a residence in Norway during the years 1834, 1835 and 1836. Made with a view to inquire into the moral and political economy of the country and the condition of its inhabitants.* 2nd. edn. London, 1851.

Langslet, Ola. *Nes Herred i Hallingdal.* Drammen, 1914.

Larsen, Karen. *A history of Norway.* Princeton, 1948.

Lassen, Aksel. *Fald og fremgang; træk af befolkningsudviklingen i Danmark 1645–1960.* Aarhus, 1965.

Lindstøl, T. *Mandtallet i Norge, 1701.* Kristiania, 1887.

Lorimer, Frank (ed.). *Culture and human fertility.* UNESCO, Paris, 1954.

Lous, J. C. *Om husmandsvæsenet.* Christiania, 1851.

Lunde, Peter. 'Kynnehuset. Vestegdske folkeminne', *Norsk Folkeminnelag*, 6. Kristiania, 1924.

Macarthur, Sir William P. 'Medical history of the famine', in R. Dudley Edwards and T. Desmond Williams (eds.), *The great famine.* Dublin, 1956.

McKeown, T. and Brown, R. G. 'Medical evidence related to English population changes in the eighteenth century', *Population Studies*, 9 (London, 1955–6), 119–41.

McKeown, T. and Record, R. G. 'Reasons for the decline of mortality in England and Wales during the nineteenth century', *Population Studies* (London, 1962), 16, 94–122.

Malm, O. *Kopper og vaccinationen i Norge.* Kristiania, 1915.

Malthus, T. R. *Essay on the principle of population.* Everyman edition, London, 1914.

Mannsåker, Dagfinn. *Det norske presteskapet i det 19 hundreåret.* Oslo, 1954.

Bibliography

Mardal, Magnus. *Norge, Sverige og den engelske trelasttoll 1817–50*. Oslo, 1957.

Marsh, David C. *The changing social structure of England and Wales 1871–1951*. London, 1958.

Marshall, T. H. 'The population problem during the industrial revolution', *Economic Journal: Economic History Supplement*, **1** (London, 1929), 429–56.

'Menigmands ven om M. Thranes arbeiderforeninger', *Morgenbladet*. Christiania, 13 November 1849.

Mohn, J. N. *Statistiske meddelelser om husmandsklassens betydning i samfundet og husmændenes økonomiske stilling*. Kristiania, 1880.

Folkemængdens forandringer i forskellige deler av riget siden 1769, delvis 1665. Kristiania, 1882.

Mohr, Otto Lous. 'Geistlige pionerer for vaksinasjonen i Norge: Nils Hertzberg og Nils Griis Alstrup Dahl', *Aftenpostens aftennummer*. Oslo, 26 and 27 July 1961.

Myklebust, Ivar. 'Svartedauden, pestår og reproduksjon', *Norsk Historisk Tidsskrift*, **37** (Oslo, 1954–6), 347–65.

Nergaard, Sigurd. 'Gard og grend: folkeminne fra Østerdalen', *Norsk Folkeminnelag*, **3** (Kristiania, 1921).

'Ufredstider: folkeminne fra Østerdalen', *Norsk Folkeminnelag*, **5** (Kristiania, 1922).

North, Douglass, C. 'The state of economic history', *American Economic Review* **55**, no. 2 (Stanford, 1965).

Ofstad, Kaare. 'Population statistics and population registration in Norway: part 3, population censuses', *Population Studies*, **3** (London, 1949–50), 66–75.

Otter, W. *The life and remains of the Rev. Edward Daniel Clarke, professor of mineralogy in the university of Cambridge*. London, 1824.

Øverland, O. A. *De norske bygdemagasiner*. Kristiania, 1913.

Palmström, H. 'The census of population in Norway, August 15th 1769', *Nordic Statistical Journal*, **8** (Stockholm, 1929).

Petersen, William. *The politics of population*. New York, 1965.

Pontoppidan, C. I. *Det sydlige Norge; efter kongelig allernaadigst Befalning ved Hielp af gode geographiske Korter og mathematiske observationer sammendraget og aflagt under bestyrelse af Hr. Conference-Raad I. Erichsen*. Kjøbenhavn, 1785.

Postan, M. M. and Titow, J. 'Heriots and prices on Winchester manors', *Economic History Review*, 2nd ser. **11** (London, 1959), 392–417.

Pram, Christian Henriksen. *Om befolkningen i Skandinavien og dens tilvæxt i tidsløbet 1769–1800*. Kjøbenhavn, 1809.

Population and Society in Norway 1735–1865

Rathke, Jens. *Afhandling om de norske fiskerier*. Kjøbenhavn, 1797–8.
'*Indberetning til commerce-collegiet om reiser (i Norge) i aarene 1800–02*, Kjøbenhavn, 1805. *Selskabet for de norske fiskeriers fremme*. Bergen, 1907.
Refsum, Helge. 'Eilert Sundt og folkemoralen', *Norsk Kultur-historie*, 4 (Oslo, 1940).
Reichborn-Kjennerud I., Grøn, F. and Kobro, I. *Medisinens historie i Norge*. Oslo, 1953.
'Vår gamle trolldomsmedisin', *Skrifter utgitt av det norske videnskaps-akademi*, Oslo, 1927, no. 6, 1933, no. 2, 1940, no. 1, 1943, no. 2.
Reinton, Lars. *Folk og fortid i Hol. ii. Frå 1815 til vår tid*. Oslo, 1943.
Rowntree, Griselda and Pierce, Rachel M. 'Birth control in Britain', *Population Studies*, 15 (London, 1961), 3–31, 121–60.
Rubin, Marcus. 'Population and birth rate, illustrated from historical statistics', *Journal of the Royal Statistical Society*, 63 (London, 1900), 596–625.
Russell, J. C. *British medieval population*. Albuquerque, New Mexico, 1948.
Sars, J. E. 'Folkemængdens bevægelse i Norge fra det 13 til det 17 Aarhundrede', *Norsk Historisk Tidsskrift*, 11, iii (Kristiania, 1881).
Schübeler, F. C. *Viridarium norvegicum. Norges vaextrige; et bidrag til nord Europas natur- og cultur historie*. Christiania, 1886–9.
Schweigaard, A. M. *Norges statistik*. Christiania, 1840.
Semmingsen, Ingrid. 'The dissolution of estate society in Norway', *Scandinavian Economic History Review*, 2, 2 (1954), 166–203.
Husmannsminner. Oslo, 1960.
Simey, T. S. and M. B. *Charles Booth. Social scientist*. Oxford, 1960.
Skappel, S. *Hedemarkens amt 1814–1914*. Kristiania, 1914.
Husmandsvæsenet i Norge. Kristiania, 1922.
Skougaard, Joh. *Det norske veivæsens historie med oversigt over statens veivæsens virksomhed i tidsrummet 1820–1896*. Kristiania, 1899.
'Skrider jordbruget i Norge fremad?', *Morgenbladet*. Christiania, 20 October 1849.
Stang, Thomas. *Den norske husmandsklasses tilstand*. Christiania, 1851.
Steen, Sverre. *Det norske folks liv og historie gjennem tidene*, VI (1720–70), Oslo, 1932 and VII (1779–1814), Oslo, 1933.
Kristiansands historie 1641–1814. Oslo, 1941.
Det gamle samfunn. Oslo, 1957.
Strøm, Hans. *Physisk og økonomisk beskrivelse over fogderiet Søndmør*. Sorøe, 1762.
Strøm, Kaare. 'The Norwegian coast', *Norsk Geografisk Tidsskrift*, 17 (Oslo, 1959–60).

Stys, W. 'The influence of economic conditions on the fertility of peasant women', *Population Studies*, **11**, 2 (London, 1957), pp. 136–48.

Sund, Oscar. 'Folketetthetsbegrepet', *Norsk Geografisk Tidsskrift*, **4** (Oslo, 1932–3).

Sundt, Eilert. *Om giftermaal i Norge: bidrag til kundskab om folkets kaar og sæder*. Christiania, 1855.

Beretning om fante- eller landstryger-folket i Norge. Et bidrag til kundskab om de laveste samfundsforholde. Christiania, 1850.

Om dødeligheden i Norge: bidrag til kundskab om folkets kaar og sæder. Christiania, 1855.

Om sædeligheds-tilstanden i Norge. Christiania, 1857.

Om Piperviken og Ruseløkbakken. Christiania, 1858.

Fiskeriets bedrift. Christiania, 1862.

Fortsatte bidrag angaaende sædeligheds-tilstanden i Norge. Christiania, 1864.

Om sædeligheds-tilstanden i Norge: tredie beretning. Christiania, 1866.

Om skab-klaaens udbredelse. Christiania, 1876.

'Bygde-Skikke', *Folkevennen*, **11** (Kristiania, 1862).

Om Ædrueligheds-tilstanden i Norge. Christiania, 1859.

'Sprogets Bygde-Skikke', *Folkevennen*, **13** (Kristiania, 1864).

'Om Vort Selskab', *Folkevennen*, **11** (Kristiania, 1862).

'Folkevennens første ti aar', *Folkevennen*, **10** (Kristiania, 1861).

'Harham. Et exempel fra fiskeri–distrikterne', *Folkevennen*, **7** (Kristiania, 1858), and *Folkevennen*, **8** (Kristiania, 1859).

'Arbeids væsen. 1. Haandsagen', *Folkevennen*, **13** (Kristiania, 1864).

'Bygde-Skikke: første Stykke', *Folkevennen*, **7** (Kristiania, 1857).

Tank, Roar. 'Studier i Christiania bys folkemengde i det syttende aarhundrede', *Norsk Historisk Tidsskrift*, 4th ser. **5** (Kristiania, 1909), 478–506.

Thaarup, F. R. *Veiledning til det Danske monarkies statistik*, 2nd ed. Kjøbenhavn, 1796.

Thomlinson, Ralph. *Population dynamics. Causes and consequences of world demographic change.* New York, 1965.

Thorsteinsson, T. 'The census of Iceland in 1703', *Nordic Statistical Journal*, **8** (Stockholm, 1929).

Tvethe, M. Braun. *Norges statistik.* Christiania, 1848.

United Nations Population Division. *The determinants and consequences of population trends.* New York, 1953.

Utterstrøm, G. 'Some population problems in pre-industrial Sweden', *Scandinavian Economic History Review*, **2**, 2 (Copenhagen, 1954), 103–65.

'Migratory labour and the herring fisheries of western Sweden in the eighteenth century', *Scandinavian Economic History Review*, **7**, i (Copenhagen, 1959), 3–40.

'Om vaccinationens tilstand i Norge i aaret 1816', *Budstikken*, **4** (Christiania, 1817).

Valen-Sendstad, Fartein. *Norske landbruks-redskaper, 1800–1850 årene.* De Sandvigske samlinger, Lillehammer, 1964.

Valstad, D. 'Et blik paa fattigvæsenet', *Morgenbladet*. Christiania, 29 July 1852.

Vig, Ole. 'Om landalmuens næringsdrift og levemaade', *Folkevennen*, **1** (Kristiania, 1852).

'Nogle ord om folketælling m.m.', *Folkevennen*, **4** (Kristiania, 1855).

Vogt, Johan. 'En generasjonsstatistikk for det norske folk', *Memorandum fra Oslo universitets sosialøkonomiske institutt*, Oslo, 29 January 1957.

Wendt, C. W. *Bidrag til børnekoppernes og vaccinationens historie i Danmark og om de sidste herskende koppeepidemier.* Kjøbenhavn, 1836.

Wiel, Ivar. 'Beskrivelse over Ringeriges og Hallingdals fogderi 1743', *Topographisk Journal for Norge*, **9** (Christiania, 1802–5), 30–2.

Woodham-Smith, Cecil. *The great hunger, Ireland 1845–49.* London, 1962.

Worm-Müller, Jakob S. *Norge gjennem nødsaarene. Den norske regjeringskommission 1807–1810.* Kristiania, 1918.

Woytinsky, W. S. and E. S. *World population and production.* New York, 1953.

Wrigley, E. A. *Industrial growth and population change.* Cambridge, 1961.

'Family limitation in pre-industrial England', *Economic History Review*, 2nd ser. **19** (London, April 1966).

X and Y (Two unknown quantities). *A long vacation ramble in Norway.* Cambridge, 1857.

Index

For the benefit of readers who know no Norwegian, å has been indexed with a, æ with ae, ø and ö with o.

Index

Biri: early cultivation of potatoes in, 55; glassworks in, 55
birth control: abortifacients, 70; condoms, 70; *see also* marriage, age at
births and birth rate, *see* fertility, population, statistics of
Bødtker, C. B., dean of Dalerne, on early marriage, 152
Borgesyssel, Mellem, Nedre, Vestre and Øvre, 5 n. 1; age at marriage in, 202
Borgund, 63 n. 5
Björkö, large families on, 83
Bornemann, O. C., bishop of Bergen, makes mistakes in return of births and deaths for 1742, 16
Borre, 63 n. 5
Børsa, 63 n. 5
Botne, 5 n. 1, 63 n. 5
Bratsberg, *see* Telemark, county
breast-feeding, duration of in various parts of Norway, 70 n. 3
Bremen, population of in 1812 and 1867, 42
Brooke, Capell, on Gudbrandsdalen, 100
Buch, Leopold von, on Nes and Ringsaker, 100-1
burden of dependency, *see* dependency, burden of
burial practices, 8-9
Buskerud (county), 56, 58, 63 n. 5, 89, 106-7, 210-11, 226-30
Byneset, 63 n. 5

Catteau-Calleville, J. P. G., 15
censuses
Denmark-Norway (1769), 2
England (1801), 2
France (1801), 2
Iceland (1703), 2
Ireland (1831), 2, (1841), 153-4
Norway (1769-1865): content of, 3-5; digital preferences in, 4; effect of tax fears on, 4, 5 n. 4, 58; effect of timing on, 4-5; efficiency of, 150, Jahn on, 6, Kiær on, 6, officials on, 5, Sundt on, 5-6; organisation of, 3-5; 89; problems of taking, 2-3, 150
Sweden (1749), 2
United States of America (1790), 2
Chartism and Marcus Thrane's labour movement, 24

Chrichton, Andrew, on Norwegian clergy, 11-12
Christiania, diocese, *see* Akershus
Christiania, town, *see* Oslo
Christians (Kristians), *see* Oppland
Christiansand, *see* Kristiansand
Church and state in Norway, close relations of, 13; *see also* clergy
Clark Daniel: on effect of eating fish on human fertility, 83; on Norwegian labourer's diet, 64; travels to Sweden with Malthus, 31
clergy
Norwegian state: German speaking, 32; hold on population, 8-13; knowledge of population conditions, 32, 152, 231-2; numbers of, relative to population, 9-10; pioneers of potato cultivation, 54; amounts of potatoes and grain on glebes of, 55-7; pioneers of inoculation and vaccination, 50-1; 'potato-priests', 65; rationalism of, 10; role in census-taking, 3, in registration of births, marriages and deaths, 7-9, 15; questionnaires on population matters, answered by, 124, 231-2; testimonials to efficiency of in civil matters, 11-12, 150
Church of England: and population returns, 11-12
Collett, John: meets Malthus, 32; on potato cultivation in Norway, 63
communications in Norway: carriage of freight, 72; difficulties of, 7, 10, 150; road mileage by 1840, 72; and spread of disease, 72
confirmation ceremony, religious in Norway: held in 'great consideration', 13; penalty for not preparing for, 13
Connaught (Irish province), age at marriage in, 153-4
Connell, K. H.: on growth of population in Ireland, 155-6; on marriage in Ireland, 152; on sources of population history, 151
Copenhagen (town), 14, 15, 30; smallpox deaths in, 53-4
cottars, Norwegian: age of, 119, 121; courtship patterns, 139-45; cultivate potatoes, 54, 63-5; household size,

246

Index

Harham, *see* Haram

harvest: effect on fertility, mortality and nuptiality, 67–71; failure of grain, 57, 59–60, measures to prevent, 66; *see also* potato in Norway

Hauge, Hans Nielsen: arrested, 13; followers of, character, 10–11, number, 10

Heckscher, Eli, on Norwegian death rate in 1742, 16 n. 3

Hedemarken,county,*see* Hedmark (county)

Hedemarken, deanery, age at marriage, 94–5, 202; fertility and nuptiality in, 199; infant mortality, 94

Hedemarken (Nes and Ringsaker) agriculture, prosperity of, 99, 101, 121 births and deaths in, 205–6 climate, 101 crofters: age of, 119, 124, 219, and of wives, 122–4, 219; children at home, 112, 122, 221; fertility of, 123; households, age and social composition, 219, relatives in, 116, 222, servants, 115, 222, size of, 108, 212, unrelated lodgers, 118, 223; life-style, 120, 148; marital age gap, 127–32, 223–6, and status, 109, 119, 128, 213, 224–5; number of in 1801, 147, 219; *see also* cottars

farmers, age of, and of wives, 110, 124, 218; children at home, 113–14, 148, 221; fertility of, 111–12; households, age and social composition of, 106–18, 212, 218, relatives in 115–16, 222, servants in, 37, 114–15, 147, 222, unrelated lodgers in, 117, 223; life-style, 120, 148; marital age gap, 127–32, 223–6, and status, 109–10, 128, 213, 224; number of in 1801, 218; *see also* farmers

fertility in, 102–4

harvest yields, 101 and n. 1

infant and child mortality, 102–4

marriage: age at, 105, 206–9; age gap in, 125–32, 223–6; bachelor–widow, 110–11, 136, 220

non-agricultural employment in, little, 101

scenery, 100–1

Hedmark (county), 55–6, 58, 63 n. 5, 89–92, 106–7, 210–11, 226–30

Hegra, 70 n. 3

heimbytte (home-exchange), prevalence of, 137; Sundt on, 137

Helgeland, age at marriage in, 204

Hemne, 70 n. 3

Herøy agriculture, backward, 96–7 births and deaths in, 205–6 climate, 96 crofters: age of, 119, 123, 215, and of wives, 123, 215; children at home, 112, 122, 221; households, age and social composition, 215, relatives in, 116, 222, servants in, 115, 222, size of, 108, 212, unrelated lodgers in, 118, 223; life-style, 120, 148; marital status, 109, 119, 213; number of in 1801, 118, 147, 215; *see also* cottars

farmers: age of, and of wives, 110, 214; children at home, 112–14, 148, 221; fertility of, 111–12; households, age and social composition of, 106–18, 212, 214, relatives in, 115–16, 119, 222, servants in, 37, 114–15, 147, 222, unrelated lodgers in, 117, 223; life-style, 120, 148; marital status, 109–10, 213; number of in 1801, 214; *see also* farmers

fertility in, 102–4

fisheries, importance of, 96–7

infant and child mortality in, 102–3

marriage: age at, 105, 206–9; bachelor–widow, 110–11, 220

Hertzberg, Nils, vaccination pioneer, 50

Hertzberg, Peter Harboe, potato cultivation, pioneer of, 54

Hillman, Arthur, on Sundt, 40

historical demography, *see under* demographic history

Hjørundfjord, 63 n. 5

Hof, 63 n. 5

Hol, size of average farm in, 98–9

Holland, population of in 1829 and 1859, 42

Hordaland (county), 56–8, 63 n. 5, 93, 97 n. 3, 106–7, 210–11, 226–30; fertility and nuptiality in 1801, 39, 89–91

household size in Norway, Malthus's views on, 36; *see also* Hallingdal, Hedemarken (Nes and Ringsaker), Herøy

Index

Setesdal, 70 n. 3
shipping: depression in during Napoleonic wars, 61; expansion in, 73, 82 and n. 2; regional importance of, xiv
Skånevik, 63 n. 5
Skjold, 125 n. 2
Skudenes, 125 n. 2
Sligo, 153–4
Smaalehnene, *see under* Østfold
Smaalenene, *see under* Østfold
Smålenene, *see under* Østfold
smallpox
  deaths from in Bergen, 51–2; Copenhagen, 53; Kristiansand, 52; Norway, 53; Sweden, 52
  incidence of not correlated with food supply, 66
  possible change in character of, 53
  see also inoculation, vaccination
Sogn: breast-feeding, duration of, in, 70 n. 3; fertility and nuptiality in, 200
Sogn, Indre and Ytre: age at marriage in, 203; infant mortality in, 94
Sogn and Fjordane (county), 56–8, 63 n. 5, 93, 97 n. 3, 106–7, 210–11, 226–30; fertility and nuptiality in, 89–91
Soløer and Oudalen, *see* Solør and Odalen
Solør, 70 n. 3
Solør and Odalen, 32, 55, 202
Solum, 5 n. 1
Søndhordland, *see* Sunnhordland
Søndhordlehn, *see* Sunnhordland
Søndre Bergenhus, *see* Hordaland
Søndre Sunnmøre, age at marriage in, 94–5
Søndre Trondhjem, *see* Sør-Trøndelag
Sør-Trøndelag, 56–8, 62, 63 n. 5, 93, 210–11, 226–30
Spain, population of (1833 and 1860), 42
spirits: distillation unrestricted, 62; per capita output, 62
Spydeberg, 5 n. 1
statistics, population, *see* population, statistics
Stavanger, county, *see* Rogaland
Stavanger, deanery: age at marriage in, 203; increase in marriages, 83; inoculation in, 51 n. 2; population growth through in-migration, 83, 86–7

still births: registration in Denmark and Norway, 13–14; effect of mode of registration on level of birth and death rates, 14
Stord, 63 n. 5
Støren, 63 n. 5
Storfosen (deanery), no return of births and deaths from in 1738, 15
Sundt, Eilert
  biography: early life, 19–20; parents of, 19–20; at university in Oslo, 20–1; friend of Henrik Wergeland, 20; supporter of 'Scandinavianism', 20, plea on to students of Nordic universities, 21; chairman of student union, 20; unwilling to enter church or academic life, 23, 25; begins career as sociologist, 23, 26; studies native and foreign scholars, 21–2; obtains parliamentary research grant for study of Norwegian gypsies, 23–4; attacks Thranism, 25; founder member of *Society for the promotion of popular enlightenment*, 27–8, becomes chairman, 28, and editor of journal *The People's Friend*, 28; writes variety of studies, 27–8, 133, antagonises public opinion, 28–9; loses grant, 28
  Hillman, Arthur, on, 40
  importance of for historical demography in Norway, xix
  research findings of: on birth rate fluctuations, 43, 45; on marriage, 27, 133, 138–44; on morality, 27, 133, 142–7; on Norwegian censuses, 5–6
  research method: belief in fieldwork, 25–6; strong historical sense, 133; use of questionnaires, 12, 124
  writings, extracts from, 134–44; style of, 133
Sunndal, 63 n. 5
Sunnfjord: age at marriage in, 203; fertility and nuptiality in, 201; infant mortality in, 94; servants from, 138
Sunnhordland: age at marriage in, 203; breast-feeding, duration of, in, 70 n. 3; fertility and nuptiality in, 200; infant mortality in, 94

Index

Sunnmøre, deanery: age at marriage in, 204; breast-feeding, duration of, in, 70 n. 3; fertility and nuptiality in, 39, 201; infant mortality in, 94

Sunnmøre (Herøy, Ullstein, Vanylven): crofters, marital age gap, 127–32, 223–6, and status, 128, 225; farmers, marital age gap, 127–32, 223–6, and status, 128, 224; marital age pattern, 125–32; widow marriage in, 136

Sweden, 31
census of 1749, 2
medical statistics of, 52, 54
population: in 1815 and 1865, 42; fall of in 1772 and 1773, 68

Switzerland, population of in 1837 and 1860, 42

Sykkylven, 63 n. 5

taxation, fears of, effect on census accuracy, 4, 5 n. 4, 58

Telemark county, 56–8, 89, 97 n. 3, 210–11, 226–30

Telemark deaneries, Nedre and Bamble, Øvre, age at marriage in, 202

Tellemarken, Nedre and Øvre, see Telemark, deaneries

Thaarup, Frederick: calculation of Norwegian birth and death rates, 37; meets Malthus, 32–3; sheriff of Solør and Odalen, 32; statistics professor at university of Copenhagen, 32

Thelemarken, Nedre and Øvre, see Telemark deaneries

Thoten and Valders, see Toten and Valdres

Thrane, Marcus: founds socialist societies, 24; imprisoned, 24–5; intellectual debt to English Chartists, 24

Throndhjem, see Trondheim

timber: depression in industry after Napoleonic wars, 61; exports of cut during Napoleonic wars, 60; location of industry, xiv, 82; population growth limited by industry, 102; rising demand for, 73

Tinn, breast-feeding, duration of, in, 70 n. 3

Tipperary, 153

Tjølling, 63 n. 5

Tolga, 125 n. 3

Torvastad, 125 n. 2

Toten and Valdres: age at marriage in, 202; fertility and nuptiality in, 200; infant mortality in, 94

Troms (county), see Troms and Finnmark

Troms and Finnmark, 56–8, 62, 93, 97, 210–11, 226–30; colonised in early nineteenth century, 87; early age at marriage in, 84–5; high fertility in, 85

Tromsø, deanery, age at marriage in, 204

Tromsø, diocese: carved out of Trondheim diocese in 1803 (location, xv), 180; in *Population and Society in Norway, 1735–1865* retained in old Trondheim diocese for reasons of comparability, 180

Trondheim, bishop of, 15

Trondheim, diocesan deanery, age at marriage in, 204

Trondheim, diocese: births and birth rate in, 48–9, 169–73, 184–8; deaths and death rate in, 46, 48–9, 173–6, 192–5; demographic crises in, 68; imports of grain into, 71; land communications in, 72; marriages and marriage rate in, 181–4, 189–91; migration, estimated, 167–9; population, growth of, 41–3, 164–7, Pram on, 17–18; potato cultivation in, 59

Trondheim, town, 31–2, 100; inoculation carried out in, 51 n. 2

Trondhjem, see Trondheim

Trysil, 125 n. 3

Tynset, 63 n. 5, 125 n. 3

Tysnes, 63 n. 5

typhus: in Akershus diocese, 72; and food supplies, 66

Ulstein, 63 n. 5, 125 n. 1

United States of America: census of 1790, 2; Norwegian emigration to, 74, 160

urban growth, in England and Norway, 9 and n. 3

vaccination: apathy towards, 50; Bergen diocese early, 50; church and, 13, 49–50; extent of (1802–60), 51; permission to marry conditional on, 13;